Risk Analysis and the Security Survey

Risk Analysis and the Security Survey

Second Edition

James F. Broder, CFE, CPP, BCFE

Boston • Oxford • Auckland • Johannesburg • Melbourne • New Delhi

Butterworth–Heinemann is an imprint of Elsevier Science.

⊗ Recognizing the importance of preserving what has been written, Elsevier Science prints its books on acid-free paper whenever possible.

Library of Congress Cataloging-in-Publication Data

Broder, James F.
    Risk analysis and the security survey / James F. Broder. — 2nd ed.
        p.   cm.
    Includes bibliographical references and index.
    ISBN 0-7506-7089-4 (alk. paper)
      1. Industries—Security measures. 2. Risk management. 3. Crime
prevention surveys. 4. Assistance in emergencies—Planning.
    I. Title.
    HV8290.B72   1999
    658.4'7—dc21   99-34309
                                                  CIP

British Library Cataloguing-in-Publication Data
A catalogue for this book is available from the British Library.

The publisher offers special discounts on bulk orders of this book.
For information, please contact:
Manager of Special Sales
Elsevier Science
200 Wheeler Road, 6th Floor
Burlington, MA 01803
Tel: 781-313-4700
Fax: 781-313-4882

For information on all Butterworth–Heinemann publications available, contact our World Wide Web homepage at: http://www.bh.com.

10 9 8 7 6 5 4

Printed in the United States of America

To my wife, Carolyn Oliver-Broder, who makes my life complete

"If you don't know where you're going, any road will get there"

Lewis Carroll
Alice in Wonderland

CONTENTS

ACKNOWLEDGMENTS

While attending the American Society for Industrial Security (ASIS) Convention in St.Louis (September 1997) the author had a meeting with an editor from Butterworth-Heinemann Publishing Company. Earlier, I had the honor of being selected to autograph copies of the first edition of this book at the ASIS Convention bookstore. We talked about writing a second edition to — among other things — update the text. It had afterall, been published in 1984 and some of the material was badly in need of updating. Notwithstanding, the book was consistently selling among the top 20 in the ASIS Catalogue, and was on the recommended reading list for the Certified Protection Professional (CPP) Review Course. I thought the editor's suggestion was worthy of serious consideration.

I then discussed the matter with several leading security professionals of my acquaintance who were also authors. Each of them without exception encouraged me to write this second edition. One of them, a close friend, with whom I have collaborated for over 25 years, provided some valuable insight. He said:

> In a profession where there are few, if any agreed upon standards, where our benchmarks are defined as "acceptable practices," there must be some principles we can turn to for guidance. In my writings, where possible, I strive to outline principles for the benefit of my readers. Your book, *Risk Analysis*, does the same thing. The principles you have codified and catalogued in your book will never change. As such you would not be serving our profession by letting your book "die of old age."

So we set forth on a labor of love to rewrite, update, and add to, hoping once again to make a small contribution to our profession; a profession which has given me more honor and benefits than anyone should expect in one lifetime.

Again, I gratefully acknowledge the help and assistance of all those who willingly and graciously gave of their professional advice, especially fellow professionals like Phillip L. Schiedermayer, CPP, and Charles Hayden, CPP. Two others, Charles A. Sennewald, CPP, and Gene Tucker, CPP, are both listed here prominently as contributing authors to this second edition.

As with the first edition my brother and friend, Donald J. Broder and my friend and colleague, Robert J. Sommers, CPP (deceased) both helped make a difficult task easier with their suggestions, guidance and support.

Finally, I want to acknowledge Laurel DeWolf, Senior Acquisitions Editor and Rita Lombard, Assistant Editor, at Butterworth-Heinemann for their encouragement, patience, and understanding of my inability to meet deadlines due to circumstances beyond my control.

INTRODUCTION

Studies by the Association of Certified Fraud Examiners report that fraud and abuse are estimated at more than 400 billion annually, cost to U.S. organizations.[1] Property and casualty insurance fraud, on the other hand, totaled 21 billion in 1996, or about ten percent of all claims.[2]

In further contrast, the Insurance Information Institute lists "The Ten Most Costly Insured Catastrophes in the United States" as follows:

The Ten Most Costly Insured Catastrophes, United States

Month/Year	Perils	Insured Loss
Aug. 1992	Hurricane Andrew	$15,500,000,000
Jan. 1994	Northridge, California earthquake	12,500,000,000
Sept. 1989	Hurricane Hugo	4,195,000,000
Oct. 1995	Hurricane Opal	2,100,000,000
Mar. 1993	20-state winter storm	1,750,000,000
Oct. 1991	Oakland, California fire	1,700,000,000
Sept. 1996	Hurricane Fran	1,600,000,000
Sept. 1992	Hurricane Iniki, Hawaii	1,600,000,000
May 1995	Wind; hail; flooding; Texas and New Mexico	1,135,000,000
Oct. 1989	Loma Prieta, California earthquake	960,000,000

The above statistics, regarding "white collar crime" and property and casualty insurance fraud, neither attempt to assess the loss in terms of human life or suffering nor do they assess the economic price society pays because of such crime. They merely attempt to place a dollar figure on the losses sustained primarily for the purpose of setting insurance rates for the future.

As stated by Senior Security Consultant Charles A. Hayden, CPP, "A company's most significant loss exposure may well be its susceptibility to

---

[1] Association of Certified Fraud Examiners, "Report to the Nation on Occupational Fraud and Abuse, 1996."

[2] Insurance Information Institute, "Insurance Issues Update," August 1998.

crime." This is especially true when one considers that loss to crime, as opposed to natural disaster, can, to a large degree, be controlled.

Knowledge of, and about crime, fraud, man-made and natural catastrophes is essential for security professionals, risk managers, design engineers, consultants and others who need to be able to assess properly the risk inherent in these hazards. A keen understanding of these factors is essential in order to assure the economic viability of any given enterprise.

The Risk Management Journal has reported that 85% of Risk Managers state that risk identification and evaluation continues to be high on their list of priorities. Next on the list of priorities is "assigning probabilities to the various consequences that can arise from an exposure to . . . loss."[3] Accurate and detailed information by necessity becomes the first order of business.

Security and risk management is principally concerned with the protection and conservation of corporate assets and resources. The task of protection continues to be an increasingly complex one in a time when technology is creating new products (and thus risk) at an explosive rate. Add this to the crime rate — now aggravated by domestic and international terrorism — the cry from some quarters for more restrictive legislation to protect privacy, and the importance of risk analysis and evaluation to design proper protection becomes self-evident.

Security, in its generic form, and the security survey/audit in its specific application, are essential elements of the risk management function. The precise role, however, that security plays will depend upon the particular business at hand. Any business plagued by continual problems of internal and external theft, can substantially improve its bottom-line profit by instituting an effective security program.

In other businesses where the need for security is less obvious, the role security plays depends largely on top management's perception of the need and importance of security within the framework of management objectives. Often one finds a big difference between what top management perceives its security (or loss control) problem to be, and what a comprehensive risk identification and analysis concludes it to be. The degree of this difference may determine a company's future—either remaining competitive in the marketplace or filing for bankruptcy.

No single source offers all the resources essential for a thorough analysis of the economic problems resulting from crime in our society. A multitude of fields—for example, private security, criminal justice, law, sociology, economics, business, accounting, and risk management—publish literature about economic crime. The unfortunate fact is that each discipline attacks the problem from within its own limited frame of reference. As an example, the

---

[3] Using Probable Risk Analysis to Improve Risk Management, Mark Jablonowski, Arm March 1996/Risk Management Magazine.

literature contains many references to the estimated 400 billion direct cost of crime to business. I emphasize the word direct because this estimate, soft as it is, does not, as far as we can tell, take into account such interrelated factors as business interruption, a figure that can far exceed the initial cost of the criminal act.

I need cite but two examples to make the point. Using a sophisticated antitamper, antiremoval fuse in a bomb, an extortionist attempted to obtain $3 million in cash from a Lake Tahoe, Nevada gambling casino. The plot failed when the payoff, complicated by weather and a nighttime helicopter delivery of the money in surrounding mountain terrain, was not successfully accomplished.

An explosive ordinance disposal team (EOD), called in to assess the situation and possibly defuse the device, decided initially to pile the sandbags around the suspected object. It soon become apparent, especially after reading the extortionist's instructions, that the device could not be moved or defused. To attempt either would cause it to explode before the allotted time. The EOD team decided that the best procedure was to attempt to control the direction of the detonation, thus minimizing the effects of the destruction.

As per the extortionists' intention, the device detonated, causing $18 million in structural damage to the hotel lobby inside of the casino. The two figures, the $3 million demand and the $18 million of structural damage, were widely reported by the media at the time of the incident. What was not reported was the amount of loss sustained by the casino because of business interruption before, during, and after the bomb exploded. Needless to say, the casino was evacuated and remained empty for a considerable period of time pending a determination by authorities that the structure was again safe for occupancy. During this period, revenue estimated to be in excess of $1 million per day was lost to the enterprise. In sum total, the structural damage, combined with the loss of revenue due to business interruption, exceeded the initial $3 million extortion demand by a ration of 10-1.

Additionally, consider the terrorist bombing of Pan American Flight 103 in 1988, which exploded over Lockerbie, Scotland. Tragic as this one incident was in terms of human loss, it also contributed significantly to Pan American Airways eventually going out of business.

Using these examples, it is obvious that for the purpose of planning for security, once risks are identified, we must evaluate and program loss control measures with a three-dimensional approach, as follows:

1. Implement sound security practices and procedures to minimize the probability of an event occurring.
2. Design plans to minimize the loss or damage if the event, notwithstanding the above procedures, does occur.

3. Develop and keep current contingent and disaster recovery plans to ensure that the enterprise is able to recover quickly enough from a sustained loss or disaster to remain in business.

A cardinal rule to remember is "Never allow yourself to assume that the preventative practices, procedures and countermeasures in place will always work to negate the threat." Remember, threats evolve, and so must the security professional. Further, management must not be allowed to become so complacent as to avoid contingency and disaster recovery planning.

The entire premise of this book rests on one principle, and that is:

The most fundamental philosophy of risk control, design and implementation has as a basic tenet making the program as self-sufficient as possible in all matters pertaining to security. This includes the two-sided coin of risk control: (1) the protection of assets by identifying, analyzing and prioritizing the risk, and (2) contingency and disaster recovery planning.

I sincerely hope that the material in this book will be of some assistance to the reader in accomplishing these objectives.

James F. Broder, CFE, CPP, FACFE
San Marino, CA 1999

1

RISK

Security is more art than science. Few formulas will cover all organizations, situations and needs, and that's the beauty and challenge of our profession. We are about probabilities.

Richard D. Sem, CPP
Are These Truths Self-Evident?
Security Management, March 1998

WHAT IS RISK?

Risk is associated with virtually every activity one can think of, but for the purpose of this text I shall limit the meaning of the word *risk* to the uncertainty of financial loss, the variations between actual and expected results, or the probability that a loss has occurred or will occur. In the insurance industry, *risk* is also used to mean "the thing insured" — for example, the XYZ Company is the risk. Risk is also the possible occurrence of an undesirable event.

Risk should not be confused with *perils*, which are the causes of risk — such things as fire, flood, and earthquake. Nor should risk be confused with hazard, which is a contributing factor to a peril. Almost anything can be a hazard — a loaded gun, a bottle of caustic acid, a bunch of oily rags, or a warehouse used for storing highly flammable products, for example. The end result of risk is loss or a decrease in value.

Risks are generally classified as "speculative" (the difference between loss or gain — for example, the risk in gambling) and "pure risk," a loss/no-loss situation, to which insurance generally applies.

For the purposes of this text, the divisions of risk are limited to three common categories:

- Personal (having to do with people assets)
- Property (having to do with material assets)
- Liability (having to do with legalities that could affect both of the above, such as errors and omissions, wrongful discharge, workplace violence, and sexual harassment, to name a few of the most current legal issues that plague the business community).

WHAT IS RISK ANALYSIS?

Risk analysis is a management tool, the standards for which are determined by whatever management decides it wants to accept in terms of actual loss. In order to proceed in a logical manner to perform a risk analysis, it is first necessary to accomplish some basic tasks:

- Identify the assets in need of being protected (money, manufactured products, and industrial processes, to name a few).
- Identify the kinds of risks (or perils) that may affect the assets involved (kidnapping, extortion, internal theft, external theft, fire, or earthquake).
- Determine the probability of risk occurrence. Here one must keep in mind that such a determination is not a science but an art — the art of projecting probabilities. Remember this rule: "Nothing is ever 100 percent secure."
- Determine the impact or effect, in dollar values if possible, if a given loss does occur.

I will discuss these subjects in detail in a later section in this chapter, "Risk Exposure Assessment."

WHAT IS A RISK ASSESSMENT ANALYSIS?

A risk assessment analysis is a rational and orderly approach, and a comprehensive solution, to problem identification and probability determination. It is also a method for estimating the expected loss from the occurrence of some adverse event. The key word here is *estimating*, because risk analysis will never be an exact science — we are discussing probabilities. Nevertheless, the answer to most, if not all, questions regarding one's security exposures can be determined by a detailed risk-assessment analysis.

WHAT CAN RISK ANALYSIS DO FOR MANAGEMENT?

Risk analysis provides management with information on which to base decisions. Is it always best to prevent the occurrence of a situation? Is it always possible? Should the policy be to contain the effect a hazardous situation may have? (This is what nuclear power plants prepare for.) Is it sufficient simply to recognize that an adverse potential exists and for now do nothing but be aware of the hazard? (The analogy is being self-insured.) The eventual goal of risk analysis is to strike an economic balance between the impact of risk on the enterprise and the cost of implementing prevention and protective measures.

A properly performed risk analysis has many benefits, a few of which are:

- The analysis will show the current security posture (profile) of the organization.
- It will highlight areas where greater (or lesser) security is needed.
- It will help to assemble some of the facts needed for the development and justification of cost effective countermeasures (safeguards).
- It will serve to increase security awareness by assessing then reporting, the strengths and weaknesses of security to all organizational levels from management to operations.

Risk analysis is not a task to be accomplished once and for all; it must be performed periodically if one is to stay abreast of changes in mission, facilities, and equipment. Also, since security measures designed at the inception of a system generally prove to be more effective than those superimposed later, risk analysis should have a place in the design or building phase of every new facility. Unfortunately, this is seldom the case.

The one major resource required for a risk analysis is trained manpower. For this reason the first analysis will be the most expensive. Subsequent analyses can be based in part on previous work history; the time required to do a survey will decrease to some extent as experience and empirical knowledge are gained.

The time allowed to accomplish the risk analysis should be compatible with its objectives. Large facilities with complex, multishift operations and many files of data will require more time than single-shift, limited-production locations. If meaningful results are to be expected, management must be willing to commit the resources necessary for accomplishing this undertaking. It is best to delay or even abandon the project unless and until the necessary resources are made available to complete it properly.

THE ROLE OF MANAGEMENT IN RISK ANALYSIS

The success of any risk-analysis undertaking will be strongly contingent on the role top management takes in the project. Management must *support* the project and express this support to all levels of the organization. Management must *delineate* the purpose and scope of risk analysis. It must *select* a qualified team and formally *delegate* authority. Finally, management must *review* the team's findings, decide which recommendations need to be implemented, and establish the order of priorities for such implementation.

Personnel who are not directly involved in the analysis process must be prepared to provide information and assistance to those who are conducting it and, in addition, to abide by any procedures and limitations of activity that may result from survey activity. Management should leave no doubt that it intends to rely on the final product and base its security decisions on the findings of the risk-analysis team. The scope of the project should be defined, and the statement of scope should specifically spell out the parameters and depth of the analysis. It is often equally important to state specifically what the analysis is not designed to accomplish or cover; this will eliminate any misunderstandings at the start of the exercise. An example might be the exclusion from a security survey of safety and evaluation procedures in hospital settings.

At this point, it may be well to define and explain two other terms that are sometimes used interchangeably with risk: threats — anything that could adversely affect the enterprise or the assets; and *vulnerability* — weaknesses or flaws, such as holes in a fence, or virtually anything that may conceivably be exploited by a threat. Threats are most easily identified and organized by placing each in one of three classifications or categories: natural hazards (such as floods), accidents (chemical spills), or intentional acts (domestic or international terrorism). Vulnerabilities are most easily identified by interviewing long-term employees, supervisors, and managers in the facility; by field observation and inspection; and by document review. In the case of hardware or electronics, tests can be conducted that are designed to highlight vulnerabilities and expose weaknesses or flaws in the design of the system. Examples would be an out-of-date key system or the introduction of a computer virus.

Threat occurrence rates and probabilities are best developed from reports of occurrences or incident reports, whenever this historical data exist. Where the information does not exist, it may be necessary to reconstruct it. This can be accomplished by conducting interviews with knowledgeable persons or by projecting data based upon educated guesses, supported by studies in like industries and locations.

RISK EXPOSURE ASSESSMENT

Before any corrective action can be considered, it is necessary to make a thorough assessment of identifiable risk exposure. In order to accomplish this, it is essential that three factors be identified and evaluated in quantitative terms. The first is to determine the types of loss or risk (perils) that can affect the assets involved. Here examples would be fire, flood, burglary, robbery, or kidnapping. If one of these were to occur (for now we will consider only single, not multiple, occurrences), what effect would the resulting disruption of operations have on the company? For example, if vital documents were destroyed by fire or flood, what would the effect be on the ability of the company to continue in operation? There is a saying common to protection professionals, "One may well survive a burglary, but one good fire can put you out of business forever." If the chief executive officer, on an overseas trip, were to be kidnapped by a terrorist group (or even suffer a serious heart attack), who would make the day-to-day operating decisions in his or her absence? What about unauthorized disclosure of trade secrets or other proprietary data? After all (or as many as possible) of the risk exposure potentials are identified, one must proceed to evaluate those identified threats that, should they occur, would produce losses in quantitative terms — fire, power failure, flood, earthquake, and unethical or dishonest employees, to name a few worthy of consideration.

To do this we proceed to the second factor: *estimate the probability of occurrence.* What are the chances that the identified risks may become actual events? For some risks, estimating probabilities can be fairly easy. This is especially true when we have documented historical data on identifiable problems. For example, how many internal and external theft cases have been investigated over the past year? Other risks are more difficult to predict. Workplace violence, embezzlement, industrial espionage, kidnapping, and civil disorder may never occur or may occur only once. The third factor is *quantifying (prioritizing) loss potential.* This is measuring the impact or severity of the risk, if in fact a loss does occur or the risk becomes an actual event. This exercise is not complete until one develops dollar values for the assets previously identified. This part of the survey is necessary to set the stage for classification evaluation and analysis, and for the comparisons necessary to the establishment of countermeasure (safeguard) priorities. Some events or kinds of risk with which business and industry are most commonly concerned are:

- Natural catastrophe (tornado, hurricane, seismic activity)
- Industrial disaster (explosion, chemical spill, structural collapse, fire)
- Civil disturbance (sabotage, labor violence, bomb threats)
- International and domestic terrorism
- Criminality (robbery, burglary, pilferage, embezzlement, fraud, industrial espionage, internal theft, hijacking)
- Conflict of interest (kickbacks, trading on inside information, commercial bribery, other unethical business practices)
- Nuclear accident (Three Mile Island, Detroit Edison's Enrico Fermi #1).

Some of the above events (risks) are unlikely to occur. Also, some are less critical to an enterprise or community than others even if they do occur (fire versus burglary, for instance). Nevertheless, *all* are possibilities and are thus deserving of consideration.

Examples include the nuclear accident at Chernobyl in the Soviet Union in 1987, and the chemical gas disaster ("breach of containment") at the Union Carbide plant in Bophal, India in 1984. Also, there exists today in the United States chemical and nerve-gas weapons stored in bunkers at military depots near populated areas. Do contingency plans exist to deal with these risks in the event of accidental fire, leak, or explosion? Are disaster drills and exercises conducted periodically to test the effectiveness of the contingency plans, if they exist? There are contingency plans for breach of containment or other industrial accident in nuclear power generating plants in the United States, and they are strictly enforced by the Nuclear Regulatory Commission (NRC), which requires periodic drills to rehearse the plans.

In the following chapters we will discuss vulnerabilities and threat identification, as well as risk measurement and quantification.

2

VULNERABILITY AND THREAT IDENTIFICATION

Before the question of security can be addressed, it is first necessary to identify those harmful events which may befall any given enterprise.
Charles A. Sennewald, CPP
Security Consultant, Author, and Lecturer

RISK IDENTIFICATION

In systems security, the primary purpose of vulnerability identification or threat (exposure) determination is to make the task of risk analysis more manageable by establishing a base from which to proceed. When the risks associated with the various systems and subsystems within a given enterprise are known, the allocation of countermeasures (resources) can be more carefully planned. The need for such planning rests on the premise that security resources, like all other resources, are limited and therefore must be allocated wisely.

Risk control begins, logically, with identification and classification of risk. To accomplish this task it is necessary to examine or survey all the activities and relationships of the enterprise in question and to develop answers to these basic considerations:

- Assets — What does the company own, operate, lease, control, have custody of or responsibility for, buy, sell, service, design, produce, manufacture, test, analyze, or maintain?
- Exposure — What is the company exposed to that could cause or contribute to damage, theft, or loss of property or other company

7

assets, or that could cause or contribute to personal injury of company employees or others?

- Losses — What empirical evidence is available to establish the frequency, magnitude, and range of past losses experienced by this and other companies located nearby, performing a like service, or manufacturing the same or a similar product?

Obviously, the answers to these questions and any additional questions that may be raised when conducting initial inquiries will be the basis for the risk identification and eventually risk evaluation of the enterprise in question.

Security professionals use many techniques to develop data for risk identification. They may review company policies, procedures (or their absence), organization, and activities to ascertain what risks have been identified and to what extent they are perceived as management responsibilities. They may review insurance and risk-related files, including claims and loss records. Interviews with the heads of departments that have experienced loss exposures can develop vital information on the organization and functioning of loss-control procedures, if in fact any exist. Conducting inspections and interviewing management and other personnel in enough locations and activities will develop a complete picture of the company's risk exposures as a basis for later evaluation of loss control procedures and their effectiveness.

The tools necessary to accomplish the above are the ability to conduct comprehensive interviews; the ability to conduct inspections and field observations of operations, procedures, manpower, and electronics in security systems; and the ability to identify, obtain, and analyze pertinent records.

Another technique is to develop asset data. To do this, one completely identifies all company assets, tangible and intangible, in terms of quantity and quality. One then locates all company assets and identifies obvious exposures that may exist at these locations. Next one must determine the value of these assets in terms of actual dollars. This should be broken into the following three categories:

- Owned assets $_____
- Leased assets $_____
- Facility losses $_____
  Total tangible assets $_____
  Total intangible assets $_____
  Grand total $_____

The identification of all company assets, coupled with a history of loss exposure for the company and other companies similarly located and engaged, will normally be sufficient to identify most of the major risks involved.

After this identification procedure, the security survey or inspection can be limited to those risks or exposures that specifically relate to the enterprise in question. These risks will usually include most, if not all, of the following:

- Crime losses, such as burglary, theft (internal and external), fraud, embezzlement, vandalism, arson, computer abuse, bomb threat, theft of trade secrets and industrial espionage, forgery, product forgery and trademark infringement, robbery, extortion, and kidnapping — to name the most common crime risks encountered by business and industry. Some others are:
- Cargo pilferage, theft, and damage.
- Emergency and disaster planning.
- Liability of officers and directors.
- Environmental controls as directed by occupational safely and health codes.
- Damage to property from fire, flood, earthquake, windstorm, explosion, building collapse, falling aircraft, and hazardous processes.
- Comprehensive general liability arising from damage caused by any activity for which the entity can be held legally liable.
- Business interruption and extra expense. An evaluation of this type of risk may require a detailed study of interdependencies connecting various segments of the entity and outside suppliers of goods and services. It may indicate the need for extensive disaster planning for reduction of the risk.
- Errors and omissions liability.
- Professional liability.
- Products liability and completed operations.

As can be seen from even a cursory review of these risks, the scope of risk identification alone, separate from risk evaluation and risk control, presupposes a degree of education and practical knowledge not often possessed by the individual security manager. This implies that the person who is charged with this responsibility should have the education, training, and practical experience necessary to seek out, recognize, and thus identify not only the risk involved but also its applicability to the enterprise in question. It goes almost without saying that the process of risk identification, evaluation, and control in any dynamic organization, public or private, requires constant attention by professionals who possess the necessary knowledge and tools to accomplish the task.

EXAMPLES OF THE PROBLEMS OF IDENTIFICATION

The author was given the assignment of conducting a security survey for a chain of fast-food restaurants. At the initial meeting with the management staff of this chain, reports from the company's internal audit division were furnished for our review. These reports showed all crime-related losses for a twelve-month period. They contained statistics that showed a disturbingly high incident rate for "robbery." One of the firm's top management people stated that he had a growing concern that a part-time high school cashier working in one of their restaurants might get shot in the course of a robbery because of the absence of procedures instructing them in how to deal with this problem.

Field inspections of a representative number of these restaurants produced evidence that their principal problem was burglary, followed closely by internal theft. "Armed robbery," or just plain robbery as perceived by management, while admittedly always a dangerous problem, was not as frequent or as serious as management had been lead to believe by the statistics in the audit reports. Further inquiry revealed that the terms *robbery* and *burglary* were being used indiscriminately and, in many cases, synonymously. It was only after properly identifying the real problem that we could proceed to develop the necessary procedures and allocate the necessary resources to address and then solve management's concern.

In another case, the author met with the management of a national corporation that, among other things, printed negotiable instruments. The purpose of the meeting was to develop a mutual agreement regarding the scope of a security survey to be conducted at one of its West Coast plants. At the outset, one of the management representatives asked, "Have you ever conducted a security survey at a plant that prints negotiable instruments?" The simple fact at the time was that I had not. Nevertheless, the answer I gave was, "No, I haven't, but that really doesn't matter. It is immaterial to me if your plant manufactures widgets or prints negotiable instruments. You will either have a security program or you will not. If you do, it will either be functional, or it will not. In either event, it can be evaluated, and we can determine if the state of the security in existence at the plant is adequate, given the unique requirements for protection that this type of production requires. If we feel the system is not functional, we will make recommendations to upgrade the quality and the quantity of the security safeguards necessary to accomplish the goal. If you have no program for security, we will design one for your consideration to meet the above requirements."

In security, as with many other disciplines, we deal in acceptable practices and principles. These remain fairly constant, regardless of the product involved. The end result is loss control. This means that one either has or does not have an adequate security system. One way to find out is to conduct a survey and identify those harmful events that may interfere with the ultimate objectives, as they are defined by the management of the enterprise in question.

SECURITY CHECKLIST

Until now I have been discussing the techniques and tools that the security professional needs in order to develop data for risk identification. Very often, security checklists are used to facilitate the gathering of pertinent information. These checklists take many forms. They can be simple lists of yes-no questions, or open-ended questions requiring narrative responses. They may be brief and narrowly focused on the specific operation or activity in question, or they may be broader in scope and cover security concerns common to all the company's operations. No matter what its appearance, the purpose of a security checklist is to provide a logical recording of information and to ensure that no important questions go unasked.

The checklist is usually the backbone of the security survey or audit. This subject is covered extensively beginning with Chapter 6.

The following is a general security checklist that is designed for companywide use; therefore, it may include many items that are appropriate in some situations but not in others. Additional checklists can be found in the appendices at the end of the book.

I. Policy and Program

1. Top management established a security policy?
   a. Policy published?
   b. Part of all managers' responsibility?
   c. Designated individual to establish and supervise security program?
2. Top manager accessible to security supervisor?
3. Any regulations published? (Attach copy)
4. Disciplinary procedures?
   a. In writing?
   b. Specify offenses and penalties.
   c. Incidents recorded?
   d. Review by management?
   e. Uniformly enforced?
5. Any policy on criminal prosecution?
   a. Number of prosecutions attempted last five years?
   b. Number of convictions?

II. Organization

1. Security supervisor full time?
   a. If part time, percent of time spent on security?
   b. Describe chain of command from security supervisor to plant manager.
2. Number of full-time security personnel?
3. Number of personnel performing security duties each shift?
   a. Do they perform nonsecurity duties concurrently?
   b. Do security duties have first priority?
4. Have security personnel received security training?
5. Are written reports made of incidents?
6. Is there follow-up investigation of incidents?
7. Background investigation of security personnel?
8. Guards
   a. Number?
   b. Employed or purchased service?
   c. If purchased service, does plant security supervisor interview and select?
   d. Is there a written contract for guard service?
   i. Management's terms and conditions included?
   e. Written guard orders? (Attach a copy)
   f. Weapons carried? (List type — for example, pistols, mace)
       i. If yes, who inspects?
       ii. Company furnished?
   g. Make watchclock tours?
   h. Guards or supervisor change clock disc/tape?
   i. Frequency of tours?
   j. Tour pattern varied?
   k. Number of clock stations?
   l. Guards submit written report each shift? (Attach copy of form)
   m. Have guards received any formal training? (Describe on reverse side)
   n. Appearance of guards?
9. Procedures
   a. Have security procedures been published?
   b. Distributed to all those affected?
   c. Revised when conditions change?
   d. Used to conduct periodic audits?
10. Does the security supervisor maintain contact with local law enforcement agencies to keep abreast of criminal activities and potential disorder in the community?

III. Control of Entry and Movement

1. Is identification required of all persons entering?
2. Are there periodic 100 percent checks of identification?
2. How often? By whom?
4. Are all visitors registered?
5. How are employees distinguishable from visitors? (Explain on reverse)
6. Are all visitors escorted at all times?
7. Is there control of employee movement between areas within the plant? (Describe on reverse)
8. Are supervisors instructed to challenge strangers in their work areas?
   a. Do they? Nearly always? Sometimes? Never?
9. Are periodic traffic counts made at all points of entry as a means of detecting need for schedule change?
10. Are identification badges issued to all employees? Wearing enforced?

IV. Barriers (Fences, Gates, Walls, etc.)

1. Is there a continuous barrier around the entire plant property?
   a. A major portion of it?
   b. Areas outside barrier? (List)
2. Fencing
   a. Eight feet high?
   b. Two-inch square mesh?
   c. Eleven-gauge or heavier wire?
   d. Topped by three strands barbed wire or selvage?
   e. In good repair?
   f. Within two inches of firm ground at all points?
   g. Securely fastened to rigidly set posts?
   h. Metal posts set in concrete?
   i. Where attached to buildings, gaps not more than four inches?
   j. Gates in good repair? (How many?)
      i. Gates same height and construction as fence?
      ii. Open only when required for operations?
      iii. Locked other times?
      iv. Equipped with alarm? (How many?)
      v. Guarded when open?
      vi. Under surveillance when open? How?
   k. At least ten feet of clear space both sides of fence?
   l. Along embankments, fence on top or twenty feet from bottom?

  2. Walls as perimeter barriers
     a. At least eight feet high?
     b. All doors equipped with alarm device or under surveillance?
     c. Means of surveillance?
     d. Windows:
        i. Permanently closed?
        ii. Accessible for removal of property?
        iii. Can be used for entry or exit?
        iv. Protected by bars or heavy screen?
        v. Equipped with alarm?
     e. Final exit (perimeter) doors:
        i. Guarded?
        ii. Alarm equipped? What type?
        iii. Controlled by security personnel? Controlled by devices?
        iv. Strong enough to resist heavy impact?
        v. Hinge pins concealed from outside or security type?

V. Lighting

  1. All of the perimeter lighted?
  2. Strip of light on both sides of fence?
  3. Illumination sufficient to detect man movement easily at one hundred yards?
  4. Lights checked for operation daily prior to darkness?
  5. Extra lighting at entry points and points of possible intrusion?
  6. Lighting repairs made promptly?
  7. Is the power supply for lights easily accessible (for tampering)?
  8. Are lighting circuit drawings available to facilitate quick repairs?
  9. Switches and controls
     a. Protected?
     b. Weatherproof and tamper resistant?
     c. Accessible to security personnel?
     d. Inaccessible from outside the perimeter barrier?
     e. Master switch(es) centrally located?
  10. Good illumination for guards on all routes inside the perimeter?
  11. Materials and equipment in receiving, shipping, and storage areas adequately lighted?
  12. Bodies of water on perimeter adequately lighted?
  13. Auxiliary source of power for protective lighting?

VI. Locks and Keys

  1. Responsibility for control of locks and keys assigned to security supervisor?

2. Does he or she control locks and keys to all buildings?
3. Does he or she have overall authority and responsibility for issues, changes, and replacements?
4. Plant manager approve formula for issuing keys?
5. Managers approve issue of keys to their area?
6. Any keys issued to nonemployees?
7. Recipient sign receipt for key?
   a. Receipt show building and room number, date, name of authorizing manager?
   b. Receipt acknowledge obligation to turn in, report loss, not to duplicate?
8. Keys issued solely because of operational need for recipient to have key?
9. Lock and key control procedures and regulations in writing? (Attach copy)
10. All keys recovered from terminating employees?
11. Master keys not marked as such?
12. Spare keys stored under double lock or in combination locked, fireproof cabinet?
13. Access to spare keys restricted to security supervisor and one other manager?
14. Locks changed immediately upon theft or loss of keys?
15. Locks on perimeter doors and gates changed annually?
16. Padlocks changed or rotated annually?
17. Manufacturer's serial number on padlocks obliterated and replaced by plant code number?
18. Padlock locked to hasp or staple when door or gate is open (to prevent substitution)?
19. Locks on inactive doors and gates checked regularly for evidence of tampering?
20. Door locks installed so that bolt extends a half-inch into jamb?
    a. Bolt covered by steel cover plate between door and jamb to prevent levering?
21. Combination locks
    a. Combination changed:
       i. Annually?
       ii. When unauthorized person may have learned?
       iii. When knowledgeable person leaves or transfers?
    b. Combination memorized? (Not written!)
    c. Combination numbers: one odd, one even, one divisible by five? (Any sequence OK)
    d. Combination disclosed on basis of operational necessity (not convenience)?
22. Perimeter doors
    a. Lock installed without keyway in outside knob?

b. Deadbolt locks in doors that must be unlocked from outside?
23. Safes
   a. Of substantial construction?
   b. Rated (labeled) for fire resistance?
   c. Rated (labeled) for burglary resistance?
   d. Lighted at night?
   e. Covered by proximity or motion detection alarm?

VII. Alarms

1. Fire alarms
   a. Water flow? Is water pressure present?
   b. Valve condition?
   c. Water temperature?
   d. Particles of combustion detection?
   e. Heat or smoke sensing?
   f. Monitored continuously by:
      i. Contract central station?
      ii. Proprietary station?
      iii. Direct connection to police or fire department?
   g. Tested regularly and tests recorded?
   h. Additional functions performed by alarm system (for example, shuts off computer power).
2. Intrusion alarms
   a. Protects all of plant perimeter?
   b. Protects high value storage areas?
   c. Protects other internal areas? (List)
   d. Types of sensors? (List)
   e. Proprietary or central station supervision?
   f. Regular recorded tests? How often?
3. Closed circuit television
   a. Used for surveillance only?
   b. Used for access control?
   c. Monitored continuously?

VIII. Communications

1. Separate communications for security and emergency use?
   a. Telephone?
   b. Radio?
2. If radio shared with other users, can security override?
3. Is there a means of contacting guard on patrol immediately? How?
4. Procedure for contacting local police and fire departments?
5. Means of alerting employees to emergency? How?

IX. Property Control (Equipment, Material, Tools, Personal Property)

1. Covered by written procedures?
2. Specified form?
   a. Serial numbered?
   b. Multipart to provide separate audit trails?
3. Signed authorization required? Approved by higher level than beneficiary?
4. All transactions monitored at exit?
5. All exits controlled?
6. All transactions audited by third party (other than security)?
7. Follow up on late returns (of borrowed items)?
8. Control points between work area and parking area?
9. Spot-checks of trucks and other vehicles?
10. All company tools (except small hand tools) marked with permanent company identification?
11. Employees sign receipt for tools and equipment issued?
12. Tools and desirable items secured in locked cages or rooms? Inventoried frequently?
13. All losses reported?
    a. Follow-up investigation?
    b. Written record?
    c. Statistics compiled? Reported to top management?
14. Shipping, receiving, and storage
    a. Guarded or within protected area?
    b. Under security of supervisor surveillance?
    c. Continuous spot-checks of complete shipments and receipts versus documents by other than shipping/receiving clerks?
    d. Outside drivers permitted inside plant?
    e. Vehicles locked?
    f. Tailgate check of existing vehicles?
    g. Storage areas under separate lock control when unattended?
    h. All withdrawals from stock recorded? Records provide separate audit trails?
    i. Continuous spot-checks of waste containers?
15. Scrap and salvage
    a. Written procedure for collection and disposal of scrap and salvage?
    b. Sealed bids required?
    c. Disposal action documented?
    d. Purchaser selected by management (other than administering employee)?
    e. Estimated annual sales of scrap and salvage?

    f. Any sold or given to employees? (Explain on reverse or attach procedure)
    g. Stored in a locked secure area?
    h. Waste spot-checked for saleable scrap and salvage?
    i. Classified and separated as to value?
    j. Spot-checked for "high grading"?
    k. Removed from premises under:
        i. Signed authorization on specified form?
        ii. Surveillance of third party employee, for example, accounting or security?
        iii. Verifies class and quantity?
        iv. Compares with purchaser's receipt?
    l. Auditors review all transactions?
    m. Are quantities within normal limits for this type operation?

X. Emergency Planning

1. Plans for reaction to imminent or actual
    a. Fire?
    b. Explosion?
    c. Flood or tidal wave?
    d. Hurricane?
    e. Earthquake?
    f. Disorder?
    g. Aircraft accident?
    h. Bomb threats and bombs?
2. Responsibilities spelled out?
3. Responsible individuals designated?
4. Organization(s) completely staffed?
5. Periodic rehearsals of:
    a. All personnel?
    b. Key personnel?
6. Have critical features of plant and equipment been identified? Protected by barriers, access control and lighting now?
7. Coordinated with local public safety and disaster organizations?
8. Include plans for postdisaster recovery?
9. Identify resources available and required?

XI. Personnel Screening

1. Written, signed employment application required? Omissions not tolerated?
2. All candidates interviewed?

3. Investigation to verify?
   a. Previous employment
      i. Employers?
      ii. Dates?
      iii. Position and duties?
      iv. Salary?
      v. Quality of performance?
   b. Education?
   c. Criminal record?
   d. Reputation?
   e. Medical record
      i. Illnesses?
      ii. Physical handicaps and limitations?
      iii. Work injuries?
      iv. Occupational illnesses?
4. Special screening of candidates for fiduciary positions? Describe.

XII. Comments

Add any information you consider useful in arriving at a realistic assessment of security in the plant. After all the significant loss potentials are identified, the next step is to evaluate the identified threats or vulnerabilities that may affect the enterprise and thus conceivably produce losses.

3

RISK MEASUREMENT

The question, "Is the system secure?" is essentially meaningless. The meaningful question is, "Is the system protected against events believed to be harmful?"

Alan Krull
IBM Information Systems,
Management Institute, Chicago, IL

Risk measurement (quantification) is an essential element for later use in determining the cost of an unfavorable event. It also aids in predicting how often such an event may occur in a given period of time. Two necessities for performing risk measurement and quantification are a quantitative means of expressing potential cost and a logical expression of frequency of occurrence. Both must admit low as well as high frequencies of event occurrence.

There is no better way to state the impact of an adverse circumstance — whether the damage or cost is actual or abstract, or the victim a person, a piece of machinery, or the entire facility — than to assign it a monetary value. Ascertaining the cost of any adverse event is the logical way to equate value in our society. For a company that is concerned with cost (and which are not?), it is the only way. As budgets and other financial matters are normally organized on a yearly basis, a year is obviously the most suitable time period to use in expressing frequency of occurrence of threats. Of course, some threats may occur only once in a period of years, such as the hundred-year flood. Others may occur daily or many times a day, such as internal theft. Each, however, can be measured in dollars as well as frequency of occurrence.

COST VALUATION AND FREQUENCY OF OCCURRENCE

It is much more difficult to say that something happens every seventy-third of a year than that it happens, say, five times a day. It is also inconvenient to work with such fractions. For this reason the transmutation of a thousand days to three years, as shown below, has been evolved. This method avoids unwieldy fractions yet maintains the flexibility of working with high-probability events in days and low-probability events in years.

In most cases, it is neither necessary nor desirable to make precise statements of impact and probability. The time needed for the analysis will be considerably reduced, and its usefulness will not be decreased, if impact (*i*) and frequency (*f*) correlations are given in factors of ten. It does not really matter to the overall estimation of threats whether the cost of the threat is valued at $110,000 or $130,000, or whether the anticipated frequency is eight or twelve times a year. If at the time of erecting safeguards it becomes necessary to refine specific items, then by all means consider it. What is necessary in the beginning is simplifying the measurement and quantification process, for reasons of efficiency and speed. This will facilitate the task by decreasing the amount of time spent on the analysis.

If the cost valuation (impact) of the event is:

$$\begin{array}{rl}
\$10, & \text{let } i = 1 \\
\$100, & \text{let } i = 2 \\
\$1{,}000, & \text{let } i = 3 \\
\$10{,}000, & \text{let } i = 4 \\
\$100{,}000, & \text{let } i = 5 \\
\$1{,}000{,}000, & \text{let } i = 6 \\
\$10{,}000{,}000, & \text{let } i = 7 \\
\$100{,}000{,}000, & \text{let } i = 8.
\end{array}$$

If the estimated frequency of occurrence is:

$$\begin{array}{ll}
\text{Once in three hundred years,} & \text{let } f = 1 \\
\text{Once in thirty years,} & \text{let } f = 2 \\
\text{Once in three years,} & \text{let } f = 3 \\
\text{Once in a hundred days,} & \text{let } f = 4 \\
\text{Once in ten days,} & \text{let } f = 5 \\
\text{Once per day,} & \text{let } f = 6 \\
\text{Ten times per day,} & \text{let } f = 7 \\
\text{A hundred times per day,} & \text{let } f = 8.
\end{array}$$

Annual loss expectancy (ALE) is the product of impact and frequency. When using the values of *f* and *i* derived from the conversion tables (listed above), you can approximate the value of ALE by the formula:

$$\text{ALE} = \frac{10^{(f+i-3)}}{3}$$

No weighting factors have been introduced into the formula; the change is only for the purpose of accommodating the converted values. An even faster way to determine ALE is to use the matrix shown in Figure 3-1, or alternatively, to develop one's own matrix. It would be impossible to list all the undesirable events that could plague any given security project. Most projects involving facilities, be they high technology, refinery, manufacturing, or service, have more things in common than one would suspect at first glance (example: fires on a cruise liner versus terrorism on the high seas). These common-origin problems have to be spliced or woven into the matrix along with events or occurrences peculiar to the particular analysis at hand.

A thorough understanding of the elements that may affect frequency estimation is one of the keys to risk measurement. The following are some common elements that deserve consideration:

- *Access* — Is access difficult, limited, or open? Can an intruder gain access easily, or is it difficult? Can any employee do the same? What are the access criteria?
- *Natural disasters* — What kind of natural disasters might realistically occur? To what degree would damage occur? How would it affect processing, stores, supplies? How would loss of power or other utilities affect the entity?
- *Environmental hazards* — What special hazards are inherent in the operation? What is nearby? Are there any explosives, gasoline, or flammable objects in the area? Unused buildings next door? What can be the aftermath of fire? Water damage? Loss of stock, material? Proximity of fire and police departments?
- *Facility housing* — What protective devices are installed, or can be installed? Burglar alarm systems, access control systems? How is the building constructed? Type of roof? Sprinklers? What kind of flooring? What is flammable?
- *Work environment* — What is the relationship between personnel and management? (Loyal? Suspicious?) What are the aggravations of employees? Past labor history? How well do supervisors know employees? What is management attitude toward employee dishonesty? (Condone? OK within bounds? Dismissal?) How are lines of communication between employees and supervisors? Supervisors and upper management?
- *Value* — How much can an intruder profit? How much damage could result in all? How much can a dishonest employee gain? How long before intrusion will be detected? What is security response capability, time?

	Values of f							
Values of i	*1*	*2*	*3*	*4*	*5*	*6*	*7*	*8*
1					$300	$ 3K	$ 30K	$300K
2				$300	3K	30K	300K	3M
3			$300	3K	30K	300K	3M	30M
4		$300	3K	30K	300K	3M	30M	300M
5	$300	3K	30K	300K	3M	30M	300M	
6	3K	30K	300K	3M	30M	300M		
7	30K	300K	3M	30M	300M			

Figure 3-1. Determination of Annual Loss Expectancy = ALE

PRINCIPLES OF PROBABILITY

At this point, some statements about the nature of risk must be expounded. What I have stated so far is a simple approach to identifying and measuring risk. *Risk* is the possible happening of an undesirable event. An *event* is something that can occur, a definable occurrence. When the event happens, it can be described. Security countermeasures are designed to protect against harmful events. For this reason, as Alan Krull has stated, the question "Is a system secure?" is meaningless. What should be asked is, "Is the system protected against events that will be harmful?"

Any event can be described in at least two ways: it may be described in terms of the damage it will present if it occurs; it may be considered in terms of the probability of its occurrence. A risk, however, should be described in terms of its potential occurrence *and* its capacity for potential loss.

The study of the possibility of occurrence is known as "probability." The principles that follow are based on philosophical (rather than mathematical) proofs derived in 1792 by the Marquis de Laplace in his *Théorie Analytique des Probabilités*. Excerpts from this classical treatise is reprinted below in part. Laplace established ten principles of probability, as quoted below.

1. Probability is defined as the ratio of the number of favorable cases to all possible cases.
2. If the cases are not equally possible then the probability is the sum of the possibilities of each favorable case.
3. When the events are independent of each other, the probability of their simultaneous occurrence is the product of their separate probabilities.
4. If two events are dependent on each other, then the probability of the combined event is the product of the probability of the occurrence of the first event and the probability that the second event will occur given the occurrence of the first event.
5. If the probability of a combined event first phase and that of the second phase is determined, then the second probability divided by the first is the probability of the expected event drawn from an observed event.
6. When an observed event is linked to a cause, the probability of the existence of the cause is the probability of the event resulting from the cause divided by the sum of the probabilities of all causes.
7. The probability that the possibility of an event falls within given limits is the sum of the fractions [#6 above] falling within these limits.
8. The definition of *mathematical hope* is the product of the potential gain and the probability of obtaining it.
9. In a series of probable events, of which some produce a benefit and the others a loss, we shall have the advantage that results from it by making a sum of the products of the probability of each favorable event by the benefit that it procures, and subtracting from this sum that of the products of the probability of each unfavorable event by the loss that is attached to it. If the second sum is greater than the first, the benefit becomes a loss and hope is changed to fear.
10. Moral hope is defined as the relation between its absolute value divided by the total assets of the involved entity. This principle deals with the relation of potential gain to potential loss and describes the basis for not exposing all assets to the same risk.

Readers and students of this text have asked the author to explain further Laplace's theory in words of one syllable. The author, unfortunately, is not astute enough to do so. The theory is merely set forth here for those readers who may desire a more precise methodology by which to arrive at probability in their unique environment or studies. For our purposes, however, the simpler the application, the better.

PROBABILITY, RISK, AND SECURITY

When security is defined as the implementation of a set of acceptable practices, procedures, and principles that, when taken as a whole, have the effect of altering the ratio of undesirable events to total events, the first principle and the importance of the probability theory becomes evident. The principal problem that security must try to deal with is that *all undesirable events are breaches of security!* The goal of security design is to decrease the ratio of unfavorable events to total events. Obviously, some events are more likely to occur than others in the same area. The risk of a flood that drowns a city would seem less likely than a transient power failure (tell this to the people of Des Moines, Iowa). Both are undesirable. Both affect the operation of the business. Where the probability of each case is different, the ratios of favorable cases are added.

Two events that have no relation to each other are considered to be *independent*. If they are not linked in any way, the probability of their simultaneous occurrence is the product of their respective probabilities. An example: What is the probability of lightning striking a second time in the same spot? It is the same as the probability of its striking the first time: the two events are independent of each other. In security, the penetration of a system and the simultaneous failure of the security system from causes other than penetration may be expressed as the product of the probabilities of the independent events. This fits the condition of Laplace's Principle 3, above. Many security (and safety) systems, such as those employed at nuclear power facilities, are based on redundancy, such that multiple failures must occur; the redundant systems do not become operational until the preceding systems have failed. Principle 4 expresses the relation between dependent events: the probability of the first event is multiplied by the probability of the second event if the second event can happen only after the first event has occurred. Breaking and entering followed by theft, to produce a burglary, is an example.

The probability of security system failure may be expressed in terms of the lower-risk multiple or backup systems. As for when two events are combined, Principle 5 expresses the idea that when dealing with events, the past does not affect the future. If we assume the risk of a security breach is a given value and that it has occurred, we may not assume that it will not occur again. Probabilities of events are not guarantees. If an event has a probability of one in a hundred, the probability of that event happening again is still one in a hundred. For example, tossing a coin for heads or tails is a fifty-fifty proposition: that is, one time out of two it should come up heads. A coin toss could come up heads ten times in succession; however, as the past cannot affect the present or the future, the chance of heads coming up each time is still fifty-fifty, and it will remain so on every toss.

Principle 6 deals with the attribution of causes to effects. It describes the relation between all causes and probable causes. This is effectively the expression of *circumstantial evidence*, as a probability leading to a conclusion but less convincing than direct evidence. Principle 7 involves the basis of *confidence limits*. To illustrate, if a random sample of one hundred variables is taken and is found to have a mean of forty and a standard deviation of eleven, it will not be possible to determine a precise mean. The best that can be established is limits within which the mean will fall with a specified probability or confidence, usually taken as 95 percent. Again we need to ask, how precise a measurement do we need?

The definition of mathematical hope is essential to the design of a secure system. This concept relates the potential gain to the probability of obtaining the gain. Principle 8 allows the utility of a procedure to be expressed in both monetary and probabilistic terms. If the potential gain from a security system was a thousand dollars and the probability of achieving this gain was one in five hundred, a value of *two* (in arbitrary units) could be assigned. Equivalent values could be assigned to other combinations to allow comparison among alternatives. But why go to all this trouble for so little gain?

Principle 9 allows for the fact that any solution to a problem introduces risk. Risk-management solutions may fail, and this must be considered in the design stage. A backup system to provide redundancy is certainly to be considered, as well as the cost/benefit ratio for doing so. This principle is extensively used in the manufacture of commercial aircraft and the space shuttle, for obvious reasons.

The condition to be considered last is the situation where one of the alternatives to positive action is to do nothing. In some cases the risks, upon analysis, become insignificant; the decision may be to accept the possibility of loss, as the potential loss will not substantially affect assets. Principle 10 relates the amount and potential of risk to the wealth of the protected entity. A very profitable company may well afford to risk assets to maximize gains. The potential losses might be too great, however, for a less prosperous company, one that may be in greater need of relief from such occurrences. In some instances, then, the most cost-effective security is simply not to implement a plan or solution; in some others, it is to cover the potential loss by insurance.

To summarize, risk can be expressed in terms of probability of occurrence. The goal of security system design is to improve the ratio of favorable events to total events, or to reduce the ratio of unfavorable events. The basic technique used is to rate risks on their probability of occurrence and to establish economic values for potential risks and potential solutions. Where possible, redundant or backup systems may be specified to provide the needed degree of security. Risk probability is not a guarantee that because an event has a low probability and has occurred once, it will not occur again.

Statistical analysis as it is used in many fields — astronomy, agriculture, engineering, or insurance — is approached by basically using the procedures enumerated above.

Again, a word of caution — no statistical procedure can, in itself, ensure there will be no mistakes, inaccuracies, faulty reasoning, or incorrect conclusions. The data must be accurate, the methods properly applied, and the results interpreted by one with a thorough understanding of the field in which they are applied. That, after all, is the hallmark of the professional.

ESTIMATING FREQUENCY OF OCCURRENCE

Where experience has provided an adequate data base, loss expectancy can be projected with a satisfactory degree of confidence. If one leaves the keys in the ignition of an unlocked car on a downtown street in a high-crime area, it is just a question of time until the car is stolen.

In new situations, however, or in situations where data has not been or cannot be collected, we have insufficient knowledge upon which to base our projections. An example would be the kidnap of a high-risk-profile businessman in the absence of any prior threats or other indications that he had been targeted for kidnapping. In such instances, quantification of risk tends to be nothing more than educated guessing. It is in cases such as this that the services of an experienced security professional are needed to reduce subjectivity to an absolute minimum and to deal with the data available, limited though it may be, in a calm, objective manner. This is also true of international and domestic terrorism and, to a lesser degree, workplace violence. Amateurs tend to become very emotional — that is to say, less objective — when faced with such dangerous issues. The services of an outside consultant or a security professional trained in such matters are essential in cases of this nature, to ensure objective analysis from the outset.

4

QUANTIFYING AND PRIORITIZING LOSS POTENTIAL

> Security is more art than science. Few formulas will cover all organizations, situations and needs, and that's the beauty and challenge of our profession.
>
> *Richard D. Sem, CPP*
> Former president,
> International Security
> Management Association

As with any complex chain of interrelated issue, overall strength is measured by the weakest link. Very strong security in one area will not compensate for very weak security in another. In order to proceed to correct conclusions and then to recommendations for corrective action, it is necessary to quantify and prioritize the loss potentials. For the professional, here lies the most difficult task in the survey process — the task of measurement, or quantification, of exposure. Given adequate historical or empirical data, loss expectancy can be projected with a satisfactory degree of confidence. On the other hand, where there are insufficient data for reliable forecasting because the data either have not or cannot be collected, one is left with the nagging suspicion that conclusions will be nothing more than exercises in educated guessing — not that there is anything wrong in that.

Many risks may be classified as things that might happen but that have not yet occurred. Such risks can either be accepted or minimized, using prescribed preventive measures. Acceptance assumes that the risk is not sufficiently serious to justify the cost of reduction, or that recovery measures will ensure survival, or that cessation of operations, if the risk should occur in its most serious magnitude, is an acceptable alternative. Minimizing the risk presupposes that it is or may be serious enough to justify the cost of eliminating or reducing the possibility of its occurrence, and that recovery measures alone will not always be effective in ensuring survival. Also, it postulates that the remaining alternative — cessation of operations — is unacceptable.

It is at this juncture that quantifying or prioritizing the loss potential becomes the hallmark of the true professional. I have often told clients that it does not take much talent to prescribe an 85 percent solution for a 15 percent problem. Real talent comes into play when one is able to diagnose client problems correctly and recommend necessary countermeasures to solve them without engaging in overkill. Granted, when we err it must be on the side of prescribing more rather than less security, but not to the level that turns a college campus, hospital, or resort hotel into a Stalag 17 prisoner of war camp.

There are always several trade-offs when one considers the implementation of a new or improved security program. Cost is the most obvious. Less obvious and often overlooked are the inconvenience new security systems cause to personnel and the probable impact on employee morale, especially if the employees perceive (rightly or wrongly) that the inconvenience caused them is greater than the threat. This "solution" can cause more harm than if management had done nothing at all. As an example, excessive access-control systems installed in a computer department of an airline reservations center resulted in employees' propping doors open for simplicity of movement during working hours. When queried, the employees regarded the inconvenience as a bigger problem than unauthorized access.

ASSESSING CRITICALITY OR SEVERITY

Some authors refer to this stage of the survey as *assessing criticality or severity of occurrence*.[1] Regardless of what one calls the process, it is vital to search for and locate the proper benchmark to adequately approximate dollar values for the loss probabilities previously identified. Once this is done, the task of comparing the cure to the disease becomes simplified. One can then design a list of meaningful solutions with priorities based on a common denominator — the dollar. One technique in use is the three-stage approach, involving prevention, control, and recovery. *Prevention* attempts to stop undesirable incidents before they get started. *Control* seeks to keep these incidents from impacting assets, or, if impact occurs, to minimize the loss. *Recovery* restores the operation after assets have been adversely affected.

---

[1] T. J. Walsh and R. J. Healy, *The Protection of Assets Manual* (Santa Monica, Calif.: Merrit, 1974).

Many professionals take the approach that prevention is sufficient, and yet they opt for the installation of various control measures. It is one thing to install fire alarms that signal a serious situation; it is another to respond to and control a fire, and then recover from its effects. Similarly, it behooves a corporation not only to have adequate security in place to prevent kidnap attempts but to design a contingency plan to deal with the kidnap event should preventive measures fail and the event becomes an actuality. In addition, nothing mentioned above — prevention, detection, control, or contingency planning — will preclude the necessity of having adequate insurance to help recover from a serious fire or successful kidnap, extortion, and ransom event.

Another technique for assessing security is to prepare a segmented schedule of overhead, installation, and operating costs for the security project. All costs identified must be directly chargeable to expected benefits. In this process it is crucial to show that the benefits (risk prevention or reduction) will outweigh the cost. This is referred to as a *cost/benefit summary*, and is useful for both existing and proposed security programs and projects. (This will be more fully discussed in Chapter 5, "The Cost/Benefit Analysis.")

THE DECISION MATRIX

Another simple technique for prioritizing loss potential is the use of a frequency and severity loss matrix as an aid in making decisions about handling risk. Figure 4-1 uses the adjectives *high, medium,* and *low* as factors to measure both frequency and severity of loss.

Figure 4-1. Decision Matrix: A Risk-Handling Decision Aid

	Frequency of Loss		
Severity of Loss	*High*	*Medium*	*Low*
High	Avoidance	Loss prevention and avoidance	Transfer via insurance
Medium	Avoidance and loss prevention	Loss prevention and Transfer via insurance	Assumption and pooling
Low	Loss prevention	Loss prevention and assumption	Assumption

The quantification and prioritizing of loss potential should take into account the fact that there are both "intuitive" security control concepts, such as the installation of a burglar alarm at a warehouse, and security control concepts based on detailed cost/benefit analysis. An example of the latter is a multiple-stage electronic card-access control system for the research and development laboratory of a computer manufacturer. The procedure for both approaches will take into full consideration the following:

- Available information resources
- Reliable probability relationships
- Minimum time and resource requirements and availability
- Maximum incentives for management cooperation
- A *realistic* evaluation of existing or planned security control effectiveness.

The means of protection designed must always be tailored to the specific risk in the real day-to-day working environment of the specific entity being studied. The application of controls simply because they are recommended by some standard or acceptable practice, without regard to risk in the real-world environment, often results in controls that are inappropriate, ineffective, and costly. Worse, as so often seen with inappropriately planned closed-circuit television (CCTV), the controls may generate a false sense of security on the part of management.

For example, the author was once asked to review the installation of a CCTV security system for a newly constructed newspaper plant in California. The CCTV system had been designed for the corporation by a building and facilities engineer. The plant was located in a newly developed industrial park. The CCTV system had apparently been planned without regard to environmental considerations. Upon review, it was determined that the CCTV system — complete with zoom, tilt, and pan lenses as well as video cassette tape-recording functions, all very costly to install and maintain — was operating in an area that had heavy fog about six months of the year during nighttime hours. Further, the fence line, at its nearest point to the building, was 350 yards away from the closest camera lens! To the question "Why install CCTV at this location?" the answer was, "We have used CCTV successfully at all our other plants and it just seemed the natural thing to do here."

They did have CCTV at their other plants, but the fact of the matter was that in the plants inspected by this author, the CCTV systems were more often than not inoperative, in whole or in part, due to constant repairs needed to cameras, monitors, and video recording units. The CCTV systems were regarded by operations personnel as expensive toys that added little to the security of the facility. Management, however, was proud of its security program, having been lulled into a false sense of security by the presence of the CCTV cameras.

The assessment of risk, using actuarial methods to handle large numbers of events or situations, will be further examined in the following chapter. This technique has become generally reliable. However, in my experience, the entire exercise of estimating risks for a specific installation or complex is at best imprecise. The definition of risks by using highly specific numbers has not always been validated by experience. Several well-known authorities have concluded that order-of-magnitude expressions, such as *low, moderate,* and *high,* to indicate relative degrees of risk are more than adequate for most risk-control surveys.

"Low," "moderate," and "high" equate roughly with probability ranges of 1–3, 4–6, and 7–10, respectively. One is cautioned here to remember that even a low risk should be taken seriously if the potential damage (or danger) is assessed as being moderate to high. An example would be the kidnap for ransom of a high-profile business executive in a foreign country. We may regard the risk to be nearly nonexistent (low), but the potential danger of such an unfavorable event should always be rated as high.

5

COST/BENEFIT ANALYSIS

The optimum reduction of risk occurs at that point at which further reduction would cost more than the benefits to be gained.

Charles E. Hayden, CPP
Senior Security Consultant (Retired),
M & M Protection Consultants

When we use the systems approach to conduct security surveys, problems are properly identified, analyzed, and quantified in terms of the seriousness of their impacts on the operation or facility. Only solutions specifically responsive to a demonstrated need or requirement are considered. Only those tools or techniques that perform the needed task most effectively at the least possible cost are designed and introduced into the system. Efficiency versus cost is, then, the first phase of balancing the cost/benefit ratio, which is essential to the proper development and design of effective security countermeasures.

The following techniques are increasingly being used to analyze, develop, and design cost-effective security. This includes procedures, hardware (electronics), and manpower utilization programs.

SYSTEM DESIGN ENGINEERING

If a facility has a security program, a good systems engineer can review it and make recommendations to consolidate, coordinate, upgrade, and improve the existing protection. If no program exists, the systems engineer will design one that properly marries the best of the following into a comprehensive and cost effective security operation:

- Procedures (written guidelines)

- Hardware (lock and key controls, card access, anti-intrusion alarms)
- Manpower (guard service or security personnel).

This can be simply done by using one of many comprehensive review techniques, such as the one set forth in Appendix A, "Security Survey Work Sheets." By asking questions and directly observing certain operations, such as the adequacy of lights at night in an employee parking lot adjacent to a plant, one can reach certain definite conclusions. Elements of the security program (lights, locks, alarms, guard coverage, and so forth) are either adequate, inadequate, or nonexistent. Obviously the two former situations are a subjective matter, while the latter leaves no room for argument.

Other, more sophisticated programs use advanced electronic techniques. An example is electronic filtering as applied to access control in security programs for highly sensitive environments, such as research and development facilities. (For an example of an electronics security system specification, see Appendix H.) Additionally, we are seeing ever-increasing use of computer programs as a tool to conduct cost/benefit ratio and computer-design analysis. Whatever technique is used to determine the cost/benefit ratio, three basic criteria must be considered before the proper procedure or countermeasure is selected: cost, reliability, and delay.

Cost

Initially we are primarily concerned with acquisition cost, but we must also consider life-cycle and replacement-cost factors. For example, the initial base cost to recore and rekey the locks of an entire facility may be fifteen thousand dollars, plus 10 percent per year for inflation, or $22,500 after a lapse of five years.

For a key-and-lock system that includes changeable cores and an in-house capability for cutting keys, the initial capital outlay of fifteen thousand dollars might well be amortized over fifteen to twenty years instead of the original five years. Here we have considered all three factors: acquisition cost, the life of the system, and replacement cost. The same exercise can be accomplished for any type of hardware or electronics equipment with only a slight variation in computation.

Reliability

Reliability is especially critical with hardware and electronic devices, such as anti-intrusion and computerized card-access systems. The state of the art in electronics systems is advancing faster than most people can imagine, much less keep track of. Consequently, units are being manufactured, distributed, and installed before being properly field tested. This inevitably leads to certain difficulties — difficulties that, unless alleviated immediately, translate into expensive electronics systems designed to solve problems that in turn, because of unreliability, create new problems, which are sometimes worse than the original ones.

I know of only one solution to this situation: build two written requirements into the contract of proposal or purchase. First, require the successful bidder to present for your inspection and to demonstrate a like unit installed on a property with the same or similar security or access-control problems. It should be one that has been functioning for a minimum of six months without problems. Second, include a clause in the purchase contract withholding the last payment (payments are usually made upon signature [one-third], upon installation [one-third], and at final system acceptance) until the system has been on line for a sufficient test period, say ninety days, to ensure that the product is problem free and all bugs have been located and eliminated. Such a clause will make it in the supplier's best interest to get the unit fully operational in as short a time as possible.

A word of caution: no legitimate electronic security supplier will object to the inclusion of the above safeguard clauses. A supplier that balks at either or both cannot or will not guarantee satisfactory results for his or her system. This being the case, it would probably be in the best interest of the buyer to look for a supplier who will. Nothing is sadder to behold than a well-meaning director of security who has finally convinced management of the necessity for an expensive electronics system that, after acquisition, continually malfunctions. Although cost, like the state of the art, is ever changing, these sophisticated, computerized systems can be extremely expensive.

Delay

Time is the third factor to consider. How long will it take, in comparison to other countermeasures that could be used, before the recommended system can become fully operational? Here we may well have to consider the possibility of having more than one countermeasure operating at the same time until the primary system renders the secondary system obsolete or less critical.

An example is the introduction of a multilevel, electronic anti-intrusion and card-access system in a facility that houses separate functions under one roof. Some of these functions — such as the research and development laboratories, and the storage area in the warehouse, which contains a six-million-dollar inventory of easy-to-conceal and easy-to-sell items — may require differing levels of protection at different times.

It is probably going to be necessary to incur manpower costs: for a guard force to secure the premises twenty-four hours a day, seven days a week, until the new access system becomes fully operational. This amounts to 168 hours of guard service coverage. If each guard works a forty-hour shift, it will take 4.2 guards (taking into account time for relief, sick time, vacation, and so forth) to accomplish this task. The cost for this service, at $9.50 per hour, is:

168 hours × $9.50 per hour = $1,596.00 per week ($228.00 per day per post),

or

$6,890 per month, or $82,680 per year (365 days),

or

average monthly cost $7,068[1]

Needless to say, a prudent, cost-conscious director of security will make every effort to phase in the anti-intrusion card-access system and phase out or reduce the manpower requirements as early as possible.

BUILDING REDUNDANCY INTO THE SYSTEM

To achieve very high levels of reliability in security programs, one should consider building redundancy into them. An example is the use of multiple smoke sensors in a computer facility to warn of the incipient stages of a potentially disastrous fire. The old saying, "One may well survive a burglary, but a good fire can put you out of business forever," has much meaning for a computer library. If we install a multiple-use smoke sensor (one that uses all three detection techniques — ionization, infrared, and the photoelectric cell), the chance of all its modes failing at the same time is statistically ten thousand to one. Yet in terms of cost, these units can be commercially obtained for less than $150 each — a small outlay compared to the cost of replacing even the least expensive computer equipment, not to mention the potential catastrophe of losing the materials stored in a computer library, due to a fire that could have been detected.

Redundancy can also be accomplished by designing a proprietary alarm system, which for a few dollars more can be remotely monitored by a

---

[1] The average monthly cost is arrived at by dividing annual dollars by twelve months. For more specific and detailed costing, the daily rate times the number of days in a given month may be used. Thus, $228 × 30 = $6,890, and 156 × 31 = $7,068. For accounting purposes one can use the same formula to compute the cost of any guard service contract.

central alarm station as an added backup, against the possibility of a power or human failure at the facility's own alarm console. The costs — a dedicated lease line and a rental (monitoring) fee — are relatively inexpensive.

In museums, multiple redundant systems are a common technique. The items on display in a museum must be readily available for the viewing public; thus, security must be as unobtrusive as possible. Many of these same items, however, are one-of-a-kind art objects and therefore priceless. Security in the daytime, functional though minimal, may include uniformed security guards, closed-circuit television, antipenetration display case alarms (local, audible, and remote), and anti-tamper or antiremoval switches behind picture frames or on wall mounts. For nighttime security, multiple anti-intrusion sensors and motion detectors may be activated to ensure that if people penetrate the perimeter barriers (such as a remain-behind burglar), their movement and presence inside the museum will be detected by multiple sensing devices. Any one of them can be circumvented or might not be fully operational; nevertheless, the odds against all of the devices failing at the same time and therefore not detecting the presence of an intruder are statistically in the thousands, virtually impossible.

The selection of the right countermeasures to control or minimize the previously identified risks will take into consideration the facts that written procedures are less expensive than hardware but hardware (including electronics) is less expensive than manpower. So when looking for the proper "fix," it is well to start with the basics and then work one's way up to the more complex and, thus more costly, fixes.

As an example, there may be no adequate substitute for the use of mechanical equipment, fences, gates, locks, safes, and vaults. In some locations, however, local real estate codes, covenants, and restrictions (known as CCRs) may prohibit the installation of a seven-foot chain-link fence with the usual three-strand barbed-wire top overhang. In these instances, not uncommon in industrial parks, one must retreat to the exterior wall of the building or buildings as the place to begin perimeter security. It may then become necessary to use electronics, alarms, a computerized console, closed-circuit television, and an exterior and interior watch-clock patrol to provide adequate security.

A SECURITY COUNTERMEASURE

If the above problem is encountered in a new industrial park, one possible solution is to prepare your security countermeasure plan in stages or increments, such as Stage 1, 2, and 3, or Increment A, B, and C. In this technique we cost out the use of each of the required systems in terms of the minimum level of security that one or more of them will provide. Then, we move up to

Stage 2 and 3, adding more security measures to the building or complex, adding ever-increasing cost to the project's countermeasures plan.

This type of program is relatively easy to explain and hence to sell to management. The underlying philosophy is, "We will try Stage 1 or Increment A first, at X dollars. Should Stage 1 (Increment A) fail to provide the needed level of security, we then move to Stage 2 (Increment B), and so on, until we solve the problem." This technique will prevent the all too commonly encountered security "overkill" situation. A security risk properly accessed as in the 15 percent range does not need an 85 percent solution, nor can management afford one. Yet given a brand-new environment, such as a recently developed industrial park in a suburban area, who is to say exactly what level of security will actually be needed? In the absence of empirical knowledge to the contrary, our system countermeasure design technique is both efficient and cost effective. What it says to top management is, "We can start out with the basics, which are the most effective for the least money, and then add to the system (at greater cost) as we develop the necessary historical data to justify spending more money."

Most cost-effective security systems use a combination of manpower and hardware (electronics) to achieve the proper countermeasures balance. The first edition of *Risk Analysis and the Security Survey*, in 1980, made the following prediction: "In the next decade we will see more use of security systems that integrate many separate functions, systems that are developed, manufactured, sold, installed, and maintained by one company. These systems will integrate security, communications, fire, life safety, building management, and energy control from one central console or command control center. The big users will be high-rise office buildings, retail stores, and shopping malls. Specialized units will be developed for use at airports, oil refineries, and electronics manufacturing plants, to name a few." This prediction became an actuality within five years.

In conclusion, even the best-designed countermeasures system must be proven to be cost effective before it can be sold to management. Only by reducing or integrating the largest cost factor, manpower, and replacing it where practical with procedures, hardware, and electronics can we achieve more effective security at less cost. This is a proven technique. Finally, whenever dealing with security vendors, be it for manpower, hardware, or electronics, obtain a minimum of three bids based on a written specification of requirements. Competitive bids are not only a proven, cost-effective technique, but they tend to keep everyone honest. Bidders should be advised of the competition, but not necessarily the identities of the other competitors. Sole-source procurement is seldom cost effective and more often than not provides fertile ground for financial manipulation, which is seldom in the client's best interest.

6

THE SECURITY SURVEY: AN OVERVIEW

> The Boy Scouts and Darwin had it right: "If you don't prepare, you won't survive!"
> *John Lay, President*
> Contingency Management Associates,
> Moraga, California

The goal of risk management — to manage risk effectively at the least possible cost — cannot be achieved without reducing, through a total management commitment, the number of incidents that lead to losses.[1] Before any risk can be eliminated (or for that matter, reduced) it must be identified. One proven method of accomplishing this task is the security survey. Charles A. Sennewald, author and security consultant, has defined the security survey as "The primary vehicle used in a security assessment is the survey. The survey is the process whereby one gathers data that reflects the who, what, how, where, when and why of the client's existing operation. The survey is the fact-finding process."[2]

WHY ARE SECURITY SURVEYS NEEDED?

The latest reports estimate that the cost of fraud and abuse to American business is in excess of forty billion dollars per year and rising. The biggest problem, and the one we see most often, is that most corporate managers do

---

[1] The field of risk management encompasses much more than security and safety. These two subjects, however, are the cornerstones of most effective risk-management programs.

[2] Charles A. Sennewald, CPP, *Security Consulting*, 2d ed. (Boston: Butterworth-Heinemann, 1996).

not even know if they have a problem. Worse, many do not even *want* to know that they have a problem! Some managers seem to prefer to keep things as they are and to regard any suggestion of a need for increased security as direct or indirect criticism of their abilities to manage their operations. Nevertheless, where fraud exists, most general business security surveys calculate losses at 6 percent of annual revenue; some surveys we have conducted have concluded that losses attributable to theft equaled or exceeded profits. This is especially likely for chain-store operations, where each individual store is regarded as a separate profit center and records of inventory shortages are kept for each location by local managers.

Crime losses far exceed the losses to business caused by fire and industrial accidents. One professional security organization estimates that the annual loss to business from fraud and abuse is twice as great as the total of all business losses due to fire and accident!

Are you really concerned about how crime may affect your business? Take a few minutes and read the 1996 Association of Certified Fraud Examiners Report, *To the Nation on Occupational Fraud and Abuse*. Then take a moment to reflect on the following estimates:

- The average organization loses more than 9 percent a day per employee to fraud and abuse.
- The average organization loses about 6 percent of its total annual revenue to fraud and abuse committed by its own employees.
- Fraud and abuse cost U.S. organizations more than $400 billion annually.

In the United States alone, estimates of the cost of fraud vary widely. No recent comprehensive studies could be found which empirically measured the economic effects of fraud and abuse. In addition to the direct economic losses to the organization from fraud and abusive behavior, there are indirect costs to be considered: The loss of productivity, legal action, increased unemployment, government intervention, and other hidden costs.

WHO NEEDS SECURITY SURVEYS?

A Stanford Research Institute report, *Business Property Security*, discussing business vulnerability to crime loss, states, "Likely victims are growing businesses where expansion occurs faster than control systems are set up and large companies where close control over branches and divisions is not feasible." This fact has been noted by many professional security consultants with whom the author has discussed the subject, but every business entity, no matter how large or small, could profit from an objective survey of their security protection. Most surveys show that the majority of business security concern is directed toward external problems, such as theft (burglary and robbery), as the most immediate priority. This situation reflects the development and growth of security in the United States, from a historical perspective: it was once thought that most, if not all, of a company's problems with theft were external in nature.

Up until World War II, before the large-scale expansion of U.S. and Canadian industry and the development of the multinational corporation, many companies in North America were what we now regard as small to medium-sized industries and businesses. Many retail enterprises were of the "Mom and Pop" variety. Because of close supervision and the personal identification between management and labor that existed, internal theft (that is, by "trusted" employees) was seldom considered, much less planned for. Hence, the fire and burglar alarm business developed and proliferated to protect these enterprises from what they considered their internal and external threats, their two "worst enemies."

With the growth of the national and multinational corporations and the almost total demise of the "Mom and Pop" commercial and variety stores, we witnessed a parallel change in business ethics and standards. These changes also affected society as a whole. As an example, in the turbulent 1960s, a new term was coined: the "Establishment." Crimes against the Establishment were then, and still are, perceived by many to be permissible, in fact not crimes at all. The lack of personal identification with a company by its employees and the dramatic dilution of ethical and moral standards among the general public combined to make internal theft by employees a simple process of rationalization. After all, who *is* General Motors, AT&T, or Safeway? "They" make gigantic profits by "ripping off" the general population (read *us*). "They won't miss one small wrench or screwdriver that I need for my workshop at home." The theft of one small item, multiplied ten thousand times each year in many large companies, adds up to an annual loss that can far exceed the total loss to external theft over the entire period of a firm's corporate existence!

Enlightened students of criminology now understand that the most predominant, certainly the most prevalent, form of business crime is employee theft in its various forms. Asset misappropriation accounts for more than four out of five employee thefts. Bribery and corruption account for about 10 percent of the offenses. Companies with a hundred or fewer employees are the most vulnerable to fraud and abuse.[3] Businesses reporting

---

[3] Association of Certified Fraud Examiners, *1996 Report to the Nation.*

a million dollars of revenue per year are particularly hard hit by crime. This is especially true for a retail enterprise that operates on a 2 percent profit margin, or a grocery store that has a 1 percent profit line. As serious students of this problem have come to realize, losses due to crime can and do have a dramatic impact on net profits.

Shoplifting, employee theft, and vandalism all cost American business billions of dollars annually. Exhibit 6-1, based on percentage of a company's net profit, illustrates how much more a company needs to sell to offset losses in stolen merchandise, equipment, and supplies. The theft of one five-hundred-dollar fax machine means the company must sell twenty-five thousand dollars' worth of merchandise to break even, if it is in the 2 percent net-profit category, $8,333 if it is in the 6 percent category. Worse yet, it is still without one fax machine. For an example of the impact of loss versus net profits, see Figure 6-1.

ATTITUDE OF BUSINESS TOWARD SECURITY

In general, we find that most businesses will take the necessary precautions to protect themselves against the entry of burglars and robbers onto their premises. Most will also give protection to high-value areas, such as computer centers, vaults, precious-metal storage areas, and any location where money is the principal product, such as banks and casinos. Many businesses,

Figure 6-1. Loss to Sales (Profit) Ratio

	If Company Operates at Net Profit of:				
Actual Loss of:	2%	3%	4%	5%	6%
	These additional sales are required to offset an actual loss:				
$ 50	$ 2,500	$ 1,666	$ 1,250	$ 1,000	$ 833
100	5,000	3,333	2,500	2,000	1,666
200	10,000	6,666	5,000	4,000	3,333
250	12,500	8,333	6,250	5,000	4,166
300	15,000	10,000	7,500	6,000	5,000
350	17,500	11,666	8,750	7,000	5,833
400	20,000	13,333	10,000	8,000	6,666
450	22,500	15,000	11,250	9,000	7,500
500	25,000	16,666	12,500	10,000	8,333

however, still do not concern themselves with protection against unauthorized access to their premises — yet 75 percent to 85 percent of external theft is directly attributable to this source. A prime example is unrestricted access at many warehouses we have surveyed to the shipping and receiving docks by nonemployee truck drivers.

Likewise, if the cost of security protection is regarded as a capital expense or a yearly expenditure, and as reducing the profit line, we can expect the person in charge of that facility to authorize only the minimum and least expensive security protection possible. If, on the other hand, security is required by corporate management or mandated by clients or the various governmental agencies overseeing industries engaged in sensitive government contracts, we find plant managers installing security protection without regard to costs (nuclear power generating plants, for example).

This latter proposition presupposes another problem. Most plant managers with whom we have worked do not have the foggiest idea what kind of security they need for adequate protection. For sensitive government-contract work, security guidelines are sometimes available. Nevertheless, many are the managers who have fallen prey to the sales pitches of security manpower and hardware salesmen who proposed package deals guaranteed to solve all problems. As a result, we constantly encounter security programs that overemphasize manpower (guards) or hardware (alarms or electronics) when the proper solution to the problem is an effective marriage of the two, coupled with adequate written procedures to deal with the most common occurrences or eventualities encountered in the real, work-a-day world. Life becomes complicated only if we allow it to.

WHAT CAN A SECURITY SURVEY ACCOMPLISH?

One approach to determining whether or not there is a need for a security survey is to find out what services an experienced security expert can provide and then seek information on security (crime)-related losses being incurred by the particular business or company. The security expert can either be in place, that is to say a member of the staff, or an outside consultant, or a combination of both.

Security-related problems might detect any of the problems mentioned in the early chapters of this book. Surveys generally, however, show that most problems encountered in the real world of security are not uncommon ones.

If the company or facility being considered has a security plan, the survey can establish whether the plan is up to date and adequate in every respect. Experience has shown that many security plans were established as the needs of the moment dictated; most were developed without regard to centralization and coordination. Upon review, many such plans are patched-up, crazy-quilt affairs. More often than not the policies, procedures, and safeguards need to be brought together and consolidated so that the component parts complement, not contradict, one another.

If the facility has no security plan, the survey can establish the need for one and develop proposals for some or all of the security services commonly found in industrial settings. By conducting a comprehensive survey of the entire facility — its operations and procedures — one can identify critical factors affecting the security of the premises or operation. The next step is to analyze the vulnerabilities and recommend cost-effective protection. The survey should also recommend, as the first order of business, the establishment of policies and procedures to, as a minimum:

- Protect against internal and external theft, including embezzlement, fraud, burglary, robbery, industrial espionage, and the theft of trade secrets and proprietary information.
- Develop access-control procedures to protect the facility perimeter as well as computer facilities and executive offices located inside.
- Establish lock and key-control procedures.
- Design, supervise, and review installation of anti-intrusion and detection systems.
- Establish a workplace violence program to help corporate personnel deal with internal and external threats.
- Provide control over the movement and identification of employees, customers, and visitors on company property.
- Review the selection, training, and deployment of security personnel, proprietary or contract.
- Assist in the establishment of emergency and disaster plans and guidelines.
- Identify the internal resources available and needed for the establishment of an effective security program.
- Develop and present instructional seminars for management and operations personnel in all the above areas.

The above list is by no means all-inclusive. It does, however, set forth some of the most frequently needed programs and systems recommended for development by security surveys this author has conducted.

WHY THE NEED FOR A SECURITY PROFESSIONAL?

Losses due to all causes continue to represent a problem of major proportions for business and industry. To the extent that the services of security professionals can help in eliminating, preventing, or controlling a company's losses, they are needed. At a security management seminar, Charles Sennewald, CPP once explained, "Crime prevention, the very essence of a security professional's existence, is another spoke in the wheel of total loss control. It is the orderly and predictive identification, abatement, and response to criminal opportunity. It is a managed process which fosters the elimination of the emotional crisis response to criminal losses and promotes the timely identification of exposures to criminality before these exposures mature to a confrontation process." The proper application of protection techniques to minimize loss opportunity promises the capability not only to improve the net profits of business but also to reduce to acceptable levels the frequency of most disruptive acts, the consequences of which often exceed the fruits of the crime.

HOW DO YOU SELL SECURITY?

As mentioned earlier in this chapter, some managers, for a variety of reasons, are reluctant even to discuss the subject of security. In the aftermath of an unsuccessful attempt to burglarize a bank vault, a bank operations manager learned that the anti-intrusion system was ten years old and somewhat anti-quated. "Why didn't the alarm company keep me advised of the necessity to upgrade my system as the state of the art improved?" he asked. The answer he received was, "The alarm system functioned adequately for ten years with no problem. Would you or the bank have authorized an expenditure of five thousand dollars to upgrade the alarm system before you had this attempted burglary?" The bank representative reluctantly admitted that he would not have. This case is typical of what we call the "knee-jerk reaction" to security. One security consultant with whom the author is acquainted describes it as locking the barn after the horse has been stolen. We all know that the only thing this protects is what the horse-thief left behind.

Nevertheless, it is not uncommon to find that management's attention is obtained only after a serious problem, one pointing to the lack of adequate protection, is brought to its attention. The first reaction is often one of overkill; the response pendulum swings from complacency to paranoia, when the facts indicate that a proper response should be somewhere in between. Given this situation, an unscrupulous alarm salesman will pre-scribe an electronics system worthy of consideration by the manager of the bullion vault at Fort Knox. The true professional will, as the first order of business, try to bring the situation into true prospective by calming the fears of the clients.

There are some things a security director or consultant can do to con-vince top corporate management that security is worth spending some money to obtain. Some methods that have proven successful are listed below.

1. Establish a meaningful dialogue with the decision makers in the management hierarchy. First, try to ascertain their feelings about security. What do they really want a security program to accomplish for them, if in fact they want anything? Do not be surprised to learn that some management personnel regard security as a necessary evil and thus worthy of little attention (that is, money or resources). Marshal the facts. Research the history of security losses experienced by the company and use this information to develop trend projections.

2. When collecting data to support your position, deal in principles, not personalities. Use the technique of nonattribution for all unpublished sources of information. With published sources, such as interoffice memos, excerpt the pertinent data if possible. Avoid internecine power struggles at all costs. Maintain a position of objective neutrality.

3. Be as professional about security as you can. The better you are at your job, the greater attention you will command from your clients. There are many avenues you can explore to develop the information you need, such as developing contacts with other security professionals who share similar problems. Don't reinvent the wheel: attend security seminars, purchase relevant books, study, and do research.

4. In making a proposal to management, hit the highlights and make your proposal as brief as possible. Save the details for later. In any proposal that will cost money, make certain you have developed the cost figures as accurately as possible. If the figures are estimated, label them as such and err on the high side.

5. It is a wise man or woman who knows his or her own limitations. If you need outside help (and who doesn't from time to time?), do not be reluctant to admit it. Such areas as electronics, computers, and sophisticated anti-intrusion alarm systems are usually beyond the capabilities of the security generalist. Do some studying. Know where to go to get the help you need.

6. Suggest that management hire an outside consultant. Competent security professionals have nothing to fear from a "second opinion." Often, the "expert from afar" has greater persuasiveness over management than do members of their own staff. More often than not the consultant will reinforce your position by reaching the same conclusions you did and making the same or similar recommendations.

7. Present your position at the right time. Recognize that management's priorities are first and foremost the generation of profit. In order to

capture management's attention, wait for the right circumstances. It is difficult to predict when this may occur; therefore, have your facts developed and be ready at a moment's notice to make your presentation. It will be too late to do the research when you are called before the board of directors without notice to explain how the breakdown in security that just happened could have occurred, and what you propose to do to solve the problem for the future.

8. Develop a program of public relations. Security represents inconvenience, even under the best of circumstances. Once you have management thinking favorably about your proposal, you will need to sell it to everyone in the organization in order for it to be successfully implemented. Most employees enjoy working in a safe and secure environment. Use this technique to convince employees that the program was designed as much for their safety and security as for the protection of the assets of the corporation.

For a comprehensive treatment of the role a professional security consultant can play and how they can help the security professionals properly define their security exposures, refer to Charles A. Sennewald's 1996 text *Security Consulting*, second edition, published by Butterworth-Heinemann. Do your homework in a thorough manner, and you cannot help but impress management with your capabilities as a security professional. Remember, be patient. Few have been able to sell 100 percent of their security programs to management the first time out of the starting blocks.

7

MANAGEMENT AUDIT TECHNIQUES AND THE PRELIMINARY SURVEY

The objective of a preliminary survey is to quickly and economically determine if a [security] survey (audit) appears to be desirable and is technically and economically feasible.

Government Accounting
Office (GAO)

AUDIT GUIDE AND PROCEDURES

Audit: Aids to Surveys

The vast majority of my colleagues found their way to the security field by way of law enforcement, military police, or intelligence activities. Many law enforcement officers have had training as investigators, but few have received training as internal auditors.

There are many similarities between auditing and investigating, but there is one important difference: the audit technique of analyzing facts, drawing conclusions, and making recommendations is absent from the investigator's background and training. Investigators are trained to obtain evidence, report objectively, and scrupulously avoid drawing conclusions or making recommendations. These they leave for their clients. The late J. Edgar Hoover, director of the Federal Bureau of Investigation, was often quoted as saying, "An investigator may be wrong in his opinions, but he must never be wrong in reporting the facts of an investigation. Opinions are best left for others to deal with."

This is not to suggest that investigators do not have opinions or draw conclusions from the results of their efforts. They have and they do, but one will look in vain for these thoughts in the investigator's reports. Investigators are taught never to editorialize but to leave opinions for "the expert witness." Such training, of course, has a real purpose: it is a proven technique for ensuring objectivity and avoiding the trap of partiality in the difficult search for the truth.

The auditor, however, is trained to appraise the truth or falsity of a proposition — not to take things for granted, jump to conclusions, or accept plausible appearance for hard fact. Audit training postulates that accepting appearance for substance is the surest way to arrive at improper conclusions. To be able to differentiate between appearance and substance and draw the proper conclusions is the heart and marrow of the auditor's task.

Both disciplines, to be sure, pursue fact — a *fact* being something that has actual existence, something that can be inferred with certainty, a proposition that is verifiable. Conjecture, on the other hand, involves propositions carrying insufficient evidence to be regarded as facts. The auditor is trained not only to adduce facts but to appraise, draw conclusions, and make recommendations from them — the very techniques the investigator is trained to avoid.

In conducting security surveys, one can and should borrow some of the techniques used by internal auditors. It can be said that most security surveys are, in the truest sense, specialized internal audits. In this context, I define internal (management) auditing as "a comprehensive review, verification, analysis, and appraisal of the various functions (operations) of an organization, as a service to management."

The auditor works with people first and things second, as does the investigator. Both auditing and investigating presuppose a degree of cooperation from the people one encounters along the path to the objective, that path usually being the obtaining of complete information and accurate data, in proper perspective. Successful professionals often obtain this cooperation through the force of their personalities and an empathetic attitude that invariably draws other people out. These individuals, by training or by instinct, understand the art and science of communication — what opens channels and what closes them. But let there be no misunderstanding: both the auditor and the investigator are often feared. Both represent a force and authority that can be a threat to liberty and security, an unknown quantity that can adversely affect one's status and well-being, even one's job and livelihood.

The first task of the professional, then, is to allay that fear, because fear is a very real impediment to communication, whereas open communication is at the heart of both a successful investigation and a successful audit. There are many techniques that can be used to allay fear, but perhaps the quickest is the use of candor — letting people know, up front, what to expect. It has been said that we often fear most that about which we know the least. Therefore, in the absence of sound justification to the contrary, there should be complete candor and rapport from the outset of the survey or audit until its conclusion. This brings us to some of the methods used by auditors in conducting successful surveys.

Field Work

The great majority of survey work, perhaps as much as 50 percent, is done in the field. The other 50 percent is usually divided equally between planning the survey and writing the final report. However, some security consultants state that they often spend as much or more time writing the survey report as they did conducting the field-work portion of the survey, especially in complicated reviews.

Field work, as considered here, consists of collecting, arraying, and analyzing data, records, and procedures wherever they are found, a process that may have an effect on the operation and thus on the results of the survey. Reduced to its simplest terms, field work is largely measurement and evaluation of the effectiveness of the security program (or the lack of one) under review.

To be meaningful, measurement must have as its basis an objective standard. By *standard* I mean a level of acceptability against which things measured can be compared. Each part of the survey must be approached with the thought that it can be effective if it determines quality in terms that can be objectively measured and compared with an acceptable practice or standard, if one exists.

Only by using these criteria can one measure intelligently and with objectivity. Where surveyors cannot measure, they must use extreme caution, because in such a case they can produce only subjective observations, not objective reports based on recognized standards or accepted practices. Where no standards or acceptable practices exist, obviously the surveyor must construct them. Likewise, where only technical standards exist, measurements obtained must be validated by one who is technically qualified to render a judgment. As surveyors apply recognized standards or acceptable practices, they must not hesitate to evaluate them to see if they are obsolete. It is no understatement to say that without standards or acceptable practices there can be no meaningful measurement; without measurement, in turn, field work becomes conjecture and not fact. Remember the saying, "If it can be measured, it's a fact; otherwise it's an opinion."

There are many methods and approaches to field work, and the one selected often depends on the individual approach of the person making the survey. Nevertheless, field work usually takes the form of observing, questioning, analyzing, verifying, investigating, and evaluating, though not necessarily in that order.

Measurements normally concern at least three aspects of the security operation: quality, reliability, and cost. (Obviously more than three aspects can be programmed into the survey, depending upon the results desired.) Regardless of how many aspects of the operation are being reviewed, the primary questions become: Is the procedure, technique, hardware, or electronic device being used effective? Does it properly address and solve the problem, with a known degree of reliability? Does it perform at less cost than others that might be just as (or more) effective with respect to the problems faced and the overall objective or results desired?

The objective of measurement is to assess the adequacy, effectiveness, and efficiency of an existing or proposed system. This is accomplished by applying six basic forms or methods of field work.

Observing. Observing is seeing, not just noticing or looking. As Sherlock Holmes was fond of saying, "You see, Watson, but you do not observe." — Arthur Conan Doyle. Observing implies a careful knowledgeable look at people, things, and how they relate one to the other. It is a visual examination with a purpose, a mental comparison with practices and standards. The ability to view and evaluate. The broader one's experience, the better one observes and the more alert one is to deviations from the norm.

Questioning. Questioning during a survey occurs at every stage of the proceeding. It may be in oral or written form. Oral questions, of course, are the most common and at times the most difficult to pose. To get the truth without upsetting people during the course of a survey is not an easy assignment. If subjects detect an attitude of cross-examination or an inquisitorial tone, they may promptly raise their defenses, which become barriers to communication. The results may be wrong or incomplete answers or, worse, no answers at all. Most successful practitioners have developed the interview technique into an art. They use this, perhaps the most common tool of our trade, with a high degree of effectiveness.

Analyzing. Analyzing is nothing more than a detailed examination of a complex entity to determine the true nature of its individual parts. It presupposes an intent to discover hidden qualities, causes, effects, motives, and other possibilities. In contrast, if one examines an operation as a whole, one cannot perceive the intricate relationships of the diverse and varied elements that make up a complex function or an unusually large activity. Any composite, no matter how large or complex, can be analyzed by division, by breaking it down into its separate elements and then observing trends, making comparisons, and isolating aberrant transactions and conditions. Frankly, the job can be done no other way.

Verifying. One verifies by attesting to the truth, accuracy, genuineness, or validity of the matter under scrutiny or inquiry. This implies a deliberate effort to establish the accuracy or truth of some affirmation, by putting it to the test. An example is a comparison with other ascertainable facts, with an original, or perhaps with another acceptable practice or standard. Verification might also include corroboration — the statement of another person or a validation by objective practices or standards, usually found elsewhere.

Investigating. An investigation is an inquiry that has as its aim the uncovering of facts and the obtaining of evidence to establish the truth. An investigation may occur as a part, or as the result, of a survey, but it is not restricted to some impropriety. If it is in fact to be restricted to an impropriety, it must be divorced immediately from the survey and referred to the proper authorities within the entity being surveyed for appropriate handling.

It is not unusual in the course of a security survey to uncover suspected fraud. Colleagues of mine and I did just that in the course of a security survey at a large hospital and medical complex. The receiving (intake) office had a thief, who had been stealing patients' valuables; the discovery necessitated a separate inquiry, which proved successful and produced a conviction. When uncovered, fraud must be dealt with outside of the scope of the review. (See Appendix B, "Danger Signs of Fraud, Embezzlement, and Theft.")

Evaluating. To evaluate is to estimate worth by arriving at a judgment. It is to weigh what has been analyzed and determining its adequacy, effectiveness, and efficiency. It is one step beyond opinion, in that it represents the conclusions drawn from accumulated facts. Evaluation, by necessity, implies professional judgment. Professional judgment is a thread that runs through the entire fabric of the security survey.

Evaluation in a survey occurs constantly throughout the duration of the project. In the beginning, one must determine which programs and procedures will be reviewed, which processes and operations are to be tested, and how big a sample must be obtained for the test to achieve the degree of sample-reliability needed. Finally, as the results of the survey accumulate, one must evaluate what the results imply — fact-finding without evaluation is a clerical, not a professional, function.

Evaluation obviously calls for judgment, and this is perhaps the real test of the true professional. There are bound to be questions and imponderables. If you find none, it may be time to leave well enough alone and get out of the game. The true art is in recognizing where the questions lie: once we identify the problem, we are well along the way toward the solution. Like a doctor making a diagnosis, only by properly identifying the problem can the security professional adequately prescribe the solution.

Mature professionals evaluate results almost intuitively, and more often than not they are correct. We of lesser experience can benefit from a more structured, formal, and organized approach to the evaluation of the results obtained. For example, in evaluating a failure to meet specific standards or acceptable practices, one might ask the following questions:

- How significant are these deviations?
- Have they or will they prevent the operation from achieving its objective or mission?
- Who or what can be hurt or injured?
- Could the injury perhaps be fatal to the enterprise?
- If corrective action is not taken, would the deviation be likely to reoccur?
- How did the problem surface in the first place?
- What were the causes? What event or combination of events caused the failure to occur?
- Will the event or combination of events cause the observed results or failure every time?

Obviously, in order to recommend corrective action, we must answer some basic questions. In following these procedures surveyors find themselves in a constant posture of evaluating. One must constantly query everything under review, with questions such as:

- What is the *real* problem? (Not necessarily what management thinks it is — what is it really?)
- What are the relevant facts? What are the processes, systems, procedures, policies, organizational structures, people? What were they in the past? What will they be in the future?
- What is presently being done about this problem at other locations within the company? At other companies?
- What are the causes? The number and variety of causes? The root cause as well as the surface cause? When and how do these causes affect the overall problem?
- What are the possible solutions, the alternatives, the cost, and the answers to the problem? What are the possible side effects, advantages, or disadvantages to the proposed solution?

Only by constant probing, questioning, analyzing, and evaluating do surveyors uncover system and performance defects, establish reliability, and develop cost-effective solutions to their clients' problems.

THE PRELIMINARY SURVEY

Definition and Purpose

The basic purpose of the preliminary survey is familiarization, based on more than a mere observation of the tasks to be reviewed. It presupposes an ability to perceive the true objectives of the operation and to locate and evaluate the key control points, if any exist. Also, one must understand the management concepts being used and the qualifications and abilities of the employees responsible for the success of the operation. (See Box 7-1 for statement of purpose.) The properly planned and implemented preliminary survey will allow one to develop a well-thought-out program, to deploy one's efforts efficiently and economically, and to form a firm foundation for the detailed examination that follows.

While a poor preliminary survey (or none at all) can easily result in a poor audit, a good preliminary survey can ensure an intelligent examination and may also substitute for many parts of the final examination. It is the simplest way to cut through the mass of detail that often obscures the objective and to get the job started quickly and on the right track. Another advantage of the preliminary survey is to test the client's sincerity and avoid misunderstandings as to the details of the project at the outset.

Many security and safety operations in large companies are extremely complex. The immediate task becomes one of not only identifying and understanding these operations but also of analyzing and evaluating them and recommending improvements designed to accomplish the job with greater efficiency and at less cost. Admittedly, this is no easy task in a large and complex industrial environment. This is especially so when one adds to the already identified internal complexity of the operation such factors as the external environment (community), legal restrictions, ecological and environmental protection procedures; public relations; employee relations; union activities; government regulations and restrictions (especially the Occupational Safety and Health Administration, or OSHA); and stockholder interest.

As complicated as the assignment may appear initially, it is well to remember that there is no mass of data so large, and no operation so complex, that it cannot be given a semblance of order and then arrayed, evaluated, and summarized in a logical, organized, methodical manner.

A preliminary survey should answer at least the following questions:

- What is the operation?
- Who or what does the operation?
- Why is it done (where and when)?
- How is the operation accomplished?

Attention: Name of Client

Reference: University of _____

The preliminary survey will be a primary overview of the university to identify major problem areas within the system affecting security. This becomes
the basis for defining the parameters of the final survey. It includes:

- Interview of officials concerned with administration of revenue
  producing and accounting programs to identify loss exposure and
  experience fully.
- A physical tour of selected campus locations to familiarize consultant with the university.
- Preliminary interviews with selected on-site operations personnel
  for basic orientation with cash handling methods and control procedures.

The agreed upon scope of the final survey will emphasize internal control procedures with physical security and emergency planning secondary. A complete evaluation will include specific recommendations for appropriate
administrative controls, hardware application and personnel to complement
the system already in use to achieve effective cost control security.

We will also provide down stream inspection to insure that agreed upon recommendations are being properly implemented.

Regards,

James F. Broder, CPP
Security Consultant

PMG

Box 7-1. Preliminary Survey — Statement of Purpose

In short, get what is important, and get it with a minimum of delay.
Focus on the highlights and forget, for the moment, the details; they will
come later. However, don't let haste interfere with order and methodology.
To go into the program's initial operation without a well-prepared agenda
may well leave the client with the impression of disorganization, the exact

opposite of what one would hope to instill at this (or any other) stage of the security review.

The author and Charles Sennewald, were once contacted to do a physical security survey of three large manufacturing plants in and near Bombay, India. The client asked for a brief proposal outlining our plan to complete this complex project. We recommended the preliminary survey approach and estimated the cost (travel, time, and expenses) to do the job and to write the preliminary survey report.

Our planned approach was well thought out; the preliminary survey was to represent about three days (that is, a total of twenty-four hours) of consulting time. Upon submission, however, our bid was rejected, because the client had expected us to absorb the cost associated with the preliminary survey, in return for the privilege of being selected (maybe) to do the big project, which would probably have taken about six months to complete.

We later learned that this was the customary way some people in that country did business. Had we known this fact beforehand, we would probably have declined to submit a proposal. Notwithstanding, we sent management a letter of thanks for the opportunity to bid on the project.

The Initial Interview

At the initial interview (or "opening conference" in audit parlance), the nature of the questions asked will vary depending on whether the survey is organizational, functional, or operational. If it is organizational, people-oriented questions will be the general rule. Functional surveys are more concerned with the actual work flow, which more often than not crosses organizational lines. In operational surveys, one is primarily interested in hardware and, to a lesser degree, in software or related procedures concerned with the effective use of the hardware being utilized. Regardless of the type of survey, the initial interview should elicit the following: What does management perceive to be the major problem areas? What does management hope the survey will accomplish in regard to solving these problems?

At the initial interview it is well to have prepared in final form a document called the *management memorandum*. This memorandum, to be signed by the highest authority possible, introduces the survey team, describes the objective of the survey, solicits the assistance and cooperation of all company employees, and authorizes access to all documents and information that may be requested in the course of the survey. Copies of this signed memorandum, where possible, should be sent to affected department heads in advance of the arrival of the survey team. In this regard, it may be well for the people doing the survey to be introduced at a meeting of all department heads.

At this meeting, the management memorandum can be read and dis-tributed, and any questions regarding operational authority can be answered. At a minimum, someone from the company must be assigned to escort and introduce members of the survey team to department heads and employees with whom they will be working. We prefer, however, the depart-ment head meeting, because such a meeting can go a long way toward estab-lishing rapport and cooperation. It also gives the department heads directly involved a chance to ask questions and receive answers, answers that ideally will allay any fears or apprehensions they brought with them to the meeting. At the very least, it serves as a vehicle to get them involved in the survey program at the outset.

After the preliminary survey has been completed, it is well to have a second meeting with the client. The purpose of this second meeting is fourfold:

1. To give the client a brief report of initial impressions obtained.
2. To explain how the surveyor perceives the objectives, activities, or functions under review.
3. To establish a meeting of the minds as to just what is to be accomplished.
4. To briefly outline to the client the general plan of attack.

It is *essential* that both parties to the survey be at this point in total agreement with regard to the objective of the project. In this way, any mis-understandings can be resolved and an agreement reached so that the prin-cipal job can move along rapidly and systematically.

Obtaining Information

What Information to Obtain. The preliminary survey, and in fact the pri-mary survey as well, will move along rapidly and systematically only if one has a clear idea of what data is needed and where to find it. Some, but by no means all, of the basic sources one should consider are as follows.

The Charter for the Operation. Copies of policy statements, directives, state-ments of functions, responsibilities, goals, and delegations of authority will be needed. In addition, one will need job descriptions of the people directly involved in the activity, if available.

Beyond the written word, it is essential to focus on the objectives of the operation — what is its *real* mission (not necessarily what the official state-ments say it is). It is not uncommon to find that official job descriptions are mere window dressing or that they have not kept pace with changing times and aims. The organization of the operation may include:

1. Organizational charts.
2. Position descriptions of the operation in the overall company structure.
3. The nature, size, and location of ancillary or satellite activities.
4. Interfacing operations and their relationship to the activity under review (safety, for instance, when the primary review is security).

Financial Information. One will want to obtain for review all financial data that have a bearing on the subject under scrutiny, either directly or indirectly.

Operating Instructions. It is essential to obtain an accurate picture of the flow of records and other data. One of the simplest ways is by flow-charting the activity. Flow charts (discussed later in this chapter) can provide a useful picture of the operation and at the same time highlight gaps and duplications in procedures, as well as pinpoint risk areas for later scrutiny.

Problem Areas. During the entire survey one should keep in mind the problems mentioned by management at the preliminary conference, as well as any deficiencies found in prior surveys, audits, or reviews. Also, focus attention on the procedures or controls that have supposedly been designed to alleviate the difficulties and problems and at the same time reduce the risks.

Matters of Special Interest. One will be especially interested in exploring any new areas mentioned during discussions with management that were of concern to them during the preliminary conference.

Sources of Information. Some, but certainly not all, of the possible sources of information available during the survey are:

1. Discussions with supervisors and employees directly engaged in the activity under review. One cannot overemphasize the importance of these people, because
   a. Not only are they usually aware of the problems, they often have worked out the solutions as well.
   b. It is essential to obtain their cooperation, because in the final analysis, these are the people who will be responsible for implementing many of the recommendations made as a result of the survey.
   c. If they feel they have played a real part in the development of solutions to the problem, they will be more inclined to work for the success of the recommendations. The reverse is, unfortunately, also true.

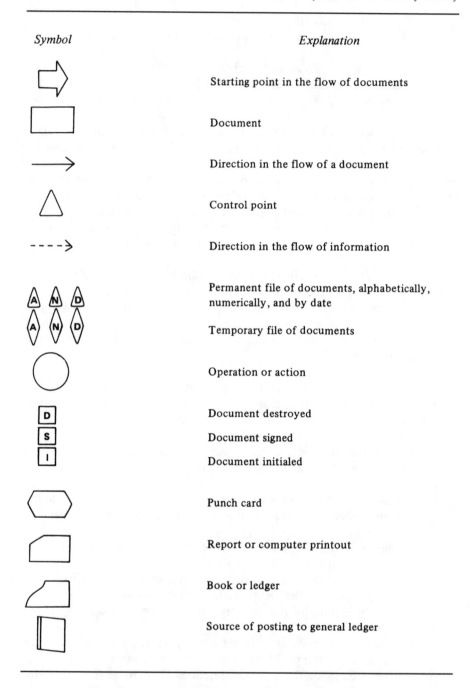

Symbol	*Explanation*
	Starting point in the flow of documents
	Document
	Direction in the flow of a document
	Control point
	Direction in the flow of information
	Permanent file of documents, alphabetically, numerically, and by date
	Temporary file of documents
	Operation or action
	Document destroyed
	Document signed
	Document initialed
	Punch card
	Report or computer printout
	Book or ledger
	Source of posting to general ledger

Figure 7-1. Standard Flow Chart Symbols

2. Discussions with supervisors downstream and upstream of the operations under review.
3. Correspondence files.
4. Prior survey, audit, or inspection reports.
5. Incident/crime reports.
6. Budget data.
7. Mission or objective statements or reports.
8. Procedural (operational) manuals.
9. Reports by or to government agencies, state and federal (OSHA, for example).

Physical Observation. Observations or inspections should be conducted in two phases. The first is a familiarization tour of the entire facility to obtain "the big picture." At this time the various departments are identified, and the managers and supervisors introduced previously are seen in their normal work environments.

Notes are made, but few questions are asked at this point. In a small operation, one tour may be sufficient to accomplish the desired objective. In a large, complex operation, it may be necessary to make a second or even a third tour before feeling comfortable with the facility and its environment. The second (or subsequent) tour may be made in connection with flow-charting various parts of the activity or operation.

Flow-Charting. Flow-charting is an art that with proper practice can become an invaluable survey tool. Making a flow chart is the easiest way to obtain a visual grasp of a system or procedure, and it is a ready means of analyzing complex operations that cannot easily be reduced to meaningful narrative description. Figure 7-1 shows some standard flow chart symbols and a legend describing each symbol used. Sometimes a simple sketch may suffice; at other times it may be necessary to use plastic overlays to describe detailed and complex operations. Figure 7-2 is an example of a formal flow chart describing a complex operation. Flow charts, however, need not be formal or greatly detailed to accomplish the task. Figure 7-3 is an example of a simple, informal flow chart.

SUMMARY

Field work is measurement — it is measuring what *is* against what *should be*. This requires both methods of measurement and the existence of acceptable practices and standards. Security surveys are usually concerned with measuring at least three basic factors: quality, reliability, and cost.

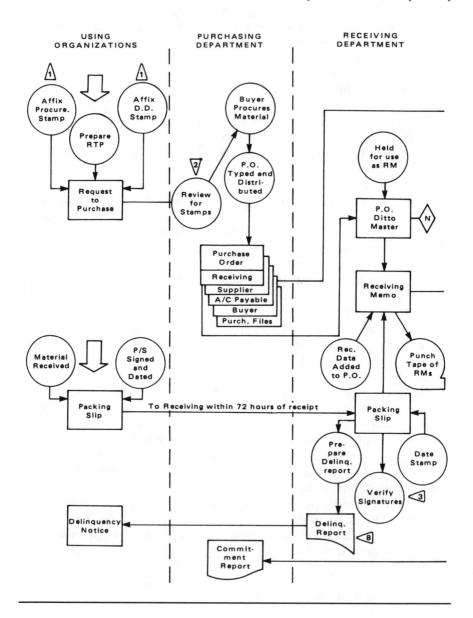

Figure 7-2. Formal Flow Chart

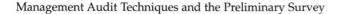

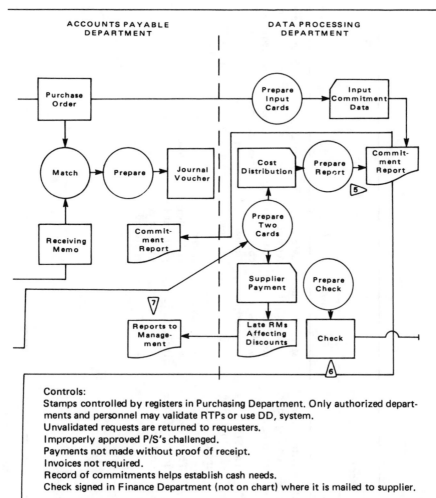

Controls:
Stamps controlled by registers in Purchasing Department. Only authorized depart-
ments and personnel may validate RTPs or use DD, system.
Unvalidated requests are returned to requesters.
Improperly approved P/S's challenged.
Payments not made without proof of receipt.
Invoices not required.
Record of commitments helps establish cash needs.
Check signed in Finance Department (not on chart) where it is mailed to supplier.

7   Reports to cognizant managers on unearned discounts monitors timeliness of processing P.O.'s, P/S's, RMs and payments to supplier.

8   Reports warn that D.D. privileges may be withdrawn.

Abbreviations:
D.D. — Direct Delivery
P.O. — Purchase Order
P/S — Packing Slip
RM — Receiving Memo
RTD — Request to Purchase

Figure 7-2. (*Continued*)

Purchasing Department	Receiving Department			A/C Payable	Inspection	Stores
	Office	Dock	Hold Area			
Purchase orders and changes are prepared and sent to: 1. Supplier 2. Accounts Payable 3. Receiving Department 4. Buyer 5. Purchasing files	The master P.O. is held in temporary files awaiting receipt of materials and shipping notice. Upon receipt of shipping notice, the receiving information is added to the ditto master of the P.O. to create the Receiving Memo.	Materials and shipping notice are received. The S/N is sent to Receiving Office. The materials are sent to the hold area.	Materials are held until the Receiving Memo is prepared. Thereupon the materials are sent to Inspection.	Evidence of receipt is matched with copy of P.O. No invoice is required. If match is satisfactory, payment to supplier is approved.	Material is inspected. Unsatisfactory material is sent to hold area. Satisfactory material is sent to stores.	Materials are stored awaiting requisitions from using departments.

Figure 7-3. Informal Flow Chart: Procurement of Materials

To measure, one must go out into the field and perform surveys or, if a program already exists to review and to test. Field work is performed using the techniques of observing, questioning, analyzing, verifying, investigating, and evaluating. The largest portion of field work is gathering data and accumulating evidence, which must then be analyzed and evaluated before recommendations can be developed. It is in the proper evaluation of the data obtained that true professionals meet their test.

The preliminary survey charts the course for the main voyage. It often provides a clear enough view of certain activities to eliminate the need for further review of these operations. The time spent on the preliminary survey is well repaid by a more efficient and economical review.

In the preliminary survey one gets to know people, understand operations, and focus on objectives, controls, and risks. One is then in a better position to perform the main survey in an intelligent, effective, and efficient manner. The preliminary survey must be considered the road map, essential for a long and difficult journey.

8

THE SURVEY REPORT

Did you ever stop to think how odd it is that you have to learn how to write your own language? Why? What is there to learn?

Rudolph Flesch and A. H. Lass
The Way to Write (New York: Harper, Row, 1963), p. 77

There is little likelihood that the average security professional was born with the writing mastery of an Ernest Hemingway. Writing is an art, and like most arts it must be constantly practiced if it is to become a useful and natural tool. While few of us can learn to write with the flow and style of a great master, we can, with a little effort, greatly improve our ability to communicate by use of the written word.

Many of us find field work the most exciting and challenging part of our daily assignments. We know many persons who are extremely competent investigators and auditors but who, when it comes to writing reports, leave much to be desired. Good writing requires good thinking. If one's concepts are confused and tangled, one's reports will reflect the same problems. If one's thoughts are muddy and don't seem to establish a bridge between cause and effect, the resulting written report is bound to reflect this confusion. Unfortunately, we are likely to be judged more often by our ability to write a good report than our ability to do good field work. Our professional ability and efficiency will be demonstrated before the eyes of many by clear, concise, complete, and accurate reporting.

I need cite but one example to make my point. We were contracted to do an investigation/audit regarding a possible kickback scheme between a vendor and a staff employee of a public agency in a large city of southern California. When we submitted our final written report to the client, we expected it to be reviewed by no more than five senior management officials. Instead, the report was reproduced, and copies were presented to the entire board of directors. Also, copies were furnished to the district attorney's office for review and possible submission to the grand jury. Many people, most of whom the writer never met, were thus in a position to judge the quality of our product by merely reading the documents. The message here is, "Every report you write bears your name. Write one bad or inaccurate report, and it will haunt you forever."

"I MUST WRITE, THEREFORE I SHALL"

What makes good writing? The answer seems to lie in good field work, a well-structured outline, copious notes or working papers, and dogged persistence. If one has done an adequate job in the field, one's notes and working papers will be full of facts and figures. Only then can one be sure that material exists for a good report. At this point it is well to remember the Chinese proverb, "A journey of a thousand miles begins with the first step." Sit down and start writing — by preparing an outline. An example of an effective reporting outline can be found in Box 8-1.

Box 8-1. Security Survey Report

I.   *Purpose.* States the reason for making the survey. Could encompass all of the subject matter in this outline or be restricted to a specific portion or spot problem. Could encompass one location or all of a large corporation.

II.   *Scope.* Describes briefly the scope of the survey effort.

    A.   Persons interviewed.
    B.   Premises visited, times, and so forth.
    C.   Categories of documents reviewed.

III.   *Findings.* This section includes findings appropriate to the purpose of the survey. For example, a survey report on physical security only would not contain findings related to purchasing, inventories, or conflicts of interest unless they have a direct impact on the physical security situation.

    A.   General: Brief description of facilities, environment, operations, products or services, and schedules.
    B.   Organization: Brief description of the organizational structure and number of employees. Details regarding the number and categories of personnel who perform security related duties.
    C.   Physical security features: Describes lock and key controls, lock hardware on exit/entrance doors, doors, fences, gates, and other structural

and natural barriers to unauthorized entry. Describes access controls including identification systems and control of identification media. Security effect of lighting. Location, type, class, installation, and monitoring of intrusion alarm and surveillance systems. Guard operations, and so forth.

D. Internal controls: Describes methods and procedures governing inventory control, shrinkage, and adjustments; identification and control of capital assets; receiving and shipping accounts receivable; purchasing and accounts payable; personnel selection; payroll; cash control and protection; sales to employees; frequency and scope of audits; division of responsibilities involving fiduciary actions; policy and practices regarding conflicts of interest; and so forth.

E. Data systems and records: Describes physical features and procedures for protecting the data center, access to EDP equipment, the media, and the data; types of application systems in use; dependency; back-up media and computer capacity; and capability for auditing through the computer. Identifies essential records and how they are protected.

F. Emergency planning: Status and extent of planning, organization, and training to react to accidental emergencies, emergencies arising from natural disasters, bombs and bomb threats, kidnap, and hostage situations, and disorders or riots. Considered in three phases: pre-emergency preparations; actions during emergencies; and post-emergency or recovery actions. Discusses coordination with and utilization of external resources, for example, other firms or government agencies.

G. Proprietary information and trade secrets: Discusses the extent to which these categories of information are recognized and how they are classified; means of protection, for example, clearance, accountability, storage, declassification, disposal; secrecy arrangements with employees, suppliers, and so forth.

IV. *Conclusions.* Evaluation of protective measures discussed in III. Findings. Identifies specific vulnerabilities and rates them as to seriousness, for example, "slight," "moderate," "serious," or similar terms of comparison.

V. *Recommendations.* Using the systems design technique, the consultant develops specific recommendations for appropriate applications of hardware, administrative controls, and person-power that will complement the protective measures already in use to provide effective controls of the vulnerabilities identified under IV. Conclusions. Cost/benefit considerations are applied to each recommendation and the structure as a whole.

Note: The client's experience is reflected in the appropriate sections of this report.

Source: Compliments of Charles E. Hayden, Assistant Vice-President and Senior Security Consultant, (Retired) M & M Protection Consultants, San Francisco, California.

If you sit around and wait for divine inspiration to give you the perfect beginning, you may well wait forever. You have to be able to develop a discipline that says, "I must write, therefore I shall," and immediately take pen to paper. It will matter little that the first passages of the draft are poorly phrased or might be worded better. Doubtless, the final report will have been reshaped and revised a number of times. The rule to remember is: "There is no such thing as good writing; there is only good rewriting." Only after painstakingly preparing dozens and dozens of reports do one's writing skills improve. Only then does the job become less painful and the product more professional. Finally, when writing truly becomes a joy, professional reports will follow. Few of us will ever reach this exalted plateau, and it is not the purpose of this text to chart a course to it. It is my purpose, however, to describe some of the time-tested methods for writing better reports, thus increasing one's ability to better serve clients and management.

Survey reports generally have two functions: first, to communicate, and second, to persuade. The findings, conclusions, and recommendations in the report are vitally important to management. For the report to communicate effectively, the channels must be clear, the medium must be incisive, and the details must be easily understood. Also, the story must be worthy of the material. Too often the skill and effort expended during the field-work portion of the survey are lost in the murky waters of a poorly written report. A dull or poorly written report will not penetrate the upper circles where the story needs to be told and where the persuasion occurs. Write your report expecting it to be read by the top decision makers in the organization, and you will always be safe.

FIVE CRITERIA OF GOOD REPORTING

The ability to write good reports can be developed. With the proper desire, the right amount of effort, the right standards, and the proper techniques, much can be accomplished. I stated earlier that field work is largely measurement, which implies the existence of acceptable practices and standards (criteria). Reports can also be measured against standards. A good report must meet the following criteria: *accuracy, clarity, conciseness, timeliness,* and *slant* (or *pitch*). To assist the reader in improving ability at writing reports, we will consider each of these criteria briefly.

Accuracy

A reader should be able to rely on the survey report, because of its documented fact and inescapable logic. Additionally, the report must be completely and scrupulously factual, based entirely on hard evidence. Likewise, the report should speak with authority. It should be written and documented so as to command belief and convey reliability. Facts and figures, as well as statements and recommendations, must be supported and supportable. Statements of fact must carry the assurance that the person doing the survey personally observed or otherwise validated them. When it is necessary to report matters not personally observed, the report should clearly identify the source. One must be careful to avoid personal attribution unless, of course, one can personally certify the existence or extent of the condition reported.

Another important facet of accuracy — and one often overlooked — is perspective, the reporting of facts in the proper light. As an example, it would be reporting out of perspective to show how one of a dozen related activities may be deficient without showing how the activities relate to each other in order of importance. This is sometimes referred to as "balance."

For a report to be accurate then, it must encompass truth, relevancy, and perspective. It must also have balance.

Clarity

One cannot write clearly about what one does not understand clearly. Clarity implies communicating from one mind to another, with few obstacles in between. In order to accomplish this, writers must have a firm grasp of the matter at hand. Until writers reach this level of understanding, they cannot take pen in hand and start to write a report. They would be better off returning to the field and continuing their activities there until they feel totally comfortable with the material under review.

Poor structure is an impediment to clarity. An orderly progression of ideas lends to clarity and thus understanding. Therefore, as most professional writers have found, one of the best aids to effective written communication is the prepared outline, as shown in Box 8-1.

Acronyms and technical jargon should be avoided where possible. If it is not possible to avoid their use, then at least give the reader at the outset an explanation of the term or initials. For example, at first mention: "Department of Defense (DOD) Bulletin #12 states . . ." not "DOD Bulletin #12 states . . . ." Do not assume that everyone reading your report will be familiar with a term, acronym (initials), or technical jargon or slang used. Quite to the contrary, good writers assume that their audiences are not familiar with these oddities and take the time to explain them in order to enhance clarity and understanding.

Likewise, reporting a finding without properly setting the stage can lead to misunderstanding. Only by reporting relevant information and background can the author expect the reader to understand the process or condition and thus appreciate the significance of the finding. If one is recommending a new procedure, one should first tell what procedure, if any, now exists and why it isn't working. This makes the client fully cognizant of the procedures in question and much better positioned to consider the proposed change favorably.

Long discussions of technical procedures muddy the waters. Here, the liberal use of flow charts, schedules, and graphs can be a real aid to clarity and ease of understanding. Be ever mindful of the old Chinese proverb, "One picture is worth a thousand words." Such aids benefit both the reader and the writer of the report. If it is axiomatic that one of the purposes of the survey report is to stimulate action along the road to change, then the report must be effective. To be effective, it must be clear!

Conciseness

To be concise means to eliminate that which is unessential. Conciseness, however, does not necessarily mean brevity. The subject matter may dictate expanded coverage. Conciseness does mean elimination of that which is superfluous, redundant, or unnecessary. In short, it is the deletion of all words, sentences, and paragraphs that do not directly relate to the subject matter in question. This is not to suggest an arbitrary, telegraphic style of writing, though in some instances this style may be appropriate. It is, however, to suggest that easy flow and continuity of thought do not depend on excessive verbiage. Short, simple, easy-to-understand sentences are the general rule to apply. Whenever one comes head-on into a long, complicated sentence, continuity of thought on the part of the reader generally is replaced by confusion. Long sentences should be dissected and rewritten to obtain a comfortable, happy medium.

Do not, however, confuse conciseness with lack of data. There must be sufficient detail in the report to make it meaningful to all levels of the audience. Both those involved in the intimate day-to-day operations and the chairman of the board of directors must have sufficient information to understand the problems reported.

Timeliness

Often it takes a while to get management to approve having a comprehensive security survey or audit initiated. Once the decision is made and the project begins, management waits impatiently for the results of the survey, the written report. The report, it is hoped, will answer all of management's needs for current information. Therefore, the report must be submitted in a timely fashion. One must be careful, though, not to be in such a hurry to communicate one's findings that the report is otherwise unacceptable. The survey report must meet all the other criteria for good writing as well.

How, then, do we meet both objectives, timeliness and thoroughness? One solution may be the interim, or progress, report. When, during the course of a survey, we come across a finding of such importance or magnitude that the details must be reported to management without delay, we can use the interim report. An example may be a safety deficiency that if not corrected immediately could lead to serious injury or death. Another example is if one uncovers the unmistakable danger signs of fraud, theft, embezzlement, or industrial espionage (See Appendix B). Interim reports communicate the need for immediate attention and, one would hope, immediate corrective action. In this regard, one would probably first communicate the deficiency to top management orally then follow up immediately with the written interim report.

Interim reports are designed to be short and to the point. They should address one subject, perhaps two at most. These reports should be clearly identified as "interim," and they must contain, usually at the bottom of the page, written disclaimers against accepting them as the final word on the subject being reported — "In the absence of a full inquiry," or words to that effect. The interim report's purpose is to give management an opportunity to focus immediately on the reported condition and get corrective action started without waiting for the final report.

Interim reports notwithstanding, the final survey report should always be submitted in a timely manner.

It is well to establish, at the outset of the project, goals and time frames, which include the issuance of reports. It has been found that schedules are necessary to keep important projects under control. The larger and more complex the project, the more important time-frame planning and scheduling become. This is especially true for those parts of the survey that are least desirable; report writing unfortunately falls into this category for many people. I have found that once the field work is completed, there is a tendency to delay the reporting part of the job. Nevertheless, the end result of the task is the written report, and management has every right to expect that reports be submitted expeditiously.

Another thought on this subject: I have seen otherwise outstanding field work totally destroyed because a report was not submitted to the client on or before an agreed deadline. A security survey can be an expensive proposition. Clients often become upset, and rightfully so, if they feel they are not getting what they are paying for, in a timely manner.

SLANT OR PITCH

Finally, the writer should consider the slant or pitch of the report. Obviously, the tone of the report should be courteous. We should also consider the effect it may have on operations personnel. It should strive for impersonality and thus not identify or highlight the mistakes of easily identified individuals, small units, or departments. The report must not be overly concerned with minor details or trivialities. It must avoid sounding narrow minded, concentrating instead on that which has real meaning and substance. The report should clearly be identified with the needs, desires, and goals of sound management. Pettiness must be avoided at all costs.

FORMAT

A report is divided into two parts. The first concerns itself with substance, the heart and soul of the project. The second is form, and form usually is dictated by the type of report being prepared, whether it is formal or informal, final or interim, written or oral.

The form of the report can also depend on those to whom the report is being directed. What do the prospective readers expect? How much time will they be able to devote to reading the report? The answers to these questions often become the deciding factors regarding the report format used.

Also, different writers employ different formats. There is no universal style or format that can be recommended to satisfy all needs. Novices will usually begin by experimenting until they find a format that best suits their style of delivery. When they find an effective format, they can modify it to meet the specific requirements and tasks at hand. The following elements are usually found in survey reports.

The Cover Letter

The cover letter can serve many purposes, not the least of which is to be a transmittal for the report. The writer may wish to include in the cover letter a brief synopsis of the findings. This would be especially helpful to members of management who are concerned only with the broad overview of the project. The writer must make certain that the details contained in the synopsis are factual extracts from the body of the report. The tendency to take poetic license and "summarize the details" must be carefully avoided, or meaning may become distorted. Whenever possible, cover letters should be limited to one page, for the benefit of the busy executive; also, anything beyond a one-page transmittal begins to invade the province of the attached report.

Body of the Report

Title. The title should fully identify the name and address, with zip code, of the entity being surveyed. It should also include the dates between which the survey was conducted, not the date the report is submitted to management — that goes on the cover letter. Also, the title should clearly state that this is a "Security Survey (Audit)," in the top center of the first page, in capital letters.

Introduction or Forward. The introduction should be brief, clear, and should invite further attention from the reader. Its purpose is to provide all the data necessary to acquaint the reader with the subject under review. At this point the writer may wish to identify the sites or departments toured, the persons interviewed, and the documents examined. One point of information that is essential here is the authority for the survey; this is usually contained in the opening sentence, for example, "This survey was conducted at the direction of the XYZ corporate management, specifically to identify and evaluate. . . ."

Purpose. The purpose section is a brief description of the objectives of the survey. It must be in sufficient detail to give the reader an understanding of what to expect as a result of the survey. The purpose should be spelled out precisely at this point, so when the findings are reported, they can be seen to conform to the statements contained in the purpose. This technique makes it easier for readers to find the substance of any particular item without reviewing the entire report. As an example, in the statement of purpose both the objectives and findings may be listed in numerical or alphabetical order, for ease in comparison between the two.

Scope. The statement of scope should be a clear delineation of exactly what areas are being reviewed and to what extent they are being examined. It sometimes helps to clarify the issue by specifically spelling out areas that are not covered in this particular survey. This is especially helpful when the title of the report is so broad or general that it may lead the reader to expect much more than the report actually delivers. In a brief report, it may be advantageous to combine the scope and purpose for the sake of brevity.

An example of a statement of scope is: "We limited our review of the purchasing department to those activities that directly relate to sole-source acquisitions. We did not review competitive bid activities in the course of this examination."

Findings. Findings are the product of field work. They are the facts produced by the interviews, examinations, observations, analyses, and investi-

gations. They are the heart and marrow of the survey project. Findings may
be positive (favorable) or negative (unfavorable). Findings can depict a satisfactory condition that needs no attention or an unsatisfactory condition
deserving of immediate correction.

Positive findings require less space in a report than negative findings.
As they do, however, represent a survey determination, it is essential that
they be included. Some writers do not report positive findings; they feel,
why burden management with matters requiring no attention? Others report
favorable findings to show objectivity and to give balance to the report. The
author favors reporting both positive and negative findings so management
can see the operation under review in total perspective.

The statement of reported findings usually includes a summary of the
findings, the criteria or standards of measurement used, the conditions
found, and, for deficiencies, their significance, causes and effects, and recommendations for corrective action.

In preparing to present a negative finding, one should be able to
answer the following questions:

- What is the problem?
- What are people (procedures) supposed to be doing about this
  problem?
- What are they actually doing, if anything?
- How was this situation allowed to happen?
- What should be done about it?
- Who is responsible to ensure that corrective action will be taken?
- What corrective action is necessary to remove the deficiency?

Using these questions as criteria, one must be able to satisfy oneself
that one has done an adequate job, in a fair and impartial manner. Only then
can the author set forth the findings in a way that will satisfy the client that
the recommendation has merit and meaning.

Statement of Opinion (Conclusions)

Not all reports contain the opinions of or conclusions reached by the members of the survey team. Those that do usually provide a capsule comment
that reflects the professional opinion and judgment of the surveyor
regarding those activities that have been reviewed. When they are reported,
comments should be both positive and negative.

Opinions are nothing more than the professional judgments of the persons making the review. Some professionals feel that management is entitled
to receive and review their opinions and conclusions. Some feel otherwise,

eliminating conclusions entirely from the report and moving instead directly to the findings and recommendations.

Regardless of the report writing technique used, when one sets forth a conclusion or an opinion, it must be supported by fact and fully justified. Also, the opinion must be responsive to the purpose of the review as set forth in an appropriate part of the report, or it may well be superfluous.

While it goes without saying that opinion more often than not finds fault, one should not hesitate to express positive opinions when compliments are deserved. This should be done not only in the interest of fairness but to lend balance to the report. An example of an opinion (conclusion): "In our opinion the procedures designed to ensure an orderly evacuation of bedridden patients in the event of fire or natural disaster were found to be adequate given the obvious limitations of a high-rise environment at this hospital."

SUMMARY

Reports will be evaluated according to their accuracy, clarity, conciseness, timeliness, and slant (or pitch). Whatever format is used (and formats come in many styles), they will include one or more of these common elements: a cover letter, and the body of the report — including a title, a forward or introduction, a purpose, a scope, findings, opinions, conclusions, and recommendations. Good writing takes constant practice and effort, but any writing can be improved by using certain techniques and adhering to established criteria or standards. Begin by preparing a logical outline, as the skeleton to which the muscle can be added later. A liberal use of flow charts, schedules, and graphs can be a real aid to clarity and understanding. Finally, remember the golden rule of writing: "There is no such thing as good writing, there is only good rewriting."

9

CRIME PREDICTION

Eugene Tucker, CFE, CPP, Contributing Author

> What will amount to adequate security varies in each individual case. No case has determined how many guards might be required or provided any other specifics as to what constitutes adequate/reasonable security.
>
> *Lopez v. McDonald's*, 193 Cal. App. 3d 495 (1987)

This chapter will examine crime as an element of hazard identification and provide some guidelines to predicting its probability and estimating its criticality. With this information, the security manager will be better equipped to justify the allocation of resources (budget) to mitigate the effects of these hazards. "By analyzing statistics and methods of operation, specific crime-conducive conditions will be obvious."[1] The risk of crime can come from within the organization, or from third parties on the outside. Because business owners owe a duty of care to employees, patrons, and guests, this chapter will also outline methods to establish whether the business or landowner is "on notice" that future crime is foreseeable and therefore required to take action to prevent the crime, to mitigate its effects, or to warn patrons and employees of the danger.

Unfortunately, there is no exact formula the security manager can use to make these determinations. This is due in part to:

- Differing laws between states.
- Differences in the duty owed and the interpretation and applicability of case law for various types of property. (Restaurants, shopping malls, and theaters, where guests are "invited," may be

---

[1] Francis James D'Addario, *Loss Prevention through Crime Analysis* (Butterworths, National Crime Prevention Institute: 1989).

treated differently by the courts than an industrial site, campus, or
doctor's office.)
- Changes in case law and decisions.
- Different interpretations regarding the assignment of responsibility. (Some courts believe that if the perpetrator of the crime is at
  least 50 percent responsible [negligent], third-party liability is dis-
  missed. Other juries have awarded victims large sums although
  they found the perpetrator only 35 percent responsible.)

The prediction of crime, like risk analysis, is an inexact science and is
often based on the professional's best educated guess. The methodologies
used to predict crime are subject to more debate than those of risk analysis.
Many factors influence criminal behavior. Precise prediction is difficult, if
not impossible. Statistical models to predict crime, such as the Brugess
method, configurational analysis, multiple regression, multidiscriminant
analysis, and log-linear analysis, are usually not required to meet the goals
of the security manager. Simple methods exist that can give the security
manager a systematic indication of future crime risk. Relying on the criminological theory that recidivism is the best predictor of future crime (though
some theories hold that age, demographics, or causation are the major pre-
dictors), we can apply this rate to individual categories of crime to estimate
the potential that crime in the surrounding community will "spill over" and
affect the safety of employees at a target location.

ANALYSIS OF INTERNAL CRIME

As in risk analysis, the prediction of internal crime relies on historical
data. We can expect past or current crime rates to continue or increase into
the future if conditions responsible for the criminal activity (opportunity,
for example) do not change. The probability of hazards and events, to a
great extent, depends upon consistent conditions over a time period sufficient to draw statistical inferences from past data. For example, if a company averages x fires per year, we can predict that the company will
probably experience close to the same number if no factors are introduced
to mitigate this risk.

Crime analysis focuses managers on the past, not the present. State or
federal Uniform Crime Reports can be used as data sources, but their information is already a year old. By the time countermeasures are devised, capital budgets approved, and service or equipment proposals submitted, we
are implement countermeasures based on data that is two or more years out
of date. Projecting crime trends will give management a better understanding of present and future crime exposure.

Given that a small percentage of employees cause the majority of crime, the arrest or departure of a single employee could radically affect future rates. Many security professionals believe internal crime, especially theft, is the result of drug and alcohol-dependent employees. The introduction of pre-employment and random drug testing, education, and treatment programs will surely affect the future projection for drug use, injuries, and theft.

If the business has already compiled adequate historical data, it becomes a simple matter to project the trends into the future. Software programs are available that sort incidents by building, site, and time. They generate incident reports and produce trend analyses by location, day, time of day, modus operandi, and other identifiers to pinpoint expected losses in specific areas, divisions, or by types of crime. If accurate records have not been maintained within the security department, check with the accounting, human resources, internal audit, and risk management departments for information. When gathering data, especially if it is anecdotal, use caution that it is not misreported or misclassified; many nonprofessionals, for instance, confuse burglary with robbery.

Adjustments must be made for factors that can influence the future occurrence of the crimes or incidents being projected. Staffing increases and changes in workforce demographics and employee attitudes (morale, job satisfaction) must be considered. How will changing rates of domestic violence against women affect the workplace if the workforce is predominantly female? Do labor contracts expire soon?

Projections can be represented as a rate; Uniform Crime Reports (UCRs) list the number of crimes per hundred thousand population or as the number of crimes expected per year. The retail department can express its rate as the number of crimes (such as robbery) for the total number of stores. The use of rates will maintain consistency in comparisons if the base (for instance, the number of stores) increases or decreases. Look for cyclical trends, such as rising theft during the holiday season or after new-product releases. Use this information to pinpoint areas of concern and to utilize limited resources in the best way. Concentrate patrols in high-crime or high-potential-crime areas of a campus, building complex, or parking lot. Focus on certain crimes, such as rape, that the projections identify as tending to occur, for example, more often during certain months of the year.

ANALYSIS OF EXTERNAL CRIME

The intent of this section is to guide policy and decision makers to realistic evaluation of the risk associated with criminal behavior from the community that may affect the health and safety of employees and assets. Its assumptions and generalities are not sufficiently focused to allow predicting the future criminal behavior of specific members of that community, or of a specific applicant, employee, contractor, or former employee. The prediction of criminal behavior is an inexact science, open to many debatable issues; errors in prediction are therefore inevitable. The security professional should evaluate the results of these predictive methods in light of the totality of the circumstances, of currently accepted criminological theory, and of the professional's experience. If adjustments seem necessary, look to the costs and personal losses that a false negative may create. Is it in the best interest of the firm to err on the side of extra protective measures against a rape, even though the analysis may indicate the probability is very low (say, one in twenty-five years), than it is to devote more resources to a higher-cost, higher-probability event, such as shoplifting?

External crime can be analyzed for three purposes. One is to determine, as accurately as possible, the true potential that crime in the surrounding community will impact the health, safety, and assets of the organization. The second purpose is to determine if the business is legally "on notice" that injury to employees, patrons, or guests by third parties is foreseeable. The third is to learn how a business should go about gathering data to support or defend a claim of negligent security after an injury has occurred — that is, how does one determine if the injury was foreseeable?

Many security managers simply determine the crime rates for their locations and benchmark the data with that of a similar organization or city with comparable demographics and population. When using crime rates or survey data from valid research, always compare apples with apples — measure parking-lot crime against parking-lot crime from other areas, and compare it to the norm for the study areas. For example, a survey found that 35 percent of restaurant industry workers admitted to taking company supplies for personal use. Unfortunately, we cannot expect all restaurant employees to follow the same pattern, because the study focused only on fast food establishments.

Prediction of the "spillover" of crime from the surrounding community is based upon many assumptions. In an industrial setting, we need to assume that the level of security protection is no different from the local standard. It makes little sense to compare burglary statistics for homes or businesses that have a minimal level of protection to those of a location that has the best locks, the highest fences, the brightest glare lighting, CCTV, and an armed security force with attack-trained dogs.

The following method is an attempt to estimate the chance of external crime affecting the workplace, absent any security measures beyond the local standard. This method is based on criminological theories and established trends, but it has not been validated in a court of law or by a professional review board. The author has found it both a useful and accurate tool to justify manpower and budget decisions based on projected needs.

1. Select the crimes to measure or predict. Include Category I ("Indexed") crimes:

- Murder
- Nonnegligent manslaughter
- Forcible rape
- Robbery
- Aggravated assault
- Burglary
- Grand theft
- Motor vehicle theft
- Arson

Include other crime exposures which would have a negative impact on the company, especially those that may result in litigation. These may include simple assault and battery, vandalism, trespassing, drug sales, and the like. Be sure to consider any special risks, such as the presence of local extremist groups.

2. Research crime rates for the offenses selected above. Data on crime rates are obtained from local, state, and federal sources. (See "How to Establish Notice," Appendix F, for specific sources.) Understand that "there are concerns that criminal justice data collection mechanisms are woefully inadequate and unstandardized across the State and Federal systems."[2]

Crime statistics are inaccurate, due to underreporting and differing interpretations of the definitions of crimes. Increases or decreases in the rates are also effected by the level and focus of enforcement (that is, targeted enforcement) and by the efficiency of the enforcement agencies. The Federal Bureau of Investigation's Uniform Crime Report summarizes crimes under the "hierarchy rule," recording only the most serious crime within an incident. The UCR is the nation's primary source of information about crime and arrest activities of local law enforcement agencies. It is relied upon by the general public as an indicator of community safety. A new system, designed to alleviate many of the current problems with the UCR, "moves beyond aggregate statistics and raw counts of crimes and arrests that comprise the summary UCR program, to individual records for each reported crime incident and its associated arrest."[3]

---

[2] James Jepp, *Domestic and Sexual Violence Data Collection: A Report to Congress under the Violence against Women Act* (Washington, DC: National Institute of Justice, 1996).

[3] Jan M. Chiaiken, Ph.D., *Implementing the National Incident-Based Reporting System: A Project Status Report* (Washington, DC: U.S. Department of Justice, July 1997).

This new program, the National Incident-Based Reporting System (NIBRS), eliminates the "hierarchy rule" and looks at detailed offense, offender, victim, property, and arrest data in twenty-two crime categories and for forty-six offenses. Implementation of this system has been slow. Only 6 percent of the population was represented by NIBRS contributing agencies as of mid-1997. There is a perception that crime rates will appear to increase if the system is adopted, due to the changes in reporting methods.

Determine the number of crimes committed for a half-mile, one-mile, or three-mile radius as appropriate, possibly adjusting for any natural boundaries that may skew the results, if the local jurisdictions maintain data at this level of detail. (Crime-tracking software used by many police departments has the ability to list, tally, and plot graphically the various types of crimes around a specific location.) If this is not available, use crime district information or, as a last resort, use citywide statistics. Extract the raw numbers from the rate by multiplying the basis by the rate. Record these numbers over time: the prior two, three, five, or ten years. Record the percentage increase/decrease in crime rates over each year for the target areas. Use this percentage for the calculation in Step 5 below.

3. Adjust the data in each category by the percentage of reported to unreported crime. Victimization and criminological studies conclude that 63 percent of violent crime went unreported in 1995. Only 16 percent of rapes are reported to the police. By adjusting the raw figures by these percentages, you should arrive at the "true" (at least a more accurate) rate of crime for each category. Compare your adjusted figures with those derived from victimization studies. This may take some research, because these numbers are also subject to change.

4. Reduce the numbers by the recidivism rate (rate of non-reoffenders). There is discussion about the validity of this weighting, because it is not clear if the 20 percent who do not return to prison have been rehabilitated or are simply evading recapture. How this adjustment will miss new offenders is not clear. Other factors that can affect recidivism include overestimation of the number of reoffenders due to political agendas and racism.

Some believe the numbers should be increased or decreased by changes in the area's overall crime. Simply adjusting overall crime rates up or down according to the recent trends does not account for the variations in the individual classes of crimes. Generally speaking, property and violent crimes are committed by younger age groups, and white collar crime is committed by older age groups. Granted, the particular trend for each individual crime can be applied to the data, but this does not consider variations in recidivism for individual crimes. Crimes of violence tend to be impulsive and therefore have lower recidivism (most homicides are one-time affairs), whereas the perpetrators of property crimes tend to continue the practice. The best result is obtained by an examination of the areas' demographics and by adjusting the data for sex and age factors.

5. Calculate the expected recurrence of crime for your location in terms of how many will occur in a certain period (five years) or in terms of full percentages, such as, "We can expect one rape in the next fifteen years, assuming no additional mitigation is introduced."

When analyzing rates, remember that certain crimes can be cyclical. For example, rapes increase in the summer months; vandalism and sabotage increase prior to and during labor disputes.

6. If possible, set probable loss figures for the predicted events. If your analysis predicts that the truck transporting finished goods from manufacturing to the warehouse will be hijacked once every five years, and the average or maximum shipment is worth $4.2 million, you can calculate the impact of this loss. Remember to subtract insurance reimbursements and to add contractual penalties for nondelivery of product, potential loss of market share, extra costs for remanufacturing, the cost of posttraumatic stress counseling, and other indirect costs. Financial loss can also result from civil litigation, loss of morale, restricted access during crime-scene investigation, clean-up costs (blood and glass), recruitment costs for a new security manager or a replacement for the injured worker, and increased worker-compensation premiums.

Consider short-term or crime-specific items, such as workplace violence or domestic violence spillover. The above method is not very useful for understanding the potential for domestic violence spillover, because the comparative "population" is different. In this case, the demographics of the workforce, compared with the rate of victimization, should provide a more accurate projection. As with comparisons discussed previously, the actual projections are affected by the number and type of formal and informal controls in place. Until studies are completed that track the amount of domestic violence spillover and establish the effectiveness of various controls, projections are mostly subjective.

Methodologies that rely exclusively on historical data or other static factors may not best protect the organization against losses from external or internal influences. Past behavior and historical data are not in themselves predictive of future behavior. The analyst must have the ability to project fundamental dynamic relationships into the future. Thus "clinical" criteria developed from the most recent trends, conditions, and the analyst's experience are needed to add practical value to the results. Reliance on purely historical data may not identify a relatively sudden rise in high-technology invasion-style robberies until the problem becomes widespread. The analyst must use great caution that subjective criteria do not add ambiguity or bias the results by unintentionally or subconsciously weighting factors to justify an agenda, and that the added variables are not redundant. More emphasis on historical and statistical data and less on "clinical" evaluations will help to avoid these problems.

INADEQUATE SECURITY

The occurrence of crime on property controlled by the business may place its owners "on notice" that the recurrence of a similar crime is "foreseeable." If a person is then injured by a third party, the victim may have a cause of action against the business or property owner for inadequate security. Management ignorance often is responsible for liability in injuries caused by third-party crime. The wise business owner will conduct a foreseeability study to estimate the level of risk and from its results determine what degree of security protection is reasonable. While there are few facts and valid studies to support expert opinion, attorneys will argue whether the presence of additional security personnel, increased lighting, attention to procedures, or other measures could have prevented an attack.

Many business owners and corporate managers are motivated to conduct a foreseeability study by fear of litigation. Absent litigation, a violent act on the property will almost certainly create an unwanted cost to the organization through reduced employee morale and customer confidence. Additional justifications for a foreseeability study include that they may:

- Lead to a summary judgment of the case;
- Pinpoint areas of concentration for guard staff and patrols;
- Lead to better utilization of resources and equipment;
- Improve overall security and financial planning;
- Help to justify security budgets and programs;
- Aid in site selection for new facilities;
- Lead to better understanding of crime risk.

Although the frequency of this litigation is increasing, cases are expensive and often difficult to win or defend. Judgments for security-related negligence often exceed insurance coverage. Firms have found themselves underinsured, despite high premiums, or not insured at all. Policies that cover the loss of customers, reputation, or future business do not exist. For plaintiffs to prevail, they must generally show that:[4]

---

[4] Exact legal requirements vary between states.

- The business or property owner had a duty to protect.
- The business or property owner breached the duty.
- The breach of the duty (crime) was the legal (proximate) cause of the injury.

Crime analysis completed for security-planning purposes is usually not sufficient for presentation to a court subsequent to a negligence (inadequate security) claim. The necessary scope of the analysis, including the type of data analyzed, will change. Property (as opposed to violent) crime, concentration on the specific cause of the injury, and the sources of the data become more important. You must match or exceed the sources of information the opposing parties intend to use in their attempt to establish notice. If the opposition bases its analysis on data that includes arrest and incident numbers, you need to do the same. (Arrest information, however, is illegal to obtain in certain states. You may be at a disadvantage if the opposition has access to police contacts, but this information may be subpoenaed or discovered by court order.) This is one of many reasons the security manager or investigator must work closely with legal counsel.

In California, the duty to protect ends at a public area, such as a sidewalk or grass strip, unless it is shown that the business or property owner took control over this public area. There are, however, notable exceptions to this rule. Control could become an issue if employees or patrons must walk across an "uncontrolled" (that is, unowned) property to get to the controlled property. The business or property owner does not always need to own, possess, *and* control the property in order to be held liable; some courts consider that control alone is sufficient, but others hold that no liability is established in this instance. In one court decision, the actual or "apparent" control over immediately adjacent property and the foreseeability of injury created a duty on the part of the property owner to protect the victim from the danger (or to warn the victim of the danger). A duty may exist if the design of the building or passageways forces employees or patrons to pass through dangerous areas.

As a security manager, use a liberal approach in the analysis. While the courts may rule in favor of the business in a given case, the time, expense, and adverse publicity of such litigation is to be avoided. The control of an area is usually a tryable fact. Additionally, courts view the issue of derived benefit to the injured person differently. At least one court takes the position that "liability does not depend upon whether the defendant derived a commercial benefit from the property" (*Princess Hotels International, Inc., v. Superior Court*, 33 Cal. App. 4th 6 45 1995). It often comes down to what testimony the judge will include or exclude in establishing control and foreseeability for a reasonable distance from the property. For planning purposes, consider crime at adjacent properties even if no legal control over the property exists. While you may not be responsible in court, an injury could have a damaging effect on your employees.

Once duty and notice are established, it becomes a matter of causation — what level of security protection is reasonable, and would it have deterred, mitigated, or prevented the offense?

There must be a causal connection (proximate cause) between the negligence to protect and the injury or attack. Proximate cause is often difficult to prove — for instance, did the lack of additional security officers or the lack of increased lighting contribute to the attack? This may be difficult to prove or disprove in court. Standards for the amount and type of security the court will find reasonable vary from one type of property to another. Where the court may find a shopping mall liable for not providing uniformed security officers, they may rule differently (find no requirement for security officers) in the case of a small business. "Standards or minimums for security can never be ironclad. Security procedures must be adapted to local conditions and changes. That is why the trial attorney requires a security expert to define security negligence."[5] The exact character of the injury is not the correct standard; rather, the question of foreseeability must be decided by the type of harm likely to be sustained.

HOW TO ESTABLISH NOTICE

Notice is based on prior *similar* incidents. A high rate of embezzlement or other type of white-collar crime does not place the business or property owner on notice for a rape. This does not mean that a high incidence of robbery does *not* put the owner on notice for rape. Courts have concluded it is not necessary to decide whether particular criminal conduct establishes notice, but that is necessary "to evaluate more generally whether the category of negligent conduct at issue is sufficiently likely to result in the kind of harm experienced that liability may appropriately be imposed on the negligent party" (*Ballard v. Uribe* [1986] 41 Cal. 3d 564, 573, fn.6). Also, "It is possible that some other circumstances such as immediate proximity to a substantially similar business establishment that has experienced violent crime on its premises could provide the requisite degree of foreseeability" (*Ann M. v. Pacific Plaza Shopping Center*, supra. 6 Cal. 4th at p. 679, fn.7). The dissent to this opinion, shared by other courts, holds that "similar" means "identical" at a very specific location (for instance, a rape next door does not put the establishment on notice for rape, only a rape that actually occurs on the premises). Recent decisions support the majority decision. The California Appellate Court in *Lisa P.* held that prior armed robberies were not similar in nature to the rape of a clerk but still had the effect of putting the defendants on notice.[6]

---

[5] Norman R. Bottom, Jr., Ph.D., *Security Loss Control Negligence* (Harrow Press, 1985).

[6] *Lisa P. v. J. Gordon Bingham*, 43 Cal. App. 4th 376 (1996).

A business or landowner who knows, or reasonably should know, that criminal behavior is occurring on or close to his or her premises must investigate to determine whether or not the criminal behavior is likely to pose a risk to those who enter the property in the future, and whether or not some aspect or feature on the property (lack of lighting, or inadequate locks) encourages the criminal conduct, or at least makes it easy to perpetrate. This seemingly negates the concept that business and property owners in some jurisdictions receive "one free crime," one for which notice is not established until the crime actually occurs on the controlled property.

Usually the crime that puts the business on notice must be relevant — examine violent crimes in comparison with prior violent crime. However, be prepared to discuss crimes, such as burglary, that, although not violent in themselves, may have a violent outcome.

To establish notice, analyze crime data over varying time periods and distances from the premises. No consistent standard or formula exists to tell the analyst what geographical area and time period to examine. The area and period is best defined by counsel. The analyst will combine the parameters provided by counsel and utilize the various sources of data available to identify the relevant incidents within these boundaries. The analyst will then examine the details of the individual cases to confirm further their relevance to the circumstances that would or would not place the business or property owners on notice. Although anecdotal evidence supplied by employees or others may not be statistically useful, it may be introduced into evidence by the opposing party and would therefore become relevant to the case. The results of the analysis are presented in a report or memo.

After-the-fact analysis of notice is a straightforward process. The challenge arises when the security manager conducts this type of study prior to any litigation. He or she must anticipate the types of incidents that would cause negligence. The analyst must examine a broader range of scenarios and draw inferences on issues of control, proximate cause, and other negligent-security issues. The analyst must consider a wide range of injury, Category I crimes as well as property crimes, for a very focused location or for multiple locations but must also compare these incidents for a more generalized area. A campus with many differing locations may have differing crime rates, security exposures, and conditions that invite crime.

Previous courts have rejected crime in the neighborhood as inadequate evidence for foreseeability inside a shopping mall. It is important to make comparisons as similar as possible — shopping malls with shopping malls, manufacturing with manufacturing. But in these cases, more is better. Include crime in the neighborhood as part of your analysis; it then becomes a matter for the courts to decide what data is relevant. Normally the incidence of crime is examined at the adjacent property or from a two-to-three-thousand-foot radius. Include a comparison to other cities, counties, states, and regions. If possible, compare individual districts within the city or similarly ranked districts in other cities with the same population.

The number of police calls for assistance in the area during the last five years can be used to show notice. Determine the ratio of calls that did or could result in violence to property, such as burglary and vandalism. The opposition will use this to prove, or try to prove, that the business knew, or reasonably should have known, of prior incidents near the business. Courts usually look at a three-year review of crime rates against persons (Category I). Crimes against people account for 99 percent of the inadequate-security litigation exposure. The courts however, may consider a five-year period as reasonable, and plaintiffs have used ten-year periods when it is to their advantage. It then becomes a matter of convincing the judge which study is the most reasonable.

SOURCES OF DATA

Local Police Departments. Check with the crime prevention bureau, department of statistics, administration, or public information officer (PIO). Some departments use software programs that will print color maps of crime incidents for selected distances around a particular address. Check with other agencies, such as transit police, for information on crimes committed in their jurisdictions.

News Media. Newspapers, TV, and radio reporters, as well as their archives, are good sources of information. These can be researched in person at the publication's office, through a local library or by using on-line searching.

Subpoena. This can include police records, crime prevention or physical security surveys completed by police, security, or insurance auditors, insurance loss runs, and electronic mail records.

State and FBI Unified Crime Reports. The FBI compiles crime data from across the nation and reports it by city, region, category, age, and other categories. A copy of *Crime in the United States* can be found at the local library or at the FBI's or other World Wide Web sites.

ATF/FBI Arson and Bomb Reports. Publications from the Bureau of Alcohol, Tobacco, and Firearms and the FBI contain information on the prevalence of arson and bombing across the United States. The National Fire Protection Association (in Avon, Massachusetts) also maintains data on suspicious fires.

Victimization Studies. Victimization studies rely not on arrest or conviction information but on surveys of the general population's experience with crime. See *National Crime Victimization Survey* (Washington, DC: Bureau of Justice Statistics).

Valid Internal or External Surveys. Survey the employee population about its experience with crime in and around the business. Ensure that the results are statistically valid.

Centers for Disease Control and Prevention (CDC). The CDC maintains information on a range of topics, including violence in the workplace, the use of firearms, and other violent crimes.

Local College Campuses. Although most college campuses are required by law to maintain crime data, crime committed on college campuses may not be reflected in local reporting sources.

Canvassing. Anecdotal information from interviews with patrons, employees, and community members is useful as a double check and can lead the investigator to sources others may miss. Speak with:

- neighbors
- competitors
- fire and ambulance crews
- union representatives
- security officers
- postal carriers
- regular delivery drivers and suppliers (Federal Express, UPS).

Public Library. Many of the sources listed above can be found at the public library. You can also research past news articles for information at the library or connect through their Web sites to clipping services.

Surrounding Businesses or Corporations. Examine their incident reports, records, interview longtime employees who would have knowledge of crime, such as the human resources director, security manager, or insurance/risk manager for insurance loss reports.

Bureau of Justice Statistics. The National Incident-Based Reporting System (NIBRS), *Criminal Victimization in the U.S.*, *Violence and Theft in the Workplace*, and *Sourcebook of Criminal Justice Statistics* are some of the useful databases and publications available from the Bureau of Justice Statistics in Washington, D.C.

INCIDENT CLASSIFICATIONS

The following list can be used to help track the occurrence of crimes and incidents. Additional subheadings or subclassifications for crimes committed by employees (internal) or for crimes committed by customers or guests (external) can be included, depending upon the needs of the firm. "Robbery" can be further divided by including theft by pickpocket (not robbery in some states), purse snatching, or other divisions.

- Arson
  Actual
  Suspected
- Assault
  Simple
  Aggravated (weapon)
- Attempted rape/rape
  by employee
  by nonemployee
  Sexual
- Burglary
  Attempted
  Forced entry
- Computer-related crimes
  Attempted break-in
  Disclosure of passwords
- Embezzlement
  Money laundering
- Kickbacks
- Technology transfer
- Extortion
- Forgery
- Counterfeiting
- Misappropriation of funds
- Domestic violence "spillover"
- Insurance (worker compensation) fraud
- Homicide
- Kidnapping
  Perpetrator known to victim
  Perpetrator unknown
  Executive or key employee
  Attempted
  Threatened
- Theft

Auto
Proprietary information
From auto
Funds
Product
Diversion
Misappropriation
Raw materials
Precious metals
Personal items
- Disturbance
- Disorderly conduct
- Sabotage
Suspected
Product tampering
- Vandalism, malicious mischief
Vehicles
Tagging, graffiti
- Suspicious circumstances
- Indecent exposure
- Possession or disclosure of objectionable material
- Sexual harassment or unwanted advances
- Tailgating
- Corporate rule violations
- Parking violations
- Vehicle violations
- Vehicle towed
- Fire access blocked
- Other vehicle code violations
- Substance abuse
Possession
Sales
Under influence
- Hit and run
- Property damage
- Robbery
Strong arm
Weapon
Force/fear
- Suicide
Actual
Attempted
Threatened

- Access control
  Attempted entry
  Unauthorized entry
  Badge missing/stolen
  Misuse of badge/card
  Loaning access control card
- Bombing
  Explosion
  Incendiary
  Threat
  Intelligence/information
- Trespassing
- Prostitution
- Gambling
- Gang activity
- Alarms
  Security
  Fire
  Environmental
  Process control
- Maintenance
  Lighting
  Fencing
  Locks/doors
  Glazing
  Doors/gates/windows open
  Shrubbery/landscaping
- Escort requests
- Police contacts
- Solicitation/special interest
- Telecommunications fraud
- Misuse of company equipment/services
- Obscene/harassing phone calls
- Demonstrations/picketers
- First aid/medical
- Safety hazards
- Terrorist threat
- Stalking

10

DETERMINING INSURANCE REQUIREMENTS

A 1996 study released by Conning and Company estimates that fraud cost the entire insurance industry $120 billion in 1995, including health care and life sectors.

Insurance Information Institute,
Update on Fraud, August 1998
Ruth Gastel, Editor

Having once been employed by what the *Wall Street Journal* described as "the world's largest insurance brokerage" makes the author aware just how little he knows about the complex business of insurance. Nevertheless, working with some of the industry's most outstanding brokers and risk managers from a number of *Fortune 500* companies does give one an appreciation for, and some insight into, the vital role insurance plays in risk control. The reader is cautioned, however, that this chapter only touches on the subject of insurance. The advice of competent insurance professionals should always be obtained before deciding on insurance issues.

RISK MANAGEMENT DEFINED

Risk management can be defined as the process by which an entity identifies its potential losses and then decides how to treat these potential losses. Once a risk is identified, analyzed, and evaluated, the optimum method of treating the risk can be chosen and put into effect. Security related losses can be due to a variety of factors, such as theft, internal crime, or vandalism. Also, losses through fire, safety problems, and product or third-party liability are some of the leading concerns of risk managers.

A properly performed risk analysis can be used for many things, but its end result is a definition of the effect risks have on a particular company, in terms of the potential for loss. The analysis should tell where, when, and how the risk is likely to be incurred. It should also indicate the extent of loss or liability if the risk is in fact incurred and how badly the company would be injured. The risk manager must then design a program to cover the company's losses, exposures, and liabilities. In dealing with most risks, the company is faced with three basic options:

- The risk can be avoided, eliminated, or reduced to manageable proportions.
- The risk can be assumed or retained.
- The risk can be transferred to a third party. (Transfer to a third party generally implies transfer of liability to an insurance carrier.)

RISK CONTROL

The process of *eliminating* or reducing risk to manageable proportions is somewhat self-explanatory. This is usually done by programming security and safety procedures to do away with problems or to reduce them to acceptable or manageable levels of severity. This is also referred to as "loss control."

By *assuming* the risk, the company makes itself liable for the loss, if any, to be incurred. If the potential loss is deemed to be within the limits of an expected and otherwise acceptable loss, the risk may be acknowledged and just left alone. No effort is made to control, eliminate, or minimize the risk. No action is taken to correct the situation, and no insurance is purchased to cover it. In some cases, a company may develop some form of self-insurance, whereby the exposure or liability is assumed by the company itself. In most instances of risk assumption or retention, the risk is perceived to be small enough that management is willing to assume total responsibility and absorb, out of operating expenses, any losses that may occur — the rationale being that the cure would be worse than the disease.

When a company *transfers* a risk, the risk manager, who usually works in conjunction with an insurance broker, endeavors to find the best insurance program available from carriers in the marketplace that provide the needed type of coverage. This is no simple task; it includes, among other things, determining the best deductible and premium payments available, which in the case of large companies often run into the hundreds of thousands of dollars annually.

Risk management is constantly faced with the problem of the selection of the best method (or if necessary, some combination of methods) of handling each identifiable risk. Regardless of the method or combination of methods used, some basic considerations affect most insurance programs. To be insurable, risks must substantially meet the following requirements:

- The risk should be worth the cost and effort to insure.
- The risks are calculable, through large numbers of similar risks.
- Losses can be clearly established as to occurrences and amounts.
- Losses must be accidental in nature, unexpected, and unintentional on the part of the insured.

CRIME INSURANCE

Crime insurance is usually obtained to supplement a company's security program. Although the presence or absence of insurance has no deterrent effect on crime, it does reimburse the company in whole or in part for losses sustained in a burglary or robbery or from internal theft. Crime insurance should, like other coverage, be tailored to meet the specific needs of the client. As one insurance broker advises, "If you want to know what your crime insurance covers, ask what it *doesn't* cover."

As a minimum, most crime insurance programs begin with "3D" — comprehensive dishonesty, disappearance, and destruction — a blanket crime or broad-form storekeepers' policy. This coverage will usually reimburse a company for losses due to employee dishonesty or counterfeit currency, as well as for loss of money, securities, or merchandise through robbery, burglary, or mysterious disappearance. These policies also generally cover certain types of check forgery and damage to the premises or equipment resulting from a break-in.

Some forms of specialized crime insurance coverage for specific needs include:

- *Mercantile safe-burglary policy:* covers loss of money, securities, and valuables from a safe or vault, and pays for damage to the container and any other property damage as a result of the burglary.
- *Mercantile open-stock policy:* mostly used by retail firms as coverage against burglary or theft of merchandise, furniture, fixtures, and equipment on premises, pays for damage to property resulting from burglary.
- *Fidelity bonds:* reimburses the employer for loss due to embezzlement and employee theft of money, securities, and other property.

(Bonds cover certain positions; employees who handle money, cash receipts, and merchandise are usually bonded.)
- *Forgery bonds:* reimburses merchants and banks for any loss sustained from the forgery of business checks.

Insurance premiums vary for these programs according to the type of business, store location, number of employees, maximum cash values, amount of security equipment (such as alarms) installed on premises, and prior losses. Merchants operating in some high-risk crime areas and thus needing insurance most are often the least able to afford the premiums. Further, it is difficult to find insurance companies willing to underwrite crime coverage in high-risk crime areas. Companies that experience a number of robberies or burglaries usually face escalating premiums, or worse, canceled policies.

For many small businesses and commercial enterprises, insurance and an antiquated burglar alarm may be the only form of protection affordable. For large companies and corporations, things are much different.

It is generally believed by knowledgeable corporate management, especially risk management, that insurance should be used for protection only against risk that cannot be avoided or controlled through the effective use of property, casualty, and security techniques. (In the insurance industry, property protection is synonymous with fire and casualty, is synonymous with safety.) This change in philosophy has come into vogue because more and more managers are getting the message that prevention, through risk avoidance, elimination, or control, is the best approach to the preservation of corporate assets. It is also recognized that most insurance programs do not fully compensate a firm for loss, regardless of the coverage.

A vice president of a large California construction company complained bitterly because the police were unable to send a detective to one of the firm's construction sites — a newly developed industrial park — to take a report and conduct an investigation into the theft of a fifteen-thousand-dollar compressor that had been delivered the day before. The police officer explained that he would have to take the report over the telephone. Further conversation with the officer revealed that little active investigation would be conducted in a case of this nature: it was regarded, the officer said, as "a problem between you and your insurance company." What the officer was not aware of, and what the vice president soon found out, was that the construction company's "3D" insurance policy had a $100,000 deductible clause — the theft of the fifteen-thousand-dollar compressor would not be covered. The big problem, the vice president lamented, was not so much the cash outlay for a new compressor as the time it would take for delivery, which was going to cause him major difficulties in meeting his construction deadline.

What this example illustrates is that management must become more interested in *avoiding loss*, not rest in the comfortable thought that it is insured against any and all eventualities. There is no insurance company I am aware of that would insure this vice president against the mental aggravation he went through; he is now, however, a believer in loss-control procedures as a solution to these kinds of problems.

A word about deductibles: these clauses are intended to reduce the cost of insurance premiums by deliberately excluding small, frequent losses while covering large, serious ones. The premiums are less expensive for two reasons: small claims are excluded if they fall under the dollar amount of the deductible, and the carrier's administrative cost of settling claims are also reduced.

It is neither the intent of this text nor the purpose of this chapter to do more than explain some basic insurance considerations that most security professionals should understand to do their job properly. Further information concerning insurance and risk management can be obtained by contacting The Insurance Information Institute, 110 William Street, 24th Floor, New York, N.Y., 10038, (212) 669-9200, or the business section of the public library. There is, however, one highly specialized form of insurance coverage that, because of historical developments and the increase in international and domestic terrorism, should be covered — kidnap, ransom, and extortion insurance.

K & R (KIDNAP AND RANSOM) COVERAGE

This form of insurance has been offered by Lloyds Underwriters for over sixty years. However, during the 1970s, as the risk and demand for coverage increased, a number of other insurers entered this market. Generally, there is little to be concerned about with respect to the financial security of such companies as the American International Group (AIG), Insurance Company of North America, the Chubb Insurance Company, and Lloyds Underwriters. Premium costs and the scope of coverage afforded under each of the companies' policies are generally the bases for deciding which to place insurance with.

Such an analysis is normally done at the time the risk manager or broker chooses to explore insuring this risk. Because there is competition in the insurance business — not only from a premium-cost standpoint but also with regard to breadth of form — any coverage comparison here would serve little purpose. Generally, the basic coverage provides reimbursement for loss of monies surrendered as a ransom payment for actual or alleged kidnapping, or following receipt of a threat to injure or kidnap an insured person. In addition, several features are usually incorporated into the policy contract:

> A *business premises extension* reimburses for any monies that must be brought in from outside for any kidnap situation if the money is lost while it is on the premises.
>
> A *transit extension* reimburses for any monies that are stolen between leaving the premises and reaching the kidnappers.
>
> A *reward extension* includes coverage for monies paid to informants whose information leads to the arrest and conviction of the individuals responsible for the kidnapping.
>
> A *personal assets extension* reimburses the insured persons for their personal assets that are used as a ransom payment if the demand is made on the insured person and not the corporation.
>
> *Negotiations, fees, and expenses* reimburse for reasonable fees and expenses incurred to secure the release of a hostage, including interest on a bank loan to pay a ransom payment.
>
> A *property damage coverage extension* provides coverage against threats to cause physical damage to property.
>
> *Defense costs, fees, and judgments* cover costs resulting from any suit for damages brought by an insured person. (The importance of this extension is underlined by an occurrence wherein a kidnapped executive later sued his employer for $185 million in damages, claiming that the employer had not exerted sufficient efforts to free him and had not taken steps to protect him from such an occurrence after being warned that the executive might be a target of abduction.)

There are some general requirements, mostly concerning secrecy concerning the fact that the company has K & R insurance coverage, of which the security professional should be aware. Here I caution that the specific details of each policy must be studied and adhered to in the event of a kidnap; otherwise the incident may be noninsurable. Some of these considerations are that:

- The ransom or extortion demand be specifically made against the named insured.
- The extortionate demand be made during the time frame of coverage as set forth in the policy.
- The company takes every reasonable precaution to ensure that the existence of the coverage is not disclosed to anyone except senior officials of the corporation.
- If a kidnap occurs, every reasonable effort is made to determine:

1. That an insured person has been abducted (note: not all policies cover all employees).
2. That the police or Federal Bureau of Investigation (FBI) have been notified *prior* to payment. That instructions and recommendations of the police and FBI in the best interest of the victim are accomplished to the extent possible.
3. That the insurance company is notified at the earliest practical time.
4. That the serial numbers of the ransom payment are recorded.

Some underwriters (insurance carriers) require that immediately upon obtaining coverage, written policy and procedural guidelines be established to eliminate the possibility of confusion with regard to the handling of these matters. Box 10-1 lists a number of topics that must be considered in establishing procedural guidelines. As will be discussed more thoroughly in Chapter 15, "Crisis Management Planning for Kidnap, Extortion, or Ransom," a more prudent course of action is to develop a crisis-management program specifically tailored to the requirements of the insured corporation. One of the benefits of such planning is to eliminate confusion before the crisis occurs: once a crisis begins, confusion usually reigns supreme if there is no well-thought-out and rehearsed plan.

Box 10-1. Executive Protection Program Outline

I. Home and Family
   A. General information
   B. Telephones
   C. Parties
   D. The executive
   E. Executive's spouse
   F. Children
      1. General information
      2. Baby sitters
      3. School(s)
   G. Residence in general—home check list
   H. Training-security awareness
   I. Doors and locks
   J. Alarm systems
   K. Lighting
      1. Exterior
      2. Interior
   L. Fence and barriers

Box 10-1. (*Continued*)

    M.   Window grilles
    N.   Dogs
    O.   Safe room

II. Office and Work
    A.   Premises—general
    B.   Access control
    C.   The executive
    D.   Executive profile
    E.   Employees—associated
        1.   Offices rules and work procedures
        2.   Meetings
    F.   Security guards
    G.   Bombs
        1.   Surveys
        2.   Target hardening
        3.   The bomb incident
        4.   Letter and package bombs
        5.   Antibomb curtaining
    H.   Threats
        1.   Telephone
        2.   Written
    I.   Hostage
    J.   Hostage calls

III. Travel
    A.   Automobile
    B.   Chauffeurs
    C.   Defensive driving
    D.   Walking
        1.   Jogging, golfing, and tennis
    E.   Elevators
    F.   Taxi cabs
    G.   Aircraft
        1.   Company
        2.   Commercial
    H.   Overseas or long distance travel
    I.   Reservations

IV. Personal Protection
    A.   Firearms—defense
        1.   Laws
    B.   Choosing a defense weapon
    C.   Firearms proficiency

Box 10-1. (*Continued*)

    D.   Weapon—method of carrying
    E.   Bodyguard
        1.   Selection
        2.   Personal qualifications
        3.   Professional qualifications
        4.   Guarding—locally
        5.   Guarding—away from home
        6.   Visitor protection
        7.   Motorcades
        8.   Public appearances
    F.   Protective clothing

V.   Crisis Management Team (CMT)
    A.   Defined
        1.   Purpose
        2.   Composition
        3.   Scope
    B.   Organization and planning
        1.   Readiness plan (prevention)
        2.   Contingency plan
            a. Worst possible case scenario
        3.   Training the team
    C.   Intelligence training
    D.   Law enforcement liaison
    E.   Public relations considerations
    F.   Ransom
        1.   Policy and procedures
        2.   Limitations
        3.   Negotiations
    G.   Civil liability considerations
        1.   Injury of employee(s)
        2.   Wrongful death claim
        3.   Stockholder suits

For serious students of risk management, or security professionals who want to understand better how insurance relates to their jobs, we recommend contacting the Risk Insurance Management Society (RIMS) Publishing, Inc., of New York City, at (212) 922-0716, and subscribing to Risk Management, a monthly magazine published by RIMS.

11

BUSINESS IMPACT ANALYSIS

Eugene Tucker, CFE, CPP
Contributing author

Companies are composed of individual business functions that work together to deliver services or products. While all functions are important during normal operations, some are more critical or time dependent than others. In most cases, not all business processes need to be recovered at the same time. Functions in an income tax software company may have an outage tolerance of just a few days in the month prior to release, but this tolerance may change to four weeks after mid-April. Functions initially less critical can become more important over time. Companies that survive after a disaster do so by focusing on the recovery of their most critical or time-dependent functions, by implementing the most cost-effective recovery strategies, and by making the best use of resources that become strained or scarce after a disaster.

A *business impact analysis* (BIA) is used to help management and the business continuity planner decide which functions are critical to the continued operation of the organization, to identify interdependencies between functions that are important to effective recovery planning, and to present management with a financial basis for selecting the most cost-effective recovery strategies. Outage tolerances or recovery time objectives are established based on the results of the analysis and the recovery priorities that are assigned.[1] Management will then understand how best to allocate recovery resources to these functions.

The business impact analysis will define the impact of a disruption over time and assist in the understanding of the amount of risk to assume, transfer, or mitigate. A common question asked of security managers and business continuity planners is: How much reduction in premium can we expect from our insurance company if we put these programs in place? The answer is usually "not much," especially when compared to the probable maximum loss,

---

[1] The outage tolerance of a function is the amount of time the organization can be without the use of that function before there is a detrimental effect on the organization. The recovery-time objective is the length of time before the organization would have the process or function back in service.

which can be avoided if the appropriate programs and resulting mitigations are in place. A risk analysis and a business impact analysis can greatly reduce the cost of insurance, by identifying and quantifying a potential loss, thereby allowing the risk manager to avoid over- or underinsuring the risk.

A BIA will allow management to make timely decisions about future business issues, and it will help the organization avoid a less than speedy recovery. Plans based on intuitive analysis are often too generalized or miss details important to an effective recovery. A comprehensive analysis often reveals interdependencies and outage tolerances that are not obvious even to those with intimate knowledge of the companies operations. This is accomplished by looking at impacts, over time, on:

- service objectives
- financial position/cash flow
- regulatory issues/contractual issues (for instance, can the organization meet milestones and commitments?)
- market share/competitive issues.

A business impact analysis will also help to:

- identify which processes and computer applications are critical to the survival of the organization;
- establish the value of each business unit as it relates to the whole, not to itself;
- identify critical resources of the organization;
- gain support for the recovery process from senior management;
- increase management's awareness of the issues and resources required for a workable program, as well as introducing a basic planning structure to the management group;
- potentially reveal inefficiencies in normal operations;
- help to justify or allocate better recovery planning budgets (cost/benefit).

A purist will advise the planner to treat the business impact analysis as a project separate from the continuity-planning phase. He or she will argue that the planner's only objective is to demonstrate the cost (impact) of a loss over time. This makes sense, in that functions are identified as critical and are prioritized in large part by their financial impact. As a practical matter, however, this is difficult, and it comes with some disadvantages. The business impact analysis will generate interest, support, and momentum in the continuity project as a whole. These advantages will diminish over time, so the planner must complete the initial phases of the project as quickly as possible. Separating the impact analysis from other elements of the continuity-planning process will often add unnecessary time and expense, which can result in failure to complete the project. Management time is often at a premium, so it is difficult to arrange more than one meeting to conduct the impact analysis, identify critical functions, and discuss recovery strategies and resource requirements. This is less of a problem in a large organization if the planner takes a top-down approach and has the opportunity to examine issues of preparedness, response, and recovery at a lower level of middle management. Unfortunately, within most organizations the best source of this information often resides only at this lower level. The planner may have only one opportunity to meet with these individuals. As a result, planners, especially those who use questionnaires extensively, include questions related to preparedness, hazard identification, and resource requirements as part of the business impact analysis meeting. Critical functions, the identification of single points of failure, and the initial selection of recovery strategies are often discussed at this juncture.

Be careful that the prioritization of functions are not based solely on their outage tolerances. Their relationship to the organization's mission is the most important factor. Impact information is also used in the cost/benefit analysis of recovery strategies. It is obviously important to decide which recovery strategies to use prior to scripting recovery instructions or steps. Often, the selection of a recovery strategy necessitates a change in policy or even the strategic plan of the company. Management may have difficulty making these decisions if the impact, solutions, and costs are not presented in a complete, positive (avoid a "savior versus doom-and-gloom") package.

RISK ANALYSIS VERSUS BUSINESS IMPACT ANALYSIS

A business impact analysis is often thought of as another name for a risk analysis. Some contingency planners believe a risk analysis is a process that focuses solely on physical assets and that a business impact analysis focuses solely on business processes. A close examination will reveal that this belief is not correct.

A business impact analysis is a means of assessing the impact of a disruption in any functional area or on the operations of the enterprise as a whole. It can be considered a subset of a risk analysis, in that it places an "asset value" on business functions and focuses on the criticality of a disruption over various time periods. The source or cause of the disruption, or a detailed understanding of the probability of its occurrence, is relatively unimportant when conducting an impact analysis and is therefore not considered. The planner has little need for chaos theory, fuzzy logic, or actuarial experience.[2]

---

[2] Is scenario planning more appropriately applied to the impact analysis, in plan and exercise development, or both? Scenario planning identifies causes, conditions, effects, and single points of failure; it also tests the availability of materials, personnel, transportation, and the like.

Therefore, the BIA focuses much less on hazard identification (some say there should be no focus on hazard identification). Listing all the hazards that might befall an operation may be useful in understanding the conditions, environment, and special needs required when selecting recovery strategies (such as the inability to move large pieces of equipment across town after an earthquake, or the amount of time required to remove bodies, complete an on-site police investigation, and remove the carnage after a workplace homicide), but it adds little to the understanding of financial or subjective loss to the operation over time. Outage tolerance is exclusive of its cause.

Again, its goal is not to rank the criticality of risks for planning purposes but to identify the impacts of the loss of business functions over time, to help identify interdependencies, and to prioritize the order of functions to recover.

The approach taken to initiate and manage a BIA is very similar to that used in a risk analysis. It must begin with senior management's commitment. Because a top-down approach provides the fastest and often most accurate results, management must emphasize this is a task not to be delegated downward in the organization. The planners' discussions with these managers in the process of collecting impact data will help to build relationships that will be useful later on if the business continuity-planning process becomes stalled, or if resistance is encountered.

The risk analysis is a more or less solitary experience, while business impact analysis is a top-down partnership with senior management. Advantages of this partnership include:

Additional Interaction with Upper Management.   For the planner or security manager to be at this level increases interaction and enhances recognition of the manager as a key member of the company. If the planner or security manager is at a lower level, bound by a tight reporting structure (as is often the case), partnership with senior management is an exceptional opportunity to familiarize oneself with their concerns. It allows senior management to recognize the value of your department and you as its leader.

Acceptance and Validity.   The data collected in this way is more often accepted. Data presented to management by an outside consultant or developed by a bottom-up approach may be met with skepticism and be examined with more scrutiny. Unless you or the consultant are intimately familiar with the financial position of the company, either may have difficulty responding to senior management's questions in a meaningful way. When the analysis is developed using a top-down approach, the management group will have had a hand developing the data and will tend to answer each other's difficult questions themselves.

Support. The partnership with senior management should generate the support needed to drive the project through the recovery planning phase. Without this support, continuity planning projects tend to bog down, die, or take so long that a great deal of time must be wasted revising information that has become outdated before the plan could be accepted.

Meaningfulness. The risk-matrix approach may be too simple and have little meaning to senior management if the results of the analysis are not in financial terms. Statistical probabilities can be confusing, and they tend to present a doom-and-gloom feeling. If statistics are used, they should be simple and accurate. Although the National Fire Protection Association (NFPA) 1600 uses the matrix approach, bear in mind that NFPA 1600 outlines minimum standards. We believe that business impact analysis or other methods that put financial data into the equation should be above this standard.

BIA METHODOLOGY

The business impact analysis, if conducted in a structured manner, can guarantee the success of the entire business continuity process. Different methods exist to accomplish this task. Whatever method is used, certain steps must be completed if the planner is to avoid obstacles commonly encountered in the analysis. The major elements of a business impact analysis include:

Project Planning
Data Collection
Data Analysis
Presentation of Data
Reanalysis

Project Planning

The initial steps to follow in the development of a business impact analysis include:

- Management commitment
- Definition of the scope of the analysis
- Identification of the participants
- Deciding how to collect the data
- Arranging interviews or distribution of questionnaires.

As stated previously, the biggest single predictor of the success or failure of the business continuity planning process is the level of senior management commitment. Most often, this commitment is gained only after management becomes fully aware of the potential harm to the company from loss of its ability to deliver service or products. These losses can be fully demonstrated through business impact analysis. The business impact analysis owes a great deal of its success to senior management support!

Which comes first, and how? Planners who have the ear of the chief executive officer (CEO) or an influential board member have little difficulty getting the needed support. Unfortunately, most planners are not blessed with this degree of leverage. To get the process started, the planner must find or convince someone in senior management to sponsor the project. Typically, this is the chief financial officer (CFO). Comprehensive financial audits increasingly mention the lack of a recovery plan. The CFO is more readily convinced of the importance of the project, due to his or her intuitive understanding of potential financial impacts on the organization. This is the person who also may be legally responsible for the protection of certain corporate documents. The CFO is usually high enough within the organization to drive the project and to help the planner both collect and interpret the data. If the planner has difficulty getting financial data from other managers, a "down and dirty" analysis can be derived from the CFO's knowledge alone.

Because the business impact analysis examines a great deal of financial data, the planner would normally maintain a close relationship with the CFO. The results of the analysis must be acceptable to management — everyone must believe that the analysis represents the true impact to the organization. The CFO should provide good insight into how the final report should be presented.

The CFO can convince the CEO and other senior managers of the need to commit themselves to the project, and of the value of a top-down approach — don't give senior managers an opportunity to delegate this task downward within the organization. Beginning the analysis at this level will help to ensure the accuracy of data, by avoiding the tendency of department managers to inflate the importance of their business units or functions. Lower managers usually do not have the "big picture" view of the impact that loss of their functions could have on the objectives of the organization.

The business impact analysis should be completed in the shortest time possible, in order to produce the most accurate results. The financial position (impact), even the organization of the company, can change rapidly; data may become outdated if it is more than three months old. Consider the use of outside consultants to assist with the interviews and analysis, if the scope of the project is sufficiently large to justify their use. The interest and momentum gained for the recovery planning process will be diminished if this phase is extended for any length of time. Enlist senior management's help in arranging to have all participants available for the study. A senior executive or the project sponsor should issue a memo to all affected personnel describing the importance of the project and introducing the project leader.

There should be agreement with senior management on the scope of the analysis, timelines for the project, the type of outcome expected (for instance, the format of the presentation), and who is to participate. Product introductions, or a pending Federal Drug Administration inspection in a biotechnology firm, are not times when full cooperation can be assumed. You will have better success when all participants are otherwise available.

Normally, the scope of the analysis will mirror that of the business continuity planning project, but management or the planner can tighten the scope to an individual division, site, or location. Many planners make the mistake of including in the analysis only those departments or business functions they believe are critical — a major goal of the business impact analysis is to determine *what* is and what is not critical. At this juncture, assume that all functions are critical at some point in time, or under certain circumstances, and include them in the analysis.

Meet with the CFO or your sponsor to determine who should participate in the analysis. Interview the highest-level manager in each functional business unit. Try to maintain consistency among the positions of the participants; that is, interview only at the director, or vice president, level. Organization charts are useful tools to guide the planner to the proper levels within the organization for interviews. As with continuity planning, many planners insist that a planning group, composed of the planner and members of management, must develop questionnaires and determine what impact the organization will suffer from disasters. They believe this is the best and only method to ensure management support and an effective planning process. In fact, planning groups can be useful, if the time allotted to do the analysis is small or the number of business units participating is very large.

Prepare an informal list of potential financial impacts that may affect the operations of the company (see pp. 117–129, "Questions and Questionnaires"). In the meeting with the project sponsor, review the types of questions and assumptions you intend to use. Discuss any additional impacts or risks the sponsor may wish to add to the list. If you are a consultant, the sponsor can ensure that terminology used in the questionnaires is consistent with that used in the company; this will help to avoid confusion or inconsistencies in the data.

Determine how best to manage the collection of the data. Data collection is accomplished through the use of interviews, questionnaires, or both. Questionnaires distributed directly to managers tend to be delegated, so avoid their exclusive use unless they are to be completed during the interview. Questionnaires are best used in a bottom-up approach to collect resource information that you will incorporate in the plan.

Schedule interviews. Give a brief presentation to the participants outlining the purpose of the analysis and giving them an opportunity to collect the information you need. It can be difficult to get managers to think in terms of the financial and operational impact of their operations, and to discuss recovery strategies, especially if they believe they will be responsible for selecting the best strategy then and there. This belief may overwhelm some managers and cause them to mentally give up on the project before it starts. Avoid this problem by clearly explaining to the manager the goals and expectations for the project prior to the interview.

In addition to the CFO, the risk manager is an important resource for the analysis. Meet with the risk manager to review insurance requirements. Determine what perils and property are excluded in existing policies. Ascertain the period of indemnity for business interruption and contingent business interruption, and estimate the time delay in reimbursement. Calculate the value of the physical assets and identify lead times for the replacement of assets. These values are often not considered, because they are subject to insurance reimbursement; however, it is important to know whether the policies call for reimbursement at replacement, or depreciated, values. (Although we will not reduce the financial impact in the analysis by the amount of reimbursement, we can add the difference in the replacement versus depreciated cost.) The loss of interest on cash reserves or on loans to secure temporary or replacement property, and extraordinary expenses during the delay between purchase and reimbursement, should also be added to the calculations.

Although it is more effective to concentrate on the restoration of critical business functions than on individual computer systems and applications, as was common in the past, critical functions can include "mission critical" processes, equipment, and applications. It is extremely important at this point to also meet with the information systems director to determine the impact of losing these functions, as well as other vital communication links within the company.

Data Collection

To obtain data that is valid, examine all current business functions and operations. Some planners suggest that only critical business functions be analyzed, but again, the purpose of this analysis is to determine which functions are critical. Any designation of a function, operation, or process as critical or noncritical prior to the analysis is merely intuitive. Intuitive estimates of potential acceptable outage tolerances or downtime can misdirect many thousands of dollars to recovery strategies that cause overplanning or unnecessary loss during a recovery situation. Data for the analysis is best collected through interviews with unit or department leaders. This approach helps to gain their buy-in for the project more effectively than if they were simply to respond in a questionnaire. During a personal interview, managers can ask questions and better understand what is expected from them.

Start the main part of the interview with the difficult financial and subjective impact questions, so that neither the planner nor manager feel the need to rush through the process as the meeting time begins to expire. If planners cannot schedule sufficient time to cover these topics adequately, they should consider postponing meetings for another time. Allow an hour to an hour and a half for each meeting, longer if nonimpact issues are discussed or if the manager is not experienced with putting impacts in financial terms. Although this is a top-down data-collection procedure, it may be necessary to meet later with the next-lower level of management to validate impacts and strategies developed.

During the interview determine:

- How the business unit fits in with the overall mission statement of the organization;
- What the primary service objectives of the business unit are;
- What the business units processes and dependencies are.

The analyst will also guide the manager to:

- Estimate the maximum loss were the function to be out of service, out of operation, or access to it were to be denied for thirty days or more. (This thirty-day period can be adjusted to fit expected outages, but it should remain consistent for all business units being evaluated. Assume that the function, or access to it, is lost at the worst possible time of the month, year, business cycle, or production schedule. Be careful that evaluation of functions is not duplicated.)
- Determine how this maximum loss is allocated over the following times: Day 1, Day 2, Day 3, Day 4, Day 5, Week 2, Week 3, Week 4. (Again, these times can be adjusted to fit the specific environment. For example, it may be more realistic for a financial institution to track its losses by the hour instead of by the day. Consult with the CFO to decide what time periods are best to use for the calculations.)
- Estimate any extraordinary expenses the unit may incur if the function is lost. (As before, indicate the maximum amount as well

as the details over a specified time. Extraordinary expenses can include costs associated with idle staff, wages paid to extra staff to handle backlogs, equipment rental, outside services, and transportation.)

- List the impact on any contractual or regulatory obligations the outage will cause. What fees, fines, penalties, or missed milestone payments will the company face?
- Indicate how cash flow will be affected by the outage.
- Rate the loss of goodwill or damage to the corporate image.

When seeking answers to these and other questions, be careful not to put participants in a defensive situation. Form questions in such a way as not to cause managers to believe they need to justify their positions within the company. Don't ask, "How valuable is your function to the organization?" Instead, ask:

- What would be the impact to the organization if this function were lost?
- How would this impact change over time?
- How would the loss of this function affect other functions within the organizations (that is, what other functions are dependent on the input to or output from this function)?

Some planners and software developers believe the best method for completing the analysis is a simple distribution of questionnaires to appropriate participants. As much as possible, avoid the use of questionnaires. Questionnaires without personal interviews will not maximize the planner's understanding of how each function fits into the overall organization and how its interdependencies relate to the whole. Managers are reluctant to put sensitive financial and other impact information "in writing" and may need additional time to answer the questions adequately. Face-to-face interviews can stimulate managers' understanding of the process and, more importantly, their ability to think through strategies and resource needs. A simple compilation of financial information from questionnaires will miss subjective information that could be important to an accurate analysis of the data.

During an interview, the analyst can ask the questions listed on the questionnaire, with the exception of items that are simply resource oriented. Have a printed or electronic (diskette) version of the questionnaire available to give to the manager after the interview. Many of the business-continuity-planning and business-impact-analysis software programs on the market have this capability. The manager fills out the questionnaire on diskette, and the analyst simply imports the data into the software, avoiding the need to input data twice.

If a questionnaire is used without an interview, meet briefly with the recipients and explain both the purpose and importance of the project. Recipients rarely complete all sections of questionnaires, necessitating follow-up questions. Questionnaires are impersonal.

Box 11-1. Sample Questions

The following are sample questions the planner should ask to obtain the type of information useful to a complete and meaningful impact analysis.

1. If your department or function generates revenue for the organization, what are the sources of this income? Sources of income can include:

- Product sales (list by product lines)
- Services rendered to outside clients
- Discounts or commissions
- Interest from investments or floats
- Incentives for on-time or ahead-of-schedule completion dates or milestones
- Tax base, if a government agency
- License and use fees
- Maintenance fees
- Other _____.

2. In addition to the loss of revenue, what other types of financial impact would there be if your department or function were lost? This may include:

- Canceled orders due to late delivery
- Penalties for late payments
- Regulatory requirements, late filings, and fines
- Contractual obligations delayed or not met
- Interest on borrowed funds
- Wages paid to idle staff
- Other _____.

3. What is your estimate of the total exposure for each item or product if the inability to function or deliver the service lasted for a thirty-day period, assuming the loss occurred during the period of its greatest negative impact? For example, if the greatest percentage of sales for your Christmas products occurs during December, use the sales figures from this month to estimate the exposure. If your greatest percentage of sales for swimwear occurs

Box 11-1. Sample Questions *(continued)*

---

during June, use the sales figures for June to estimate loss of sales potential for swimwear. Combine these two (or more) totals to arrive at the exposure for a thirty-day period.

List the cumulative minimum and maximum loss for the Days 1, 2, 3, 4, and 5 of the outage for each exposure. If your organization includes retail sales, list the daily sales volume for a seven-day period. Continue by calculating and listing the exposure for Weeks 2, 3, and 4 of the outage. Again, use a time period that is significant to your business. (Recovery times are often thought of in weeks and months, but impacts in certain institutions, such as a bank, can increase dramatically in a few hours and days. In banking, the organization may cease to exist long before the end of a thirty-day period. These organizations must therefore calculate their losses by hours, not days.)

It is useful to list these figures in table format, for ease of input onto a spreadsheet or into a database program that can combine and report the totals.

Exposures may include:

- Lost sales (total or by product)
- Delayed milestone payments
- Other _____.

4. What types of extraordinary expenses are necessary to implement expected or projected recovery strategies for your business functions? These expenses may include:

	Day 1		Day 2		Day 3		Day 4	
Exposure	*Min*	*Max*	*Min*	*Max*	*Min*	*Max*	*Min*	*Max*
Lost Sales	0	0	5000	5000	7500	10000	10000	20000
Canceled order	0	0	1000	1000	2500	3000	75000	100000

	Day 5		Week 2		Week 3		Week 4	
Exposure	*Min*	*Max*	*Min*	*Max*	*Min*	*Max*	*Min*	*Max*
Lost Sales	20000	30000	75000	125000	350000	500000	750000	950000
Canceled order	100000	250000	450000	750000	750000	750000	750000	750000

Table 11-1. *Example of BIA Input Table*

Box 11-1. Sample Questions *(continued)*

- Transportation costs
- Rent for alternative space
- Contract services
- Emergency requisitions
- Temporary relocation of employees
- Temporary employees to catch up backlogged work
- Equipment rental
- Additional supplies
- Other _____.

Determine the minimum and maximum extraordinary expenses over time and list them as described in Question 3.

5. At what times of the week, month, year, or business cycle is processing or production especially critical? In other words, when can an outage hurt you the most? This information is useful to the management team in making strategic "corrections" or modifications to the recovery plan made necessary by the timing of the disaster. It can illustrate changing priorities and allow decision makers to redirect resources to where they are needed most, and when.

> Critical times are typically the end of each quarter or year, or some significant product-related event. A toy manufacturer may list the months of September, October, and November as its most critical time, preceding the Christmas season. When requesting answers via questionnaire, allow respondents to provide free-forms. Some questionnaires and business-impact-analysis software programs only allow for the selection of individual months. Although this monthly period may be sufficient for the analysis, it may not be sufficiently focused for recovery purposes. As pointed out above, a financial institution may not be able to recover from a month's outage. Later, this information is matrixed in the continuity plan.

6. What other business impacts may result from the loss of your business functions? The financial loss due to reduced customer service or technical support, tarnished public image, or the loss of future business is difficult, if not impossible, to predict or measure. Some impacts may be purely subjective, or difficult to state in direct financial terms. These impacts can have the greatest effect on the survivability of the company, and they should always be included in the analysis. This questions asks respondents to list what these impacts may be. Examples include:

Box 11-1. Sample Questions *(continued)*

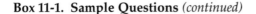

- Loss of competitive advantage or market position
- Loss of shareholder confidence
- Increased liability
- Decreased employee morale
- Cash-flow difficulties
- Reduced public image or confidence
- Reduced customer service
- Contractual consequences
- Regulatory violations and consequences
- Loss of key personnel.

7. How would you rate the severity of the above impacts if your business functions were lost? On a five-tiered scale, rate the estimated potential severities of the impacts if the outage were to occur during the worst possible moment. A value of 1 represents a minor impact, while a 5 represents a severe or fatal impact upon the function or the organization. (Any wider range of choices, such as a scale of one to ten, adds ambiguity to the evaluation.)

Some analysts attempt to assign specific definitions to each value. Although the definitions vary, the following is typical:

1 = Minor or no impact (the function or operation is easily handled, not affected, or is not an issue);

2 = Somewhat critical (although the problem is still easily handled, some degradation in the image, service provided by the function, or ability to meet requirements will occur);

3 = Moderate (nearly all of the functionality or ability to meet requirements is degraded);

4 = Serious (continuation of the function or ability to meet requirements is extremely difficult);

5 = Severe (the function or ability to meet requirements ceases).

The criticality categories listed elsewhere in this publication can also be used to express the severity of the impact. Use these impacts to help to determine which functions are critical to the organization and to demonstrate to management the consequences of the loss of certain functions. The severity ratings are combined by type of impact for each function, and then by type of impact for the entire company. This can be reported in a table or matrix format, but again, a graphical representation is easier to understand.

8. How much time would be required to reconstruct records or backlogged work once your function was back in operation? This question seems redun-

Box 11-1. **Sample Questions** (*continued*)

---

dant to the calculation of certain extraordinary recovery expenses, but it will help determine outage tolerances and recovery-time objectives. Based on a reasonable or expected duration of an outage, estimate the amount of time required to catch up, considering that normal operations are concurrent.

> Allow the respondent to give an open-ended response to this question, as the range of possibilities can be great. For some functions, the time required can be a few hours; in others it can be a number of years (and yes, you should discuss proper backup procedures in this instance).

9.   What short and long-term resources will your function require to operate at a minimally acceptable level while returning to normal operations? This question is intended to give the analyst an overview of critical systems and equipment to help determine outage tolerances and interdependencies. The respondents should detail their resource needs on resource forms or questionnaires after the interview. Questions such as this, and others that ask about the criticality of systems, equipment requirements, application tolerances, and dependencies, are also useful to the issues of critical-function recovery and recovery prioritization. Keep in mind that software applications and systems (servers) are not critical functions for the purpose of a business impact analysis—they *support* critical functions. If a server or application is lost, its impact is the loss of the critical functions it supports. Be careful that such factors are not counted more than once in the calculation of losses.

10.   What are the lead times for the replacement and installation of the equipment and systems listed above? This is an important question, one that can drastically affect the selection of recovery strategies. High-technology equipment can have lead times of six months or more. Even if the equipment can be quickly replaced, the re-creation of its environment and support systems can take a long time.

OTHER QUESTIONS FOR THE IMPACT ANALYSIS

The following questions are commonly listed on questionnaires or asked during the business impact interview. They can help the analyst maximize the use of time while gaining information for an effective analysis and continuity plan.

- What is the name of your department, unit, or function? Please describe its function. Include an overview of what your depart-

Box 11-1. **Sample Questions** *(continued)*

ment or team must do to recover from a disaster (you will be asked to list detailed instructions later).

- How long can your department, unit, or function be out of service without adversely affecting the overall operation of the company?
- What are the most critical functions of your department or unit? Which of these functions would need to be recovered first, either at an alternative site or reconstructed at the original site?
- What tasks would be necessary to recover these functions?
- If these tasks for the recovery of the various functions are dissimilar, how many separate recovery teams would be necessary to implement these tasks?
- Who would you select as team leaders and alternates for these teams?
- What customers (internal or external) or other business activities would be impacted by the inability to deliver or perform your function? Describe the extent of the impact and estimate the amount of time before the impact would affect the customer.
- What other areas or functions of the company are you dependent upon to operate effectively, and how would their inability to deliver service or products affect your operations? How would an areawide disaster affect the physical delivery of this service or product?
- What other needed services, products, or raw materials would be available if access to your present supplier ceased?
- Is your function directly involved with billing, collection, or the processing of revenue? If yes, please describe.
- Have any arrangements or agreements been made with your vendors for emergency delivery of critical resources?
- Where would or could the organization go to perform this function if employees were unable to gain access to the current location? Are similar functions performed at other company locations, on whose resources you could depend on an interim basis? Please state the names of the units, sites, and office locations.
- Indicate the estimated square footage required to house disaster-recovery operations for both a short and long-term (or permanent) relocation of your business unit. Attach a copy of any special floor plans needed.
- What computer support systems (that is, HP, IBM, stand-alone PC, or LAN) are necessary for the continued operation of your unit?

Box 11-1. Sample Questions *(continued)*

What is the maximum amount of time these support systems could be unavailable before their loss would have a negative impact on the company? Rank these systems in order of priority and indicate what configurations are necessary. Are these systems maintained by the Information Systems Department or by your department?

- Do your critical vendors have tested recovery plans in place, and is their recovery time consistent with your needs?

RESOURCE QUESTIONNAIRES AND FORMS

Ideally, the resources required to implement the recovery strategies are best determined subsequent to the selection of the strategies themselves. Most often, however, questionnaires are distributed after the interview to give the respondent time to list the short and long-term resources they would need to recover their operations based on only the preliminary discussion of strategies. Resources are selected from the following categories:

- Employees and consultants
- Internal and external contacts
- Customers
- Software and applications
- Equipment
- Forms and supplies
- Vital records
- Other _____.

Employees

Not all employees on your staff are generally needed during the initial recovery phase. After a disaster, space and resources may be limited. List the names, titles, addresses (optional), and contact phone numbers for the employees assigned to your team. Set up call trees if desired. List as many numbers as practical (home, office, cellular, pager, fax, and e-mail addresses) and use a consistent format, such as: (415) 555-1212.

Identify at what point during the recovery process the individual is required, according to the following:

Box 11-1. Sample Questions *(continued)*

Figure 11-1-1. Sample Employee Resource Questionnaire Form

---

*Function:*_____

			Contact Information				
Employee	Title*	Address	Home	Cellular	Pager	Priority	Called by:

* Title, position, or recovery function.

1 = required within the first twenty-four hours;
2 = required after twenty-four to seventy-two hours;
3 = required after three to five days;
4 = remain on standby until advised.

Internal and External Contacts

List the names, addresses, and phone numbers of vendors, suppliers, con-sultants, or other persons and groups, either internal or external, you may need to contact to assist with the recovery, the replacement of supplies, equipment, or raw material, or to provide technical support. This list should be complete but as short as possible. Bear in mind that your original list of contacts (phone books, vendor lists, etc.) may be buried under tons of debris after a disaster.

Briefly describe (one or two words, if possible) the type of service each contact provides and list any account numbers, passwords, or other type of authorizations required. If there are contact persons within a vendor company, you may list those names also. Examples of these con-tacts include:

Box 11-1. Sample Questions *(continued)*

Figure 11-1-2. Sample Internal/External Contact Resource Questionnaire Form

---

*Function:*_____

Contact/ Vendor	Name	Represen- tative	Address	Primary Phone	Alternate Phone	Category	Account Number	Password or Other

- Plumbers
- Electricians
- Seismic or structural engineers
- Janitorial service
- Security service
- Food service vendor
- Payroll processing
- Hot site providers
- Portable toilet/showers
- Insurance broker
- Bank manager
- Federal or regulatory agencies
- Media contacts
- Equipment/systems suppliers.

CUSTOMERS

Although customers may be listed under "internal/external contacts," you may want to list separately certain customers or contacts you would wish to inform of a disaster, in order to let them know of major delays and when you expect to

Box 11-1. Sample Questions *(continued)*

Figure 11-1-3. Sample Software Resource Questionnaire Form

---

*Function:*_____

Software Description	*Version #*	*Serial #*	*# of copies required*	*Source*	*Required by (day)*	*Environment (PC, Mac, HP)*

return to normal. If your organization is unaffected by a regional disaster, you may need to affirm to these customers your ability to continue to serve them.

Software

List all software applications utilized by the unit or team that would be required in a recovery situation. List the name and version number of the application or operating system and at what point during the recovery it is required (that is, first twenty-four hours, by Day 2, by the end of Week 2, for example). Record the location of backup copies (source).

Equipment

List the critical equipment your unit will need to function after the disaster. This should include, but is not limited to: desktop or personal computers (if possible, state configuration or hardware requirements, that is, amount of random access memory [RAM], hard disk, processor speed, CD-ROM drives, special attachments), terminals, printers, fax machines, calculators, phones, modems, tables, chairs, soldering irons, microscopes, shovels, and like equipment. Include model numbers and enter the quantity required for

Box 11-1. Sample Questions *(continued)*

Figure 11-1-4. Sample Equipment Resource Questionnaire Form

*Function:*_____

Equipment Description	Make or Model	Configu- ration	Short Term Requirements	Long Term Requirements	Lead Time	Environment (PC, Mac, HP)

a short-term outage (usually defined as less than five days) and also for a long-term outage. Estimate lead time for the replacement of equipment.

Forms and Supplies

List all forms and supplies that would be required to conduct business for both a short and long-term outage (for instance, letterheads, vouchers, diskettes, and special forms). Regular office supplies, such as paper, pens, or staplers, do not have to be included, as they should be readily available. Include such supplies as food, glassware, shipping cartons, and raw materials. Indicate where these supplies are stored or can be obtained.

Vital Records

Please list the critical records or reports on which your unit depends—records that must be available to send to regulators or that are necessary to conduct normal operations. Examples include accounts receivable, floor plans, corporate minutes, technical manuals, and the disaster-recovery plan.

Box 11-1. Sample Questions *(continued)*

Figure 11-1-5. Sample Forms and Supplies Resource Questionnaire Form

---

*Function:*_____

Description	Make, Model or unit #	Location	Short Term Requirements	Long Term Requirements	Lead Time	Quantity on Hand

Figure 11-1-6. Sample Software Resource Questionnaire Form

---

*Function:*_____

Description	Media type	Internal Location	External Location	Form or Box Number

Indicate where these records are stored or located within the company and on what type of media (paper, microfiche, or computer tape, etc.). If the record is in off-site storage, or at a law firm, identify the company and its location on this form and in the plan.

Data Analysis

The information gained from the interviews and questionnaires is analyzed according to the scope and goals of the project. Data is combined from all business functions, to allow the planner and management to decide which of them are critical to the continued operation of the organization and which are dependent upon others. Their outage tolerances are determined, and recovery priorities for both the individual business functions and support systems, such as computer applications, are assigned. When drawing these conclusions, the planner must keep the following guidelines in mind.

Outage tolerances and critical functions are not determined solely on the numerical data. For one thing, their designations may change. Also, while the analysis may indicate that product A generates the most income, it may also carry the highest recovery cost; management may decide to recover product B first because it has the lowest recovery cost, or is a product they wish to emphasize at the time. In most cases it is readily apparent from the data which functions are the most important, but the planner must obtain early verification of this from the sponsor.

Again, account for impacts only once each; be careful of duplicates. In a large or complex organization, it is easy to add the loss of a dependent function more than once when calculating the overall impact.

Do not deduct insurance coverage or expected claims reimbursement from the loss figures. While it is possible to predict (assume) the maximum amount of reimbursement for claims, it is more difficult to predict when the reimbursements will actually be paid or how the total amount will be distributed over the life of the claim. During a recovery situation, claims are usually not filed all at once — the extent of the loss, the amount of documentation, the varying procedures between insurance companies, and the added workload on the claims departments during an areawide disaster will delay or extend the process. Small and medium-sized companies have little tolerance of an interruption in cash flow caused by a disruption; for them, anything less than a rapid reimbursement may have fatal consequences. Figures adjusted for expected reimbursement may not adequately warn of this danger.

After the data from the interviews and the questionnaires are analyzed, verify the results with business unit management and with the CFO. This verification is important for keeping the data credible throughout the process.

Establish outage tolerances both within the critical processing time windows and during "normal process times" — that is, not end of month or end of quarter. List both in the recovery plan.

Presentation of the Data

Because business impact analyses are often used to gain management support for the continuity planning program or to justify program budgets, their results are presented to senior management. This presentation could be the most important step in the impact analysis. If it is successful, the planner will gain the political and financial support needed to complete the project. If not, the planner will have wasted many hours of valuable time and will face needless delay and frustration, and may produce a plan that is less than effective.

The analysis presented to management must be credible. As stated earlier, a top-down approach will result in the greatest degree of success. If this approach is used, the planner will have few problems with the acceptance of the analysis. When presenting the results, ensure that figures are accurate and not misleading, and that the data and the presentation are short and simple. Matrices, tables, and statistics tend to bore and confuse people, even at the senior management level. Slides with contain spectacular pictures of disasters and natural phenomena for background tend either to distract or cause the graphics to be remembered only for their scenery. Relationships and financial data are better represented graphically, either by pie, bar, or other types of charts. Whenever possible don't present expected occurrences in terms of probability — state them as a fact. For example, if the local Office of Emergency Services or the United States Geological Survey predicts that the probability of a major earthquake is 82 percent in the next ten years, report, "I believe there will be a major earthquake during the life of our strategic plan" (assuming it is a ten-year plan).

Distribute a written report that includes supporting data, the impacts for the individual functions or units, and the combined impacts for the organization. Unless it is important to the understanding of interdependencies or other relationships to mention others, discuss only the impacts of the major functions and the impact to the organization as a whole. During the presentation, outline why you are there and what you expect the group to decide or to do as a result of the analysis.

Reanalysis

Finally, business impact analysis should not be a "one shot deal." The information in recovery plans must be updated regularly and the basic strategic framework of the plan reviewed annually. It is logical that the impact to the organization will change as the structure and strategic direction of the business change. The impact analysis will help to identify these changes.

REVIEW

Risk analysis looks at the probability and criticality of risk to assets, while the business impact analysis addresses the value of assets or functions over time. The BIA is not concerned with specific events or probabilities. It identifies the financial and subjective consequences for the organization of the loss of individual functions.

Note: See Appendix D, sample business impact analysis introduction letter, and Appendix I, sample introduction letter, disaster recovery planning.

It may be appropriate to include scenario planning in a risk analysis to help identify hazards, and its detailed cause and effect approach is very useful to find a single point of failure in a complex system such as a manufacturing process or electronic control equipment, but its use in the Business Impact Analysis is somewhat counterproductive. Remember that in a BIA, we are concerned with the impact of a loss over time, not what caused the loss.

12

BUSINESS CONTINUITY PLANNING

Eugene Tucker, CFE, CPP
Contributing author

> A plan is nothing, planning is everything.
> *Dwight Eisenhower*

Business continuity planning is defined in many different ways, each reflecting its author's particular slant on contingency planning. Many of these definitions attempt to combine the definitions of continuity *planning* and of a continuity *plan*. There is an important distinction between the two.

Business continuity planning is a process that identifies the critical functions of an organization, that develops strategies to minimize the effects of an outage or loss of service provided by these functions. The most common strategies involve alternative facilities, where backup systems, procedures, and equipment would be available to restore operations to a minimally acceptable level. Disaster recovery planning is really synonymous with business continuity planning, but the term is a product of the data center. It represents the idea that recovery planning is important only to telecommunications and data centers. Business continuity planning implies recovery planning for all the critical functions or business units of an organization.

A business continuity plan is a comprehensive statement of consistent action taken before, during, and after a disaster or outage. The plan is designed for a worst-case scenario but should be flexible enough to address the more common, localized emergencies, such as power outages, server crashes, and fires. Although the actions listed in the plan contain sufficient detail to implement strategies designed to recover critical functions, they are more guides than inflexible dictates. Because it is not practical to plan for every type of contingency, and because each disaster has its own set of conditions, the ability to modify the plan must be incorporated.

Although a recovery plan is important, it is the planning process that returns the greatest value. This distinction is often missed by both planners and by the end users of recovery plans. The identification of critical functions, the thought and analysis behind the development of the strategies designed to recover the functions, and the knowledge of why one particular strategy was selected over another are not always apparent from simply reading the plan. This is valuable knowledge when last-minute decisions are required to adapt the plan to a particular situation. The planning process is also a training exercise. The participants must think through contingencies, so that the actions required to recover from them will be already familiar. Reading the plan for the first or second time just after the disaster will provide for a less than effective recovery. This is assuming, of course, that the plan is not buried under a hundred tons of rubble.

WHY PLAN?

Responsibility for contingency planning often resides with the risk manager, the chief financial officer (CFO), or with the data center manager. Security managers are, however, increasingly taking the role of plan developers. Their experience with the protection of assets, involvement in the identification and the mitigation of risk, and their emergency-response duties make them logical choices for this role. The ability to work effectively with all levels of management is a required trait for security managers, a trait that all the successful ones possess.

Some types of businesses, such as financial institutions and industries regulated by toxics laws, are required to maintain continuity plans. It is generally agreed that the Foreign Corrupt Practices Act of 1977 (FCPA) requires executives of public companies to take reasonable precautions to preserve records from destruction. This requirement is often satisfied with a continuity plan. The Securities and Exchange Commission can seek injunctive relief for noncompliance, even institute criminal proceedings against executives. Intent is not a required element of this statute. *Banking Circular 177*, first issued by the Comptroller of the Currency, requires all financial institutions to maintain corporationwide contingency plans. Although it directly applies only to banks and other financial institutions, it sets a standard for all organizations with fiduciary responsibilities. It is significant to others also, because it includes a suggested planning methodology.

In any case, even in the absence of regulatory requirements, it makes good business sense to maintain a continuity plan. The cost of downtime, the cost of reconstructing lost data, and the loss of cash flow can severely damage many organizations, even beyond their ability to recover. If they are unable to operate, retail and transportation operations can lose an average of over $100,000 per hour, high-technology manufacturing $200,000 per hour, and financial brokerages over five million dollars per hour. The costs of rebuilding twenty megabytes of data include:[1]

Function	Time Required	Cost
Sales/Marketing	19 days	$20,000
Accounting	21 days	$22,000
Engineering	42 days	$114,000

Without continuity planning, the organization may lose its competitive advantage, valuable employees, and future research. Organizations cannot insure against lost customers or a diminished public (customer) image. History consistently shows that between 35 to 50 percent of businesses never recover after major disasters. Other rationales for continuity planning include:

- Requirement by financial auditors
- Prevent the loss of market share
- Capitalize on the lack of planning by the competition
- Fiscal responsibility
- Stockholder liability
- Regulatory requirement
- Retain key employees
- Prevent the loss of research
- Help ensure the safety of employees
- Preserve customer confidence
- Assist in the overall economic recovery of the community
- Assists in a quick and orderly recovery after a disaster
- Minimize the economic loss (devaluation) to the firm.

THE PLANNING PROCESS

The basic steps involved in business continuity planning are simple, although their implementation can be complex and time consuming. The critical functions of the organization are identified and ranked according to

---

[1] *NSCA News 1990* figures adjusted for 1995 inflation, from a presentation by Roger N. Farnsworth, Business Recovery Managers Association, 1996. Note: 20 MB of information is not a large amount of data.

their value to the organization or to their interdependencies with other critical components. Cost-effective strategies for recovering the critical functions to a minimally acceptable level are evaluated. Once the recovery strategies are chosen, a plan is developed to implement the strategies. The plan is tested (the proper term is "exercised," or "simulated" — see Chapter 13), and provision for maintenance of the plan is established.

Before these steps commence, it is important to identify physical or procedural hazards that could cause an outage or that may delay the recovery process. When dealing with multiple sites, the planner should visit each location and conduct an inspection for these hazards. This inspection should identify single points of failure in critical systems, and it should produce a set of recommendations to mitigate the results of the hazards identified in the business impact or risk analysis.

Next, the organization must prepare to respond to the disaster or to the emergency when it happens. The goal of emergency response is to protect the health and safety of employees, guests, and the community, and to minimize damage to the organization by stabilizing the situation as quickly as possible. Response planning is not recovery planning, but the two plans should be integrated so there will be a smooth transition from response to recovery.

Once the disaster or emergency is stabilized, recovery and restoration will begin. The terms *recovery, resumption,* and *restoration* refer to separate phases of the organization's return to predisaster service levels (although some planners use them interchangeably). Resumption embraces the initial, short-term strategies and steps to get back into production as quickly as possible. Moving to a *hot site* (a separate building or office area with duplicate, or equivalent, equipment already installed, waiting for emergency use) and transfering production to a satellite facility are examples. Recovery and restoration refer to the long-term strategies and steps the company will follow to reestablish its normal goals, service, or production levels. The replacement of a production line, installation and testing of replacement equipment, and the construction of new facilities are examples. In this text we will use these two terms interchangeably.

PROJECT MANAGEMENT

Business continuity planning projects, if not properly managed, will lose momentum, languish, and die, or assume such a negative tone that the participants become hesitant to complete the project. Information and the strategic mission of an organization can rapidly change, so once the project is started, any significant delay will cause the end product — a business continuity plan — to be outdated before it is completed.

Project management is a major skill, and it is required of anyone who undertakes responsibility for business continuity planning. It is a partnership between members of management, outside services and vendors, employees, and sometimes regulatory agencies. The ability to schedule and manage resources, time, and people will bring the project to a successful conclusion.[2]

In broad terms, the following steps are followed to produce an effective plan:[3]

1. Identify the planning coordinator;
2. Obtain management support and resources;
3. Define the scope and planning methodology;
4. Conduct risk identification and mitigation inspections;
5. Conduct a business impact analysis;
6. Identify critical functions;
7. Develop recovery strategies;
8. Setup recovery teams;
9. Develop team recovery instructions;
10. Collect resource information;
11. Document the plan;
12. Train recovery teams;
13. Exercise the plan;
14. Maintain the plan.

1. Identify the Planning Coordinator

A person within the organization is designated as the planning manager, coordinator, leader (or other appropriate title). This person is responsible for the management of the project (that is, the completion of the plan) and possibly for coordinating or leading the recovery effort subsequent to a disaster. The coordinator may also have major responsibilities for plan activation. Ideally, this person should be a management-level employee who has good people and project management skills, a good understanding of the organization, and is detail oriented. A vast technical knowledge of risk, computer, and telecommunications systems is not necessary, but it can be helpful.

---

[2] Business continuity planning is an ongoing project of maintaining resource information and reexamining the basic strategies used to develop the plan. The plans must be "living" documents; the project is never "concluded."

[3] The Disaster Recovery Institute (DRI), in an attempt to standardize planning methodologies, has issued a common body of knowledge, which may list steps different from those listed here. See appendix C.

2. Obtain Management Support and Resources

No planning effort or project will be successful without the support of upper management. This support must be communicated to all levels of management. Most agree that the development of a business continuity plan is a noble project, but all too often other priorities tend to take precedence if participants are not held accountable to time lines and milestones. Its timely completion should be included in the goals and objectives for all expected participants. While the best results are obtained by motivating participants in a positive manner to complete their development tasks, it always helps to carry the big stick of upper management support behind your back.

In situations where the driving force behind the project is not senior management, the results of a business impact analysis should demonstrate to senior management the potential impact to the organization if all or a portion of the company could not operate. Their support is often obtained as a result of this demonstration. Before conducting the business impact analysis, you may need to define the scope of the project.

3. Define the Scope and Planning Methodology

It can be a daunting, if not impossible, task to produce plans for a large, worldwide corporate structure unless the job is accomplished in small pieces. Narrow the scope of the project to a single division, site, or building, something small enough to allow a positive outcome. A successful project will add momentum for the completion of subsequent projects throughout the remainder of the organization.

The selection of a starting point may be dependent purely upon need or upon the degree of risk. The risk or business impact analysis will show where the planners energy are best directed. Be prepared to go beyond the established scope when identifying interdependencies and strategies. The scope of the project may be to develop recovery plans for a manufacturing site in California, but the best strategies may involve the transfer of administrative functions and financial computing to the company's site in Illinois, and the transfer of manufacturing to Nevada.

Many methods exist to manage the project. These include:

- Planning standards for the business units or divisions
- Steering or planning committee
- Facilitation of internal development
- Use of template plans.

In large organizations, corporate continuity planning policies and procedures are developed and instituted. Planning standards can be successfully developed even when the scope of the project involves many locations or business units. Persons responsible for planning at each location or division are chosen. Planning guidelines, methods, and templates are developed and distributed. The corporate planner then trains these persons in the expectations of the project, monitors their progress, and helps to implement the plans. When this method is used, plans for the entire organization are developed quickly (usually a two-year process). Greatest success is achieved when the corporate planner develops the "basic plan" (see Chapter13, "Plan Documentation") and allows the divisions to concentrate on planning for only themselves.

Many businesses form a planning or steering committee composed of the company's or division's top managers to discuss business impacts and select strategies, and they assign the documentation of the plan to individual functional mangers. The business continuity planner will coordinate the efforts of the committee, business units, and outside consultants. A variation of this method is often applied at the business-unit level, where a committee is formed to identify critical functions and strategies. Steering committees work best when the organization or planner has little knowledge of continuity planning principles and strategies or cannot gain an understanding of the operation or needs of the business unit.

The use of planning committees is suggested in *Banking Circular 177*, Comptroller of the Currency, and NFPA 1600. Many planners insist that committees are the best way to produce effective continuity plans. Fundamental problems, however, can arise with the committee approach. Committees can delay decisions, and corporate policies can dilute the effectiveness of the process. Often, much time is wasted discussing administrative issues.

The best planning method places the planner in the role of a facilitator. The planner must bring his or her project and people management skills together to assist each individual business unit to develop its own plans. Each unit or recovery team must "own" its portion of the plan and become familiar with its contents. Working as a facilitator, the planner can tap the individual managers' or business unit leaders' technical knowledge and experience to guide the creation of their own plans, while keeping them consistent in direction and format with the overall planning structure. As opposed to a committee, working with these individuals helps the planner or senior management meet milestones and hold responsible those who do not.

Many business continuity planning consultants promise to come in and develop a plan for your organization within three months, or sell you a template plan in which you just fill in the blanks, but your organization will gain very little from their product. The individuals responsible for its implementation will have little familiarity with or commitment to its contents. It becomes the consultant's plan, not your plan. Consultant should act as facilitators, and as advisors about the most effective strategies, if they are to deliver effective plans.

Use great caution when using templates (for instance, external or internal plans from other organizations). They are meaningless if not adapted to local conditions and needs. They do not require the "thought process" necessary to provide the training needed to execute the plan effectively after a disaster.

Once the scope and methodology are determined, select the managers who will participate in the process. This may be the same group that participated in the business impact analysis. In most cases, they will be the functional or department heads. Schedule interviews of at least one hour's duration to discuss:

- Business impacts;
- Critical functions;
- Recovery strategies;
- Expectations and needs of the manager;
- Description of the project;
- Questionnaires or resource forms;
- How the function operates under normal conditions and how the product or service is delivered; or produced;
- Interdependencies — for instance, where the input comes from and who gets the function's output. (For example, a manufacturing line might get its input from raw materials stores. Its output goes to Quality Assurance. If raw materials stores are not recovered, or are not recovered first, manufacturing may have difficulty with its recovery. If a particular software application stops processing, other applications that depend on its output may stop or return inaccurate results.)

Schedule meetings over a two or three–day period with:

- Management information systems (MIS) or the local area network (LAN) administrator
- Human Resources
- Legal
- Facilities
- Management or site manager
- Manufacturing/Operations
- Finance (accounts receivable and payable, cash management, and payroll)

- Telecommunications
- Risk and insurance manager
- Security and safety
- Other pertinent functions.

Prior to the meetings, issue a letter or memo to the participants to introduce yourself and let them know what you expect. Briefly outline the process so they can begin to think about their responses.

4. Conduct Risk Identification and Mitigation Inspections

The more hazards and risks that can be identified and mitigated beforehand, the less severe will be the disaster and the faster the recovery.

Inspect the buildings, grounds, and community for any hazard that may injure employees, damage equipment or facilities, or cut off the supply of materials, resources or services. When searching for these hazards, the techniques learned from scenario planning are useful. Think through the causes and effects of likely scenarios and offer recommendations to mitigate their effect. For example, some of the typical effects following a major earthquake may include:

- Structural damage and displacement
- Posttraumatic stress
- Loss of utilities (gas, water, electrical power)
- Disruption of communications
- Transportation difficulties
- Inflated prices for goods and services (in a cash economy)
- Human resource problems
- Overloaded and nonresponsive governmental services
- Victims trapped under structures and debris
- Fatalities, shortage of hospital beds and medical assistance
- Disruption of routines
- Difficulty obtaining food and water
- Uncontrolled fires
- Increased illnesses
- Damaged or destroyed product and raw materials
- Canceled orders
- Loss of vital records.

A review of the literature on the effects of a flood would make clear the need to control mold, mildew, and snake bites, but such benefits of experience may not be available in print on the results of a failure of a proprietary process or a hazardous-substance spill. Scenario planning will help you foresee the postdisaster conditions that must be considered.

Question the general manager, facilities manager, or other appropriate people on what could prevent emergencies, outages, and disasters. Does the company have an evacuation procedure? Are first aid, food, and water supplies stockpiled? Are critical systems or equipment connected to an uninterruptible power supply? Are computer files backed up on a regular basis and stored off site?

5. Conduct a Business Impact Analysis

When relevant risks and hazards have been identified, submit a report to the steering committee, senior management, or the sponsor of the project outlining recommendations to mitigate the hazards. This report can be combined with the results of the business impact analysis, especially if the analysis has been completed informally, as is too often the case.

6. Identify Critical Functions

The identification of critical functions is a major result of the business impact analysis. Many planners believe it is a waste of time, effort, and resources to include in the plan functions that are not critical to the organization. Equipment and space at a hot site or other alternative location is expensive and limited; therefore, priority there is given to the most important functions and employees. Remember that recovery operations are time sensitive. There must be a logical sequence (order) of recovery actions, to minimize recovery time. Others argue that if a function is not critical, it should not be a part of the organization in the first place.

Generally speaking, a critical function can be a process, service, equipment, or duty that would have one of the following impacts on the company if the function were lost or if access to it were denied:

- Affect the financial position of the company
- Have a regulatory impact
- Reduce or destroy public/customer image/confidence or sales.

7. Develop Recovery Strategies

The heart of the business continuity planning process is the selection of the best recovery strategy for each critical function of the business. This is where the planner or consultant can provide the most value to the organization.

In many plans, the major strategies include the transfer of one or more functions or business units to alternative locations. Ideally, this is accomplished quickly and transparently. The selection of the best strategy, especially those used to recover technical functions — such as mainframe computers, servers, and telecommunications — can be complicated and can change according to many factors. If the planner does not have the technical knowledge or if the expertise is not available internally, it is best at this point to bring in consultants. Many recovery strategies involve large expenditures, so it is important that the solution does not become the problem — that is, the strategies must be cost-effective.

During the interviews with managers, discuss options they believe can reestablish temporary (short-term) operations. Also discuss how the managers expect to implement the options and how long it will take. Repeat this process for a long-term outage. Very often the function leader has been through some type of outage or knows someone who has. What did they do to reestablish operations? Discuss the feasibility of other strategies, and pick the ones that will work best, based on recovery needs and requirements (for instance, outage tolerance).

Complete a cost/benefit analysis for each strategy, using information from the business impact analysis. If the loss of the function will cost the company $100,000 after ten days, it makes little sense to spend $300,000 on a strategy that will put it back in operation in one day, especially if less expensive strategies exist to resume at least partial operations in, say, eight days. Once the analysis is completed, select the best recovery strategy.

Recovery strategies can be multifaceted for a single business unit or function. The actions required for recovery may be different from those required for restoration. If operations are transferred to an alternative location, at some point they need to be transferred back to a new, permanent location. The strategies developed are limited only by cost, the planner's creativity, and the strategic direction of the organization. It is important, of course, that a strategy can be reliably implemented. If the recovery strategy for a West Coast technical support center is to transfer support calls to a center on the East Coast, be sure that:

- Its telephone equipment has the capacity to handle the extra volume of calls.
- The East Coast support staff is knowledgeable about the products supported by the West Coast center.
- Provisions are made for the difference in time zones.
- Extra staff is available on the East Coast.
- Manuals and documents are available.

The following list represents a small number of strategies the planner can select to recover critical functions, data, and equipment. It is by no means exhaustive, and each one should be researched by the planner to determine if it is the best strategy suited to the situation. During the hazard inspection or business impact analysis, determine to what extent any of these strategies or redundancies are already implemented:

- Revert to manual methods
- Alternative power sources
- Alternative communications modes (cellular, satellite, other)
- Alternative processing sites
- Third-party manufacturing
- Purchase of material from competitors
- Records management
- Facilities salvage and restoration.

Revert to Manual Methods.   More and more functions rely on automated systems to perform their work. When the automated systems fail, businesses can revert to the manual methods used before the system was automated. For example, a mail order electronics distributor types an order into a form that resides on a computer. The computer sends the "pick list" to the warehouse, deducts the item from inventory, and sends a report to accounting after it has billed the customer. If the computer fails, the person who takes the order fills out a three-page NCR (No Carbon Required) form and physically sends a copy to the warehouse, inventory control, and accounting. When the computer or server is repaired, automated methods resume, and temporary employees are brought in to input the NCR forms into the system.

Unfortunately, with high turnover in many organizations, few employees remember how the job was done before automated methods were used. Often "new" manual methods are developed, and recovery teams are trained in their use. Many high-technology companies, however, cannot use manual methods to manufacture their products.

Alternative Power Sources.   Power surges, spikes, and drops account for the more common "disasters." These utility problems damage or destroy sensitive computer systems, research, and production equipment. Important data files can be corrupted. If power is lost, work in progress can be lost. Power losses over wide areas are expected to increase over the years as more demand is placed on the power grids and as companies adjust to deregulation.

The most common and least expensive mitigation to this risk is to install an individual uninterruptible power supply on each piece of critical equipment. A UPS is basically a device that delivers "conditioned" power (current protected from significant spikes or drops) to the equipment. It also contains a battery that, in case of a complete loss of power, will allow the unit to continue operation until a backup generator takes the load or the equipment can save its data and executes its shutdown routine. Some high-technology equipment can be damaged if it is simply shut off without going through this routine.

If the loss of electrical power will have a serious impact, consider bringing in redundant power from a different grid. This will prevent power losses caused by local conditions, such as lightning strikes or downed lines. Feed the power from a different direction and to a different part of the site.

Another common mitigation and strategy is to install a backup generator capable of running critical (or emergency) systems as long as a fuel supply is available. If possible, have extra fuel on hand (if electrical power is out, the pumps at the local gas station will not work). Generators are powered by diesel, natural gas, or by gasoline. Those supplied by natural gas might also be fed by separate sources or routes. Smaller generators mounted on trailers can be rented and brought on site. If this is the strategy selected, consider the installation of a "quick fit" device outside the building. This device would be hardwired to the electrical distribution panel; the generator is simply plugged into the building, saving many hours of connection time.

Power supplies and generators should be tested regularly under load conditions.

Telecommunications.   Most organizations are highly dependent on communications for voice and data transmission. The loss of voice and data can quickly have a severe impact on the organization. Equipment failure, software glitches, cable cuts, hackers, and fires in cable vaults or central stations can cause the loss of this function for days. Phone companies devote a tremendous amount of resources to ensuring the reliability of their networks, but after a disaster, communications becomes the most quickly affected function. Due to increased demand, the telephone network can become overloaded and cease to work, even if the equipment is working properly. This can even happen internally, for instance, if a well publicized event causes a sudden influx of calls, overloading the switchboard's ability to handle the traffic.

Strategies to mitigate damage to the communications system and to recover its function include:

- Service and replacement agreements
- Bypass circuits and fax lines
- Divergent routing
- Cellular backup
- Satellite systems
- Hot/cold sites
- Third-party call centers.

When equipment fails or is damaged or destroyed, it will need replacement. However, organizations cannot afford to be without communications for the time required to reorder, deliver, and install new systems. Most communications vendors offer twenty-four-hour emergency-equipment replacement agreements for an up-front additional cost, with annual renewals of the agreement. If the impact of the loss of communications is severe or time dependent (such as in a catalogue sales operation), the organization may use a telecommunications hot or cold site. A *cold site* is a separate building or office area that does not have the equipment installed but has sufficient space to accommodate at least the minimum number of employees needed to conduct business. A call to the telephone company will transfer the company's lines to the hot site so that the move will be transparent to the customers. Like hot or cold sites for computer systems (discussed below and in Chapter 13), there are subscription, setup, declaration, and user fees involved. Modern call centers have operators on standby to answer questions or take messages until the firm is set up in the hot site. This initial switch over can take less than fifteen minutes if the company is faced with a local (not regional) disaster.

Many systems are equipped with a number of "power failure" circuits that bypass the phone switch (your main on-site phone-switching equipment) and directly access an outside line. This capability, and the location of these circuits, should be confirmed, and used when necessary. If a fax server is not in use, phone lines for facsimile machines can be "borrowed" for voice or data communication. Check to see if your handsets are compatible (digital versus analog) with these circuits.

Voice and data are transmitted around the world through a variety of modes — overhead cable and fiber, underground cable and fiber, microwave, and satellite, to name a few. One of the more common causes of communications failure is a cable cut by a contractor digging a trench. Landslides and bridge collapses also disrupt communication cables. *Diverse routing* is one method used to protect against these dangers. With diverse routing, your main circuits may pass through southern states while your secondary or diverse circuits use cables located in northern states. Unfortunately, diverse routing can in reality mean only that your circuits use separate pipes — buried right next to each other. This can be true even if your primary and secondary cables are carried by different communications providers.

After the Loma Prieta earthquake in California, interest in *cellular* communications for emergency and recovery operations increased. Cellular systems minimize the use of ground-based cable, and the abundance of cell antennas adds redundancy to the system. Many believe they would be more survivable during and after a disaster. The switch to digital cellular makes data transmission and portable Internet access over the cellular system an acceptable strategy for a portion of the organization's recovery needs. The planner should use this strategy with the caution, however; as in land-based systems, the increased number of users will congest the network even during nondisaster times. We see this occurring now in large metropolitan areas like Los Angeles. To add a degree of reliability, consider subscribing to two different providers, if this option is available in your area.

Microwave is a form of high-frequency radio transmission beamed from point to point. Microwave transmissions can be used to reestablish communications between buildings across a campus, city, or wider area. They can provide diversity in both voice and data communications, and they are not very susceptible to cable cuts. The use of microwave for diverse routing can be expensive, but it easily spans difficult terrain and provides large bandwidth capabilities.[4] Transmission towers, however, are susceptible to destruction or misalignment by high winds and earthquakes.

Satellite transmission is used for primary or diverse routing, or as a backup communications channel. It is especially useful for continuity planning, in that mobile transmitters can be connected to the site and used to reestablish communications very quickly. Their failure rate is very low, and they are affected only by the difficulty with transportation after a disaster. Bandwidth and security are very good. Cellular phones are now using satellites as their cell antennas.

Two-way radio is becoming more popular as a primary means of connectivity between desktop components and servers, especially for networks in a campus environment. It saves the cost of wiring the networks together, and it is more tolerant of structural damage. However, security, bandwidth, and range limitations can become problems.

Third-party call centers and answering services, used for overflow customer support or order entry, can also be primary call centers after a disaster. Investigate the ability of their equipment and staff to handle the increased call volume. Consider sending some of your staff members who are familiar with the product and company to assist or train the center's staff.

Alternate Sites and Data Recovery. Virtually all organizations rely heavily on data systems for all aspects of the business. The extent of this reliance is often not realized until a server crashes, a major data base becomes corrupt,

---

[4] The term "bandwidth" is used frequently when discussing continuity planning strategies for data and communication systems. It refers to the amount of information that can be effectively transmitted along a particular medium. It is measured by transmission speed. Think of bandwidth as a pipe: you can easily fit a quarter-inch dowel down a half-inch pipe, but if you have a one-inch dowel and only a half-inch pipe, you need a bigger pipe, or you need to cut the dowel and send smaller pieces down the pipe. The same is true for data and telecommunications. You can only fit a certain-sized signal down a given size of wire.

or access to the office is denied. As functions become more automated and paperless, they simply stop functioning when complex equipment, environment, or connectivity fail. The tasks required to recover data operations can be complex even in a small organization, especially if platforms (the type of equipment used, such as mainframes and servers), firmware (operating systems), applications (user programs), and connectivity (by which desktop systems communicate with servers and mainframes) are not integrated: equipment must be repaired or replaced, configured, and installed; connectivity must be reestablished or rebuilt. Strategies can become further complicated when different parts of the organization "own" and maintain separate networks or data centers. The planner must work very closely with the data center managers or consultants to identify recovery priorities and strategies. The more common data center strategies include the following:

Replacement Agreements. The destruction of a building full of desktop computers would represent not only a monetary loss of equipment, work in progress, and possibly the data residing in the computers but a major delay in recovery — because of the need to purchase, deliver, set up, reconfigure, and reload each computer. Once computers are installed and connected to the network server, reinstallation of the applications can be accomplished somewhat automatically. But even this, if it is possible, could require a lot of time. If the loss of the equipment is the result of an areawide disaster, you will be competing with other large companies for replacement equipment. To avoid these delays, you can enter into agreements with computer manufacturers to deliver large numbers of preconfigured computers within twenty-four hours to your primary or alternative location. The same applies to server repair and replacement. Your applications, configured to your environment, in this way are installed by the vendor prior to shipment, saving you valuable time and resources.

Servers that are on the same network (or can be easily connected) and that have excess capacity can be pressed into service to rescue a server that has failed. Some organizations keep spare, preconfigured servers in storage for immediate replacement if a primary fails. Unfortunately, this is a very costly strategy.

Hot and Cold Sites. A hot site, as discussed above, is an alternative recovery location prepared ahead of time, in this case with computers, servers, a mainframe, and related equipment such as hardware and telecommunications. Hot site vendors exist to provide this service on a first-come, first-served basis. The hot sites typically include a limited number of workstations and both data and voice communications infrastructure, enabling the organization to relocate employees temporarily. Organizations pay a subscription fee to the vendor and, when the hot site is needed, pay an additional "declaration fee" — to "declare a disaster" to reserve a system and space ahead of other possible claimants. The company brings its latest backup data tapes (has them shipped or electronically transferred to the site), loads its programs, and quickly resumes operations at the hot site. Daily use fees are usually payable, as long as the hot site is occupied.

Recovery plans should detail the step-by-step instructions required to transfer operations to the hot site and list the employees who are to occupy the site. Most hot site vendors have personnel on staff to assist with developing the transfer plan.

Duplicate systems — capable of processing normal operations, installed within the organization, and used to run test programs or other noncritical processes — can be pressed into service if a main system fails. Few managers, however, can justify the expense of such duplicate systems. The supply of commercial hot sites is limited and could easily be saturated in a regional disaster, leaving the organization without a system or location with which to recover. An *internal* hot site, if located in a region away from the disaster, will eliminate this danger.

A cold site, in this connection, consists of an empty facility or leased space where computer hardware, telecommunications and furniture would be delivered to construct a temporary processing capability. At a cold site, nothing is prewired or ready for immediate operation. Obviously, this is a less expensive strategy, but because of the time required for setup, it may not be a practical solution.

Mirrored Data or Remote Journaling.   When computer systems fail or are destroyed, data is lost. The computer system and facilities may well be in perfect working order, but if access to them or to data were restricted due to a bomb threat or fire on another floor of the building (or at a neighboring company), the data on the system since the latest backup would be inaccessible and therefore unusable. Organizations that cannot afford such a delay in processing can use data recovery strategies that automatically back up data and send it to an alternate site. Depending on the criticality of the data, this can be done in *batch* form (backup data is stored until transmitted all at once, at certain time intervals), or by *remote journaling* (information is transmitted and stored on a remote computer as it is processed).

When analyzing a firm's network systems, question the MIS manager about redundancies built into the equipment. Most server equipment contains separate hard drives that mirror all data that is stored on the primary and will switch to the backup drive if the primary fails.

Policies and Procedures.   Most "data" disasters are caused by people, not by equipment failure or natural catastrophes. Policies and procedures regarding data systems must be identified, implemented, and enforced to ensure a smooth and effective recovery. A data backup policy is an obvious starting point, but backup policies cannot be completely effective if the client does not store its data on the server. Most client/server architectures allow users to access two areas to store data — locally on the user's C-drive and also on the server. Although there are programs that back up the user's local drive (if the user's computer is running), this is a time-consuming operation and may back up unnecessary files. To avoid this, all users should store their data files on the server. Policies that restrict unauthorized installation of personal software or downloading material from the Internet will help to avoid disasters resulting from computer viruses.

Data Backup.   Most organizations can afford to lose a day or two of data or can tolerate the time required to reconstruct a small amount of lost work-in-progress. The primary strategy used in these organizations involves the nightly backup of each day's transactions onto magnetic tape. This is often done in spite of a lack of a policy establishing its need. Each organization must develop a data backup policy that requires:

- Nightly incremental backup of the server
- Weekly full backup
- Monthly archiving
- Yearly archiving.

Backup tapes should ideally be taken each day off site to a storage facility that specializes in the safe and secure storage of computer backup media. Offsite storage facilities should be audited annually to ensure:

- Good physical security.
- That authorization lists are up to date and enforced.
- That good fire prevention measures are in place.
- That the building is structurally sound.
- That it can find and deliver tapes and manuals in a reasonable time.

If this is not possible, try to store tapes in a fire-resistant cabinet located in a separate building. During an evacuation, take the tapes (or whatever media is used) with you, if this can be done safely. At the very least, backup tapes should be sent off-site weekly and the previous weeks tapes returned and recycled.

Third-Party Manufacturing.   Many firms is the United States and Japan were directly affected by the Kobe earthquake, because their only sources of raw materials or parts were in that region. Inability to get parts required these companies to reduce production, find and qualify alternative suppliers, order new parts at inflated prices, and suffer through delayed delivery schedules. The solution: Identify sole-source suppliers and take action to find alternatives far ahead of such problems. If the operation uses "just in time" manufacturing, arrange to warehouse a sufficient quality of material to allow for delay caused by a disaster or contingent interruption. Some distributors will warehouse materials at your location, retaining ownership until the material is removed and used.

Another concern is the loss of manufacturing equipment, facilities, or personnel due to labor action, inclement weather conditions, or natural disasters. As outlined previously, manufacturing operations may be transferred to other locations and shifted within the organization. If this is not feasible, approach a contract manufacturing facility and make arrangements for it to manufacture your product temporarily.

As the world becomes more data oriented, consider a backup plan that involves some form of virtual manufacturing.

Purchase of Material from Competitors. In an effort to maintain market share, some companies purchase finished product from their competitors and repackage it under their own brand.

Records Management. Many business that have not recovered after disasters have considered the loss of their business records the primary cause. Most regulations affecting business continuity planning refer to record retention and recovery. It should be apparent that a major focus of business continuity planning is the preservation and recovery of vital records. The insurance industry refers to these records as "important papers." The loss of customer, accounts receivable, and asset lists can severely damage future sales, cash flow, and insurance reimbursements. Also, failure to protect corporate records could in some instances bring criminal sanctions against management.

Records are identified as vital if they are important to the continued and future operation of the company. Their loss will have a severe impact or make it difficult to remain in operation. Some firms distinguish records as either *vital* or *important*, depending on how much they would be needed after a disaster. Vital records are those absolutely required to recover and restore operations; important, or key, documents are those that will reduce recovery time. Examples include:

Customer lists	Articles of incorporation
Securities and stock records	By-laws
Corporate minutes	Other corporate financial records
Deeds	Leases

Patents and trademarks   License agreements
Accounts receivable   Banking statements
Tax documents   Treasury records
Payroll and benefits information Research & development (R&D)
Information and specifications   Insurance policies
 as-built drawings   Clinical trial results
Federal Drug Administration   Security files
 (FDA) filings   Business continuity plan
Negotiations   Records that support regulatory
Asset lists   requirements
Laboratory notebooks

Once records are categorized, there are a number of options for safe-guarding against their destruction, if they cannot be quickly recreated from their sources. The type of media they are stored on, and the time dependency of the information, may effect your recovery strategy. Most records are paper documents stored on site. At the very least, they should be stored in locked, fire-resistant cabinets. The most important documents should be photo-copied and stored off site at a facility that specializes in document storage. As with data storage, always audit the security, fire safety, rapid retrieval, and environmental controls used by the storage company. Copies can also be stored at off-site locations within the organization. Document tracking and rapid retrieval can, however, become a problem when storage is internal.

Many records are copied onto microfiche, a technology that is becoming less popular with the increased use and lower costs of document scanning. Document scanning decreases retrieval time and reduces storage space. The documents are stored electronically on diskette, magnetic tape, disk packs, compact disks (CD), digital video disk (DVD), or optical disk. They can be sent directly to electronic vault facilities for storage and returned to recovery locations via the phone system.

Once vital records are identified, it is important to implement policies and procedures that ensure their routine backup. Not all documents need backup; many can be recreated from the originals at vendors, customers, or at regulatory agencies. Back up those documents that cannot be recreated without difficulty and those for which the delay required for their re-creation cannot be tolerated.

Facilities Salvage and Restoration. A general recovery strategy that leads organizations to identify alternative processing and manufacturing facilities prior to a disaster, and to develop plans that allow for the rapid transfer of operations to these facilities, is typically very effective in getting back to some level of service. The goal of restoration is to return the organization to a predisaster state or to a defined strategic position. This cannot be done, however, in a temporary facility. The damaged facility must be rebuilt, relocated, or repaired. The rebuilding or permanent relocation of the organization is an issue to be addressed by the management team subsequent to a disaster. The planner will discuss these possibilities with management ahead of time and arrange for agreements and resources to expedite the search for new facilities — during conditions in which, inevitably, space would be scarce and prices inflated.

Most organizations return to their original facilities after a disaster, especially if the buildings are structurally sound. Before this can happen, the facility must be cleaned and made habitable. In the aftermath of a fire there will be heat and soot damage to equipment. Smoke from a fire is acrid and corrodes sensitive electronic components, even after the fire is out. Water from sprinklers or firefighting hoses can damage documents and cause dangerous molds to grow. The drying and dehumidification of buildings requires specialized equipment and techniques. These services are provided by "restoration" companies, which either do the work themselves or subcontract to companies that specialize in:

- Salvage and debris removal
- Electronic component cleaning and repair
- Soot removal
- Dehumidification and drying
- Document drying and recovery
- Reconstruction (painting, plumbing, masonry, and drywall)
- Water extraction and moisture control.

The safe recovery of vital records and books, and the prevention of disease from water damage caused by flood, fire sprinklers, or roof collapse requires special expertise and equipment. Restoration companies that specialize in a particular type of damage have expertise, experience, and equipment not generally available to internal facilities staff or to general contractors. Most general contractors can clean and rebuild a facility after a fire, but they may be unaware of the techniques used to eliminate the odor of smoke.

It can be very expensive to scrap damaged equipment, especially if it is unique or replacement lead times are extensive. Insurance policies may not pay the full replacement value of the damaged equipment. According to companies that specialize in the decontamination of equipment, restoration can save up to 75 percent over replacement costs, and restoration can be completed in a few weeks instead of the months potentially needed for replacement.

Most restoration companies will, for no charge, inventory assets and maintain construction plans off site. The use of these services can expedite the recovery process and allow management to concentrate on other recovery issues. In areas susceptible to earthquakes (that is, virtually every part of the country), one of the first tasks necessary is the cosmetic repair of cracks and other damage. A large part of the psychological healing after a disaster is the return to normal surroundings. Employees staring at cracks in the wall are reminded of the disaster; restoration companies, if agreements are reached ahead of time, can erase the reminders that hinder a return to normalcy.

Other Steps to Produce an Effective Plan

The remainder of the steps to produce an effective plan (steps 8–14) are described in other chapters.

REVIEW

Business continuity planning is a process that identifies the critical functions of the company, develops cost-effective strategies to recover these functions, and gathers or lists the people and resources needed to implement the strategies.

It is in the planning process itself that the true value of continuity planning is realized. Although some planning methodologies are more effective than others, each must be adapted to fit the corporate environment and culture. In most companies, the planner will not be successful without the committed support of top management.

Business continuity consultants can be used to facilitate the project and advise the company on the best recovery strategies. The more common strategies include data backup; prioritization of systems, applications, functions and equipment; and transfer of these operations to an alternative location. Strategies and plans must then be devised to repair, rebuild, or relocate the business. Do not forget to devise plans to move out of the alternative location and back into a permanent facility.

13

PLAN DOCUMENTATION

Eugene Tucker, CFE, CPP
Contributing author

The planning process delivers value to the organization by forcing its members to identify critical functions, place a value on the loss of these functions, and to think through the most effective recovery strategies. The importance of documenting these efforts is fundamental to the Business Continuity process. The lack of a plan will add delays to the organization's fight to recover, cause the misuse of scarce resources, and may ultimately set the stage for the failure of the business.

Eugene Tucker, CFE, CPP

REQUIRED ELEMENTS OF THE PLAN

Business continuity planning can take many forms, depending upon the applicability of regulations, the organization's culture and document-control procedures, and its level of sophistication (or limitations) in the use of technology (such as having interactive plans on CD ROM). Absent regulatory issues, the best format to use is one that the planner is comfortable with and that satisfies the following conditions:

- The plan must be organized in a logical sequence.
- It must be "clean" and easy to follow. (Information that is difficult to find under stressful circumstances is useless.)
- It must be complete but not overly detailed. (It must contain sufficient information to allow someone who did not participate in the

planning process to understand what is required to recover the business. It should not contain information irrelevant to the task at hand, such as hazard identification, mitigation recommendations, or justifications for the program.)

- It must contain a glossary defining any terms used.
- It must facilitate a smooth, seamless transition from response to recovery.
- It must assign responsibility for planning to individuals within the organization and describe the emergency lines of authority.
- It must outline specific resources and tasks required to carry out recovery operations.
- It must be flexible enough to address unforeseen events. (No two disasters are exactly the same; neither is their response and recovery. The plan must allow for midcourse correction and adaptation.)
- It must contain references to other plans or documents. (While all the information necessary to the recovery effort must reside in the plan, the plan should not contain a restatement of detailed operating procedures or instructions, such as the multivolume Novell Operating System installation set. Necessary documents, references, and other plans that are not immediately required and cannot be included in the plan should be listed in the vital records section. These must be duplicated and stored off site for later retrieval.)
- It must state assumptions upon which the plan is based or by which it is constrained.

MULTIHAZARD FUNCTIONAL PLANNING

Multihazard functional planning is a format the Federal Emergency Management Agency (FEMA) suggests that governmental agencies use to develop their emergency operations plans.[1] An effective business continuity plan follows the multihazard functional format, especially if a recovery team methodology is used. More recently known as "all-hazard emergency operations planning," it is based on the premise that although the causes of emergencies and disasters vary, almost three-quarters of them produce common response requirements. The jurisdictions can then develop task-based plans around these requirements or functions rather than around each anticipated hazard. Some hazards do produce unique needs; these needs, requirements, and responses are appended to the "basic plan," under this methodology.

---

[1] It is of interest to recovery planners who develop their plans under the National Fire Protection Association's (NFPA) guidelines number 1600 or who wish to be consistent with governmental planning methodologies.

The main part of the plan — known as the *basic plan* — outlines the overall emergency organization, its policies, assumptions, activation, and lines of authority. Its primary audience is the jurisdiction's executive and management level staff.

Functional annexes are subplans that focus on specific functions the jurisdiction will perform in response to the disaster. Shelter management, evacuation, and search and rescue are examples. Each annex may contain its own appendix of tasks and requirements for dealing with the specifics of a particular hazard. Standard operating procedures (SOPs) and checklists may be included in the annex.

CONTENTS OF THE BASIC PLAN

The basic plan should contain the following elements or sections: [2]

- Introductory material:
    - Promulgation document (outlines the authority and responsibility for the plan; usually signed by the chief executive officer)
    - Signature page (demonstrates that all response organizations have participated in its development and are committed to its success)
    - Dated title and revisions page
    - Distribution list
    - Table of contents
- Purpose statement.
- Situation and assumptions. (This section will include the scope of the response and the assumptions upon which the plan and response are based. "Situation" refers to a description of the justification or necessity for the plan.)
- Concept of operations. (Describes the overall strategy or approach to the response, activation of the plan, and coordination with other agencies.)
- Organization and assignment of responsibilities. (Delineates the emergency organization and reporting hierarchy. Each position is listed, along with an overview of its duties and responsibilities.)
- Administration and logistics. (Defines the general administrative policies, such as financial and purchasing controls and procedures, resource management, and mutual-aid agreements.)

---

[2] FEMA, Guide for All-Hazard Emergency Operations Planning, SLG101, 1996-723-006/83312 (Washington, DC: Government Printing Office, September 1996).

- Plan development and maintenance. (Describes the overall approach to the plan — in contrast to the approach to the response above. Explains responsibilities of the planners, and the planning process and includes the requirements for plan maintenance and exercising.)
- Authorities and references. (Highlights enabling laws and the legal basis for emergency operations, refers to other documents with relevant information.)

RECOVERY TEAMS

Some organizations rely upon a single team of executives and key employees to direct recovery operations after a disaster. Sometimes referred to as the *crisis management team*, it decides what individuals or departments within the organization will do to effect the recovery. Their decisions may be based upon detailed preplanning or upon a loose set of recovery strategies.

A more effective recovery method involves the formation of individual recovery teams arranged along departmental lines or drawn from several departments with similar functions (and therefore with similar recovery strategies). Large departments or teams may contain support teams, or subteams, that focus on particular functions or resources.

Each team is composed of a leader, and alternate leader, and essential personnel. Recovery teams reporting hierarchy extends to a management team through the recovery coordinator (see Figure 13-1).

Figure 13-1. Crisis Management Recovery Team

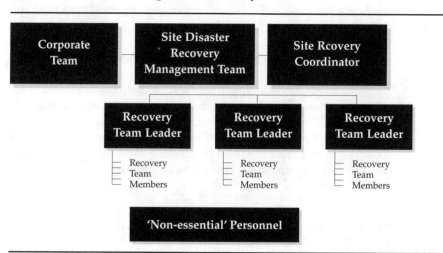

This structure allows for a response that is selective (not all teams need to be activated in every recovery situation), coordinated (information flows efficiently up, down, and across the recovery organization), and focused.

A *corporate team* may exist in organizations with many divisions or multiple geographical locations. The corporate team is responsible for making strategic business decisions and will direct the recovery process on a regional basis. Team members will include top management and the business recovery coordinator. Other responsibilities may include:

- The safety of all personnel;
- Assisting the site disaster recovery management team to decide if an alternative work site is required;
- Projecting and tracking the financial impact of the disaster;
- Determine the need to review the strategic position of the company based on any change or expected change in financial position, production capacity, corporate image, or sales;
- Working with the public relations director to develop messages and positions, and communicating the necessary management decisions to the public relations team — that is, activating the crisis management plan;
- Resolving conflicts with the allocation of resource requirements between multiple sites affected by the disaster;
- Ensure insurance claims are filed in a timely manner;
- Monitoring the recovery operations and recovery expenses;
- Keeping the Board of Directors updated on the position of the company and on the progress of the recovery operations;
- Monitor and assist the site disaster recovery management teams, local recovery coordinators, or facilities teams with building restoration, relocation, and the acquisition of temporary or permanent replacement facilities.

The *site disaster recovery management team* is responsible for the coordination of the restoration efforts of the local recovery teams. In smaller organizations, it may assume many of the duties of the corporate team.

One member of the disaster recovery management team is designated as the *recovery coordinator*. The recovery coordinator is responsible for the overall operation of the recovery. The recovery coordinator activates teams as necessary if they have not self-activated and acts as the liaison between team leaders, the disaster recovery management team, and with the corporate team.

The team leaders activate their plans and notify their team members. They are responsible for overseeing the implementation of their teams' recovery instructions. The qualities of a good team leader include the ability to take charge in an emergency situation, familiarity with the operations of the functions to be restored, and freedom from other significant recovery duties that may interrupt focus. For political reasons, the department manager is most often selected as the team leader.

Only employees "critical" to an operation are selected for the recovery team. "Nonessential" personnel are assigned to other duties, to other teams as needed, or are temporarily furloughed. In today's business environment, where staffing is lean, fewer employees (and business functions) are considered nonessential. The duties imposed on the team members by the recovery instructions must closely match the members' normal skills and scopes of responsibility. If members are to perform special functions outside their normal duties, they should receive training in these new skills beforehand.

PLAN ORGANIZATION AND STRUCTURE

Like the multihazard functional plan, the business continuity plan consists of a basic plan and departmental or team plans (similar to annexes). The basic plan contains administrative and descriptive details required to implement the plan, as well as information that is common to the recovery effort of two or more (or all) teams.

The basic plan may contain the following sections:

- Table of contents
- Policy
- Scope
- Objectives
- Assumptions
- Activation procedures and authority
- Emergency telephone numbers
- Alternate locations and allocations
- Recovery priorities
- Plan distribution
- Training
- Exercising
- Plan maintenance
- Appendix
- Team recovery plans

Policy. The plan can briefly outline or reference the existence of management's policy to develop, exercise, and maintain the plan. Ideally, it will include a full policy statement, signed by the CEO. Some planners include a brief description of the responsibilities of separate divisions, sites, or departments for developing their own plans.

Scope.   The dimension of the recovery process encompassed by the plan is briefly but completely discussed. If the plan pertains to a single building or site, refer to it by building numbers, site name, and exact street address. Inform the reader of any pertinent functions, locations, or contingencies not included in the plan. If the plan includes crisis management and response issues, bring them to the attention of the reader.

Objectives.   What, in general terms, will the plan accomplish? Objectives can include:

- Ensuring the safety of employees and assets;
- Minimizing economic losses resulting from interruptions to business functions;
- Providing a plan of action for an orderly recovery of business operations.

Assumptions.   List any assumptions upon which the plan is based or by which it is limited. It is nearly impossible to plan for the absolute worse-case scenario, where everything ceases to exist. Most of us now know that California will not fall into the ocean (or worse, see all its residents move east). Common assumptions include that:

- Buildings will be either partially or totally damaged or inaccessible.
- Most key personnel identified in the plan are available following a disaster.
- Alternate facilities identified in the plan are available for use in a disaster.
- Backup data and valuable papers located in off-site storage will be readily available.
- Critical resources will be available.
- Most employees are trained on facility evacuation procedures.

Activation Authority and Procedures.   List the persons or circumstances who have the authority to activate the entire plan, individual team plans, or multiple team plans. Typically, any member of the management team or the recovery coordinator can activate the entire or any portion of the plan, while team leaders can independently activate their individual teams, with notification to the recovery coordinator.

Some plans allow for a graduated activation (Level I, II, III); some, in an effort to get to the head of the line when competing for space at a hot site, will let the type of disaster dictate how the plan is activated. For example, in a localized disaster, such as a fire in the data center, the team will first assess damage before declaring a disaster. However, if the disaster is regional, such as an earthquake, and the data center is damaged, the Activation Authority will immediately declare a disaster to the hot site, pay the declaration fee, and then assess the damage and only then decide if there is a need to relocate to the hot site.

Disaster levels can be defined as:

Level I Disaster.   A Level I disaster is one resulting in facility inaccessibility or loss of power or other critical services for an expected period of up to forty-eight hours (this time factor can change according to the recovery time objective).

Damage from a Level I disaster is not large in scale. It may consist of minor damage to one or more buildings, lack of access due to weather or city infrastructure conditions, or hardware and software problems.

Level II Disaster.   A Level II disaster exists when the outage is expected to last from two to five business days.

Damage from a Level II disaster is more serious than Level I and may result in heavier losses to equipment and documentation (files, reports, contracts) due to a prolonged event, such as a fire or flooding.

Level III Disaster.   A Level III disaster is one in which the disaster results in outage anticipated to last in excess of five days.

A Level III disaster is severe and could include the total destruction of one or more buildings, or service within the buildings, requiring significant facility restoration or replacement.

Data-centric or information systems team plans may use a different activation sequence, each of which may involve a specific response by a different group of people. If a disruption is expected to last less that two hours, a "Stage 1" situation is declared, the team leader or shift supervisor is notified, and instructions are implemented by the on-duty personnel. If the outage is not resolved within this time frame, or if it is apparent that more time is required, the response will escalate to a Stage 2 or 3. This will invoke an additional set of instructions, notifications, or full recovery-team activation.

Alternative Locations and Allocations.   Virtually all recovery plans include an alternative location to which the team can transfer its operations to reestablish critical functions and resume the delivery of service. Common alternate locations include:

- Hot/cold site
- Vacant or shared space in another portion of the building, site, or corporation
- Hotel conference rooms
- Mobile trailers
- Third-party contract manufacturers
- Training centers
- Vendors and suppliers
- Competitors
- Home

Although the company may have an overall relocation strategy, certain teams may relocate to different locations. All alternative locations should be listed in this section.

Allocation refers to the number of team members that will relocate. Not all employees are needed during the initial phases of a recovery. This number will indicate how many employees or team members are needed to arrange resources and space. Some planners include the total head count and the short and long-term space requirements (square footage) in this section, but this is best left in the facilities, real estate, or other team plan.

Hot site or relocation floor plans may be included to expedite the setup of work stations, communications, and systems.

Recovery Priorities. The recovery priorities section is a listing, usually in tabular form, of the organization's departments, teams, or critical functions in order of importance as determined by the business impact analysis. The recovery time objective, as well as any times of the year, quarter, month, or other business cycle during which the loss of these functions is especially critical, are also listed. This information is useful to the management team if a decision to reallocate resources becomes necessary.

Plan Distribution. List plan recipients in this section.

Training. All affected employees should be aware of the existence of the plan, the methods the company and employees will use to communicate with each other, and their responsibilities after a disaster. Although the planning process is itself an educational tool, team members must understand how the overall recovery will work. The importance of record keeping, lines of authority, and team structure must be emphasized. Outline the methods used to deliver this training.

Exercising. *Exercising* is a term used to describe the various levels or methods used to test certain or all elements of the plan. The term "testing" is no longer used, because it connotes a pass/fail mentality; most planners believe their overall efforts are best served by promoting a positive outcome, and therefore they offer a better motivation for the participants. Simulation is probably a better term, because to many of us, exercise is not something done willingly.

Many publications exist that guide the reader through the steps of a table-top, departmental, functional, and full-scale simulation. The plan should present the company's policy and time lines for simulations. All portions of the plan must be simulated. It is best to start small and graduate to full-scale simulations, in which major portions of the plan are included. Attempt to include city, county, or state agencies in a full-scale simulation. At a minimum, plans should be simulated annually.

Plan Maintenance.   The persons responsible for maintaining the plans are identified, along with the method and frequency of updates. These plans must be "living documents." Employee and vendor contact numbers change often and must be kept current in the plan. This information must be reviewed quarterly. The plans must be reviewed annually to determine if they still match the overall strategic direction of the organization, and be changed accordingly.

Appendix.   The appendix will contain the glossary, forms common to most teams, supporting information, and common documents.

Team Recovery Plans.   Business continuity plans, especially those for large organizations, can be many pages long, rivaling the size of most large metropolitan area phone books. The mere size of these plans will cause most people to place it forever on their bookshelves, to be read only by an auditor. In fact, however, access to all information in the plan is required only by the recovery coordinator, possibly the management information systems director, and just a few others. It is best to distribute to each individual recovery team only the portion of the plan that is meaningful to it.

The recovery team plan will contain at least the following information:

- Review of pertinent information from the basic plan
- Overview of the team plan
- Team-member contact list
- Scripted continuity instructions
- Resource listings
- Blank forms, contracts, and other documents

Information from the Basic Plan.   Activation procedures, communications, organization and structure are summarized in the team plan. The duties and responsibilities of the team leader and how the team relates to the recovery are discussed. This will allow the team plans to function independently of the basic plan, keeping the information focused and the size of the plan manageable.

Overview of the Team Plan.   A review of the general business functions of the department or team, along with its critical functions, continuity or relocation strategies, are listed here. Briefly include other relevant information.

Team-Member Contact List.   A listing of the team members is given, detailing their titles or positions, and emergency contact numbers (work, home, cellular, and pager). Call trees, if used, are placed in this section. It is possible that all team members will not be needed during the early stages of the recovery. Indicate at what phase or day they should be called.

Scripted Continuity Instructions.   Include the instructions or tasks the team must follow to implement its continuity (recovery) strategies. Separate instructions can exist for the team leader and team members; they can be further separated by time (initial twenty-four hours, initial forty-eight hours, greater than five days), by phase (response, restoration, recovery), or by whatever period is most practical. As stated before, these instructions should be brief but complete. They should be understood by someone reasonably familiar with the type of operation the team is attempting to recover; avoid, however, technical terms, abbreviations, and acronyms. The instructions should minimize the need for decision making after the disaster.

Resource Listings.   Vendors (internal and external contacts), customers, equipment requirements, forms, supplies, software and applications, vital records, and other resources are listed in this section. Model numbers, configurations, floor plans, cabling diagrams, tax tables, milestones, and other due dates, along with both the short and long-term quantities required, are listed.

Blank Forms.   Forms that are needed by the team and included in the appendix are also found here. Copies of contracts or agreements with vendors should appear in the team plan.

14

RESPONSE PLANNING

Eugene Tucker, CFE, CPP
Contributing author

> Worrying about possible disasters can cause
> many sleepless nights for senior executives and
> board members, and prompt the creation of com-
> prehensive contingency plans to help ease these
> worries. It is important, however, to maintain a
> delicate balance between overplanning for events
> that may never happen and being adequately
> prepared to respond if disaster does strike.
>
> *Jack E. Cox and Robert L. Barber,*
> "Practical Contingency Planning,"
> Risk Management Magazine,
> March 1996

Organizations should be able to respond to situations they can reasonably
anticipate during a disaster. An effective response will reduce injuries, protect assets, and position the organization for a smooth and rapid recovery.
Emergency services provided by local jurisdictions (police, fire, ambulance,
and hospitals) may not be available. When the demand for these resources
must be prioritized, businesses are virtually always at the bottom of the list;
government believes that the business community has the resources to be
self-sufficient and that other organizations, such as public schools, are more
in need of its services.

An emergency-response capability is required by the 29 CFR (Code of
Federal Regulations) 1910.38 for all organizations. This FedOSHA
(Occupational Safety and Health Administration) regulation sets the minimum standard for response planning. It requires all employers to maintain
emergency action and fire prevention plans. These plans must be in writing
if there are more than ten employees. Section 1910.120 further defines requirements for all emergency response operations required by parts 1910 and 1926.

The National Fire Protection Association (NFPA) of 1996, section 1600, entitled "Standard for Disaster Management," addresses codes and standards. This section outlines a minimum standard for the design and implementation of both response and recovery programs. While at the time of this printing NFPA 1600 is a guideline, many expect it to be reissued as a directive.

State and local jurisdictions may impose additional requirements on the business community to develop a response capability. These requirements supersede federal standards if the local regulations are more stringent. Most of these regulations are matters of law and industry standards; accordingly, managers can be held liable in civil and criminal court if the programs they require are not implemented. Additionally, violation of these laws is excluded from liability insurance coverage for "errors and omissions" and "directors and officers."

Significant elements of these standards and regulations include the use of the Incident Command System, hazard-based planning (multihazard functional planning — see Chapter 13), and coordinated response (unified command).

THE INCIDENT COMMAND SYSTEM

The Incident Command System (ICS) is a hierarchical management structure used by governmental agencies (fire and police) to respond to emergencies. It is primarily a field-response management system, but it has been adapted for use in an emergency operations center (EOC). Devised by the fire service in 1971, it provides guidelines for common multi-agency operating procedures, terminology, communications, and management. Its modular structure allows for a consistent and coordinated response to incidents of all types and complexity. Because of the growing interdependency between the response organizations of industry, business, and governmental agencies, the use of the incident command system by business and industry is unavoidable, other federal and state mandates not withstanding.

The Incident Command System as a management tool relies heavily on the concept of "management by objectives" (MBO). Response objectives are set by the senior responder, the incident commander (IC), and are delegated to subordinate positions after agreement that the objectives can be met. By using this approach, the incident commander can coordinate the response to complex and technical incidents without unreasonable expectations. The system is also sensitive to the basic management principal of "span of control," which limits the ratio of subordinates to supervisors. If the incident is small and the response is relatively simple, the ratio is eight subordinates to one supervisor. If the crisis expands and becomes more complex, the span of control is reduced, in order to provide the most effective leadership. Some believe the span of control in an emergency situation is five or less.

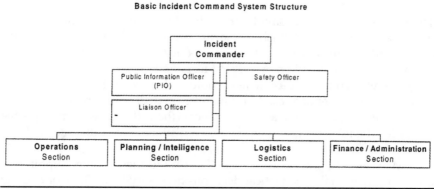

Figure 14-1. Basic Incident Command System Structure

The Incident Command System is divided into five major functional units. (The fire service version is expandable to thirty-six positions, but most of them are not relevant to business responses.) The five units or sections are (see Figure 14-1):

- Incident command
- Operations
- Planning and intelligence
- Logistics
- Finance and administration

Emergency response teams (ERTs) or "industrial fire brigades" may be required by law or industry standards to utilize the ICS. If the organization's response requirements do not warrant the use of an ERT, business owners and responsible managers (including recovery planners) must still be aware of the ICS methods and protocols used by the local jurisdictions.

For small incidents, it is not necessary to establish all units (sections) of the ICS. In this case, the incident commander (see below) directly manages or assumes the duties of each of the units or activates them as additional personnel arrive. Operational need is the primary factor in determining what is activated.[1] Each unit is headed by a section chief and may be further divided into subsections as required by the complexity of the incident or need to maintain proper span of control. [2]

---

[1] *ICS for Executives: Standard Emergency Management System Executive Course, Student Reference Manual* (State of California, August 1995).

[2] The law enforcement version of ICS uses the term "officer in charge" (OIC) instead of section chief.

Incident Commander

The IC has overall responsibility at the incident or event. He or she determines objectives and establishes priorities based on the nature of the incident, available resources, and agency policy.[3] The role of the incident commander is usually filled by the first responder to arrive at the scene; that person is relieved of this duty when a more senior responder or a designated incident commander arrives. A command post (CP) is set up near the location of the emergency (at a safe distance); there the IC will manage the response. The IC is usually identified by a distinctive vest marked with the words "Incident Commander."

Management must delegate *ahead of time* to the incident commander the authority to make the tactical decisions necessary to stabilize or end the emergency without interference. Management's place is in the emergency operations center, making strategic decisions based on developments and allocating resources between multiple incidents. The incident commander follows preexisting policy set by management.

Some of the specific duties of the incident commander include:

- Overall field management of the emergency
- Coordination with the EOC or other ICs (the IC of the firm's ERT should colocate with the fire or police department IC — see Unified Command, below)
- Ultimate responsibility for the safety of responders
- Approval of all plans and resources
- Situational analysis
- Setting of objectives and priorities
- Delegation of authority as necessary
- Responsibility as primary responder until others arrive.

If the size of the emergency warrants, the following assistants to the IC should be appointed: an *information officer, safety officer,* and *liaison officer.*

Information Officer.   The information officer (or public information officer [PIO]) is the news media contact for the event. In a business environment, the public relations representative fills this role but should be less (or not at all) subordinate to the IC as he or she would be under the government's version.

Safety Officer.   The safety officer monitors safety conditions, ensures compliance with safety regulations, and develops measures to assure the safety

---

[3] Ibid.

of all assigned personnel.[4] The safety officer is often responsible for evaluating changing conditions and should have the authority to withdraw responders or suspend an operation without clearance from the incident commander.

Liaison Officer.   The liaison officer assists the IC in large incidents to which other agencies may also respond, by coordinating their involvement and providing necessary information on conditions, objectives, and resources.

Operations

The operations section implements the "incident action plans" according to objectives issued by the IC. Its members are the "doers" of the response effort. They participate in the selection and "reality checking" of goals and direct all resources necessary to carry out the response. A constant flow of situational and information milestone-achievement information goes back to the incident commander.

Planning and Intelligence

The planning and intelligence section develops action plans to implement the goals and objectives of the incident commander. As part of its planning, this section determines what resources are needed to accomplish each task. Members of this section must gather information about the incident before they can devise a meaningful plan. For example, the incident commander might issue a command (set a goal) to extinguish the fire. The planning section determines that the fire is small in origin, involves general combustibles, and will require dousing with water by one hose team. The operations section will then grab a hose and put out the fire. This accomplishment is noted by the IC and the planning section, which is also responsible for tracking any resources used. This example may be simplistic; in a large scale incident this section will:

- Collect intelligence (analyze conditions and the scope of the incident)
- Project or predict changing conditions
- Prepare action plans
- Prepare contingency plans if conditions, events, or resources change
- Track resources available, in service, and used.

---

[4] Ibid.

Technical advisors are included in the planning section to provide expert advice when needed. Chemists, safety engineers, toxicologists, industrial hygienists, meteorologists, and structural engineers are examples of the types of experts that might be included in the response.

Logistics

The logistics section obtains all resources and services needed to manage the incident. Personnel, equipment, food and supplies, and restroom and shower facilities are delivered by this section. The logistics section simply supplies resources; the operations section is responsible for their management and use.

Finance and Administration

The finance and administration section maintains records and documents the history of the response. It projects, tracks, and approves expenditures by the logistics section, and it completes a final cost analysis of the response. Documentation of times, events, and actions is important to the postincident analysis, insurance reimbursement, criminal prosecution, or in defense of a civil action.

EMERGENCY OPERATIONS CENTER

The EOC is a location where the management team members or emergency managers meet to direct or coordinate the response to a large-scale incident or to begin the business's recovery. Often the original EOC is damaged or access to it is restricted; the business recovery leaders must then meet at an interim location to decide where to set up an alternate EOC. To the business continuity planner, the EOC or command center is where management coordinates the actions of the individual recovery teams, monitors the progress of the recovery, and passes requests and information up, down, and across the structure of the recovery organization. Although its primary function is strategic, the EOC can make such tactical decisions as the allocation of resources between competing teams, incidents, or plans.

The organization must anticipate the complexity of its response and recovery, and design an EOC that accommodates its operational requirements. From the business perspective, the physical and operational layout can be as simple as a conference or hotel room. Companies with numerous sites in different geographical areas need (as do governmental agencies) to design theater-style complexes that have adjoining rooms and integrated audio-visual, computer network, and communications systems and support personnel. The EOC should be located in a secure, structurally safe building that is centrally located and easily accessible to the responders even when transportation systems are disrupted. An alternate EOC, such as a mobile trailer, located a distance from the main site, should always be available.

The EOC centralizes control of disaster response among individual recovery teams or among multiple governmental agencies. Large EOCs utilize an ICS structure internally and actually configure the seating or work space along functional lines.

The primary functions of a governmental EOC are to:

- Coordinate the response to large or multiple events
- Create or refine policy
- Allocate resources
- Collect and manage information about the incident, responses, and decisions
- Release information to the public
- Maintain appropriate records.

For most businesses, the EOC is a large conference room that has a sufficient number of phone jacks, room for status boards, and separate work space for the management team leader and recovery coordinator. The phone jacks should be wired to allow the firm's phone switch to be bypassed in case of power failure or the destruction of communications equipment. Extra phone sets and fax machines, as well as all supplies needed to operate the EOC (radios, extra batteries, overhead projectors, whiteboards, forms, and office supplies) should be stored in the room or close by. Duplicate supplies and equipment should be stored in the alternate EOC if possible.

The flow of information, both from outside and within the EOC, is critical to the decisions made during a crisis, especially in a large-scale operation. Technology, such as computer networks and multimedia displays with colorful graphics, will speed the delivery of accurate information to decision makers and will greatly reduce fatigue. There are several software programs on the market that are designed for use in an EOC and can help to satisfy these requirements. External information must flow between the incident commander (or recovery team leaders) and the EOC. Situational or conditional reports must be available. The EOC must have the ability to communicate with the outside world even when power and normal modes of communication are disrupted. Backup communications, such as cellular or satellite telephones and amateur ratio, should be utilized.

Other considerations for the EOC include:

- Don't overwork the EOC staff. Decisions made under stressful conditions are often less effective. Add long hours to the stress, and the quality of the decisions can deteriorate even more. Shifts should not exceed twelve hours. Arrange for rest periods, breaks, professional massages, and plenty of food and water.
- Access control (security) is important, especially in a large EOC. Unauthorized visitors, media personnel, and managers not directly involved in the EOC operations must be denied access to the center. Consider a badging system to help control access to the EOC.
- A video conferencing capability is useful, as is an ability to monitor ATV (amateur television) broadcasts. In a recent California flood, the local ATV club rented a helicopter and sent live video back to an EOC.
- All EOC operations, rooms, and equipment should be connected to backup power generators.
- The EOC must be "user friendly" with respect to both comfort and functionality. Poor lighting, high noise levels, difficult-to-read visuals, poor ergonomics, and other negative "human factors" will tend to fatigue the staff sooner and adversely affect its ability to make intelligent decisions.
- The EOC must be designed to support multishift staffing and to operate continuously for extended periods.
- Keep operations as quiet as possible. Establish separate meeting rooms and a soundproof radio room; deliver TV audio through headphones, and use telephones that light instead of ring.

UNIFIED COMMAND

Unified command is used when multiple agencies or jurisdictions are involved in the response to an incident. Its structure is that of the Incident Command System, but unified command planning combines the objectives of all incident commanders so that the overall response can operate as if it were a single-agency incident. Resources are shared, but participating agencies do not have the authority to approve or disapprove the objectives of others.

EMERGENCY RESPONSE TEAMS

An ERT is an internal organization of employees designed to respond to emergencies before the arrival of public agencies. Although membership in the team is usually voluntary, employees from certain departments are generally necessary to ensure an effective response. This includes security (access control, communication), facilities (resources, equipment shutdown), and environmental health and safety (technical support).

An emergency response team can help the company to:

- Intervene and stabilize emergencies with less delay
- Reduce injuries and loss
- Prevent adverse publicity
- Demonstrate management concern and support for the safety of employees
- Minimize the impact on the environment
- Help comply with regulatory requirements to mitigate hazardous materials incidents (Fed OSHA, Cal OSHA, Uniform Fire Code, Environmental Protection Agency)
- Become the sole response in a disaster situation when public agencies do not have the ability to respond.

Some basic steps required to form an ERT include:

Management Acceptance and Support.   The effective and safe operation of an ERT involves a large commitment of time, money, and resources for training and equipment. The time required for training even a small ERT in a low-hazard environment should be no less than eight hours each quarter, much more in a larger, risk-intensive environment. The type of hazards the team may respond to will also affect the minimum training and equipment requirements. Teams involved in higher levels of "hazwoper" (hazardous waste operations) require a minimum of forty hours of training. This specialized training and equipment, and the "lost" time of members away from their normal duties, can add up to a significant expense for most organizations.

Duties and Responsibilities.   What is the scope of the team's duties and responsibilities — that is, what type of incidents are they expected to respond to? This will often define recruitment standards, equipment requirements, and training levels. Medical examinations and inoculations may be required.

Planning.   Develop response plans, team structure (conforming to the Incident Command System), policies, and procedures.

Determine Equipment and Resource Needs.   Budget for short and long-term requirements. Don't forget to include communications equipment. Two-way radios, pagers, police and fire scanners form a basic response-communications system.

Recruit Team Members.   Include sufficient numbers to field full teams for all shifts, to meet the staffing demands of each type of incident, and to allow for a reserve force to substitute for sick or injured team members. Provide incentives to create interest.

Develop Training Programs.   The training must fit the scope of the team's duties and regulatory requirements. It may be necessary to bring in outside consultants or to have the local fire department assist with training.

Conduct Regular Drills.   Practice, practice, practice. Arrange joint drills with public agencies.

Advertise.   Let employees and the community know about the capabilities of the team. This will increase confidence in the organization's ability to respond to emergencies, and it should elicit better cooperation from employees.

EMERGENCY PROCEDURES

The following sections provide guidelines the reader may use to plan their response to emergencies. The guidelines are generic and are not intended to list all foreseeable emergencies, or all measures the organization should take to prepare for, respond to, and recover from an incident, natural hazard, or disaster. Many of the guidelines and conditions apply to multiple types of disasters, though they are listed here only with the section they are most associated with. In all cases, always assess the situation before formulating a response.

Evacuation Considerations

Although people tend not to panic in emergency or disaster situations, evacuation planning and drills will reduce injury and confusion.[5] Experience has shown that people tend to leave by the door from which they entered the building or airplane, even if they are just a few feet away from a more appropriate exit. All evacuation planning should include visitors, vendors, contractors, and guests.

Prevention and Preparedness

1. Determine who will plan, coordinate, and authorize evacuations. Assign an alternate for this person. Employees should be trained to activate fire alarms if this method can be used to initiate an evacuation.

---

[5] Fischer et. al.

2. Develop unobstructed emergency escape routes that comply with local regulations and do not lead to or through hazardous areas. Ensure that your plan is consistent with legal requirements, such as for proper signage (illuminated exit signs), posted evacuation route maps, and numbers of exits. Never nail doors shut; clearly mark any doors and hallways that are not exits. If the emergency is minor, it may be necessary only to relocate employees to a safe location within the building. In high-rise buildings, it may be appropriate to evacuate only the three floors above the incident and the two floors below.

3. Devise special procedures for employees to stay behind and shut down equipment or perform critical operations. However, delaying the evacuation of employees should be minimized, if not eliminated.

4. Select *evacuation monitors* or *floor wardens* and clearly define their duties. Floor wardens typically confirm that everyone in their assigned area evacuates, ensure that the escape route is safe, and assist where needed.

5. List methods used to notify employees of an evacuation. This can include activation of the fire alarm or other distinctive audio/visual warning (be certain that warnings can be heard in all locations of the facility), public-address system announcements (develop scripted warning messages that can be adapted to the immediate situation), or by word of mouth (using floor wardens or supervisors).

6. Identify employees with handicaps who may need assistance with evacuations. Assign "buddies" or floor wardens to assist these people. Purchase special equipment, such as evacuation chairs, to assist with their removal from the building. Train potential users of this equipment on its location and operation. Wheelchairs should not be taken into stairwells.

7. Establish assembly points. Show the assembly points in the Emergency Action Guide (if required) or on wall maps.[6] If feasible, place a sign, placard, or bright painted markings on the ground to indicate where employees are to assemble. Assembly points should be a reasonable distance from the building, so that employees and guests are not injured by the emergency or other dangers. They should not be located where they could impede emergency operations or equipment.

8. Devise a method to account for employees and guests. This can be accomplished through a sign-in log or by having area supervisors taking roll calls of their employees and guests.

---

[6] Some states require employers to provide employees with written instructions to follow during an emergency.

9. Establish procedures and guidelines to follow when returning to the building. This should include a method to check whether the building is safe to reoccupy. Designate who has the authority to notify evacuees when it is safe to reenter.
10. Document your plan. Include the procedures in your Emergency Action Guide or list them on wall-mounted evacuation maps.

Response Considerations

1. If it can be done safely, shut down hazardous processes prior to evacuation.
2. Train all employees to recognize the evacuation signal and to follow evacuation procedures. Include the following instructions:
   - All employees are to leave immediately by the nearest exit.
   - Do not return to the work area to obtain personal effects.
   - Do not use elevators.
   - Assist the disabled.
   - Go directly to the assembly point unless instructed otherwise (do not stop to talk with friends or to get something from a vehicle).
   - Do not reenter the building until the "all clear" is given.
   - Ensure that all employees and guests evacuate. Floor wardens will sweep an assigned area to check that all have evacuated and to help the disabled evacuate.
   - Notify emergency officials if anyone is not accounted for.

Recovery Considerations

1. Establish several methods to disseminate return-to-work instructions with employees if they are released to go home.
2. Keep the evacuation plan up to date.
3. Review the plan and procedures at least annually or after any major change in the configuration of the building. Provide for the training of newly hired or transferred employees.

FIRES

Sixty-four to 70 percent of businesses that have major fires never recover. They go out of business for good, primarily due to the loss of vital business records. Fire is also a major cause of accidental death in the United States. Injuries and burns from fires are often so hideous that their victims become reclusive; they do not want to be seen in public. The healing process from serious burns is said to be the most painful of any trauma. Property and indirect losses from fires are so large that they are figured in whole percentage points of the gross domestic product.

Prevention and Preparedness

1. Establish a written fire prevention plan. The plan should as a minimum include the following elements:[7]

   - A list of potential fire hazards and their proper handling and storage procedures, potential ignition sources (such as welding, smoking and others) and their control procedures, the type of fire protection equipment or systems that can control a fire involving the hazards.
   - Names or regular job titles of those responsible for maintenance of equipment and systems installed to prevent or control ignitions or fires; and
   - Names or regular job titles of those responsible for the control of accumulation of flammable or combustible waste materials.
   - Housekeeping. The company must control accumulations of flammable and combustible waste materials and residues so that they do not contribute to a fire emergency. The housekeeping procedures shall be included in the written fire prevention plan.
   - The company shall apprise employees of the fire hazards of the materials and processes to which they are exposed.
   - The company shall review with each employee upon initial assignment those parts of the fire prevention plan which the employee must know to protect the employee in the event of an emergency. The written plan shall be kept in the workplace and made available for employee review.
   - Maintenance. The company shall regularly and properly maintain, according to established procedures, equipment and systems installed in the workplace to prevent accidental ignition of combustible materials.

2. Install automatic fire detection, suppression and warning systems (UL-listed monitored fire alarm systems with smoke detectors and sprinklers).
3. Install fire extinguishers on every floor and near hazardous areas.
4. Establish guidelines and other written material for employees. Train employees in fire safety and evacuation.
5. Conduct regular fire prevention inspections and immediately correct any hazards identified.

---

[7] Adapted from California Code of Regulations, Title 8.

6. Maintain all fire control devices and equipment in good working order and up to local codes and standards.
7. Establish a vegetation "clear zone" extending at least a hundred feet from brush, fields, or forests. Use fire-resistant landscaping and building materials.
8. Shut off utilities, processes, and electronic systems if evacuation is anticipated. Be aware that some utilities cannot simply be turned back on without inspection. Never delay evacuation if this cannot be done safely.
9. In the case of a wild land-fire, place escape vehicles in position before evacuation is ordered.
10. Ensure that the address of the business is clearly marked and that the fire department is aware of the locations of shut-off valves and hazardous materials. Work with the fire department ahead of time to develop "prefire" plans.
11. Control traffic and parking so emergency vehicles have access to the facility.

Response

1. Obtain basic information about the location, type, and size of the fire if it is reported to you. Record the time, name, and extension number of the person reporting the fire. Ask if personnel have evacuated the area and if anyone is trapped or injured by the fire or smoke.
2. Evacuate the immediate area. If it can be done safely and quickly, open windows and close doors. Don't use elevators. If floor wardens are used to verify that everybody has evacuated, leave your office door open so he or she can check that everybody has left. Stay low, near to the floor, if smoke and heat are strong.
3. Dial 911 or the number that directly accesses the fire department dispatch center. Remain on the line until the dispatcher hangs up. Some organizations will first send a member of management, security, or the emergency response team to evaluate the need to notify the fire department. This can be a dangerous and costly approach, as fires can get out of control quickly.
4. Fight the fire, if you are qualified to do so. In many jurisdictions, the equipment and training required to fight a fire beyond the incipient stage (nonstructural, preflashover) is extensive.
5. Shut off heating, ventilation, and air conditioning systems if a potential for bringing smoke from the outside into the building exists.
6. Dispatch one or more people to meet the fire department and direct them to the location of the fire. The less obvious the route, the more personnel should be assigned to this task.

7. Remove any vehicles or other impediments to responding equipment.
8. If the building is sprinklered, assign a person to monitor the post indicator valve (PIV). This person should verify that the valve is functional and in the open position. Remain at this position to ensure that the valve is not prematurely shut.
9. Assign a person to check or start the fire pump, if one is utilized.
10. Determine whether equipment or hazardous processes should be shut down. Do so only if it is safe.
11. Move flammable or hazardous materials away from the area. Do so only if it is safe.

Recovery

1. Contact a restoration service that can repair smoke-damaged equipment, clean up water, and control mold and odor.
2. Prevent further damage to facilities and equipment from rain, theft, and other fire-related problems.
3. Restrict access to the damaged area.
4. Contact insurance carrier or broker.
5. Determine if the fire will affect production schedules or the functions dependent on any equipment, materials, or product destroyed by the fire.
6. Ask the fire department if it or disaster recovery teams can remove critical equipment or records not damaged in the fire. Some companies place large red or yellow dots on this equipment so it can be quickly located and removed if access to the building is restricted.
7. Recreate any lost vital records.
8. Provide status reports to major customers and employees.
9. Quickly replace or replenish used fire control equipment or devices.
10. Begin relocation and reconstruction.

LIGHTNING

Lightning develops as a result of interactions in the atmosphere between charged particles, interactions that produce an intense electrical field (up to a hundred million volts) within a thunderstorm. These bolts produce so much heat (fifty thousand degrees) that the air explodes into rumbling shock waves. Lightning kills more people across the United States each year than tornadoes; it is second only to flooding in weather-related deaths. Lightning is one of the leading causes of interruptions and other power-quality disturbances. The amount of lightning activity an area receives is measured in terms of "flash density," the number of cloud-to-ground lightning strikes per square mile during a year.

Of all weather-related phenomena, lighting is associated with the greatest number of myths. Lighting can and often does strike in the same place twice, and it seeks the best conductor to ground, not necessarily the tallest object. The tires of an automobile do not protect it from lightning; the metal body will conduct the charge away from its occupants — convertibles excepted, but why would someone drive with the top down in the rain? You can be struck by lightning from a storm many miles away, even if the sky overhead is clear. A software engineer in Silicon Valley, an area of California where lightning is uncommon, was injured when his computer exploded. The engineer was on the ground floor of a high-rise building that was struck by lightning.

Prevention and Preparedness

1. Monitor the storm's conditions. The National Weather Service broadcasts continuous weather and warning information over the National Oceanic and Atmospheric Administration (NOAA) weather radio stations. Internet sites provide weather conditions and information, and local stations often broadcast severe-weather information.
2. Install line conditioners that reduce the effects of power surges on sensitive or critical equipment, and connect critical equipment to uninterruptible power supplies.
3. Instruct employees to stay indoors. Outdoor activities should be discontinued immediately.
4. Avoid contact with pipes, railings, wire fences, telephones, other electrical equipment and appliances, including faucets and showers.
5. Train employees to avoid open areas if outside and to seek low ground in a wooded area (not under single tree). Employees should crouch close to the ground on the balls of their feet, but they should not lie down. Stay clear of metal objects; if in a group, they should move away from each other. Include first aid as a part of the training.
6. Maintain scheduled backups of computer, telecommunications, and other data systems.
7. Establish twenty-four-hour guaranteed-service or equipment-replacement agreements with vendors.
8. Shut down systems if feasible.

Response

1. Dial 911.
2. Treat injured victims. Remove them from danger. Cardiopulmonary distress, broken bones, and burns are the most common lightning-related injuries. Look for entry and exit wounds.

3. Check for and extinguish fires.
4. If power is lost, shut down equipment.

Recovery

1. Log all events, actions, decisions, and expenses.
2. Activate response teams as required.
3. Assess and document damage.
4. Reestablish utilities.
5. Test and replace damaged equipment and connectivity. Restore data if any is lost.

FLOOD/HEAVY RAIN

On a worldwide basis, floods account for 39 percent more loss of life than earthquakes. The onset of a flood can be gradual or sudden, and it can occur in areas where they are not normally expected. Heavy rains are usually the root cause. A summer storm in Colorado was responsible in 1976 for the deaths of a hundred campers and vacationers — water came rushing down a river without warning. Floods of this type can reach heights of thirty feet or more; they can result from the collapse of a dam formed by a landslide, ice, or a debris jam. Flooding can also result from the structural failure of permanent dams during an earthquake. High seas produced by major storms or storm surge can also cause flooding, especially in low-lying areas.

Floods are usually easy to predict. Flash floods generally reoccur in the same location, but can happen within minutes of a storm. Where floods are prevalent, NOAA maintains River Forecast Centers and provides reports on river levels, rainfall, and predicted weather. Up-to-the-minute information is also obtained from firsthand observations, monitoring police and emergency services radio communications, and river-level Web sites. Some jurisdictions prone to flash flooding have installed horns and sirens to warn people of impending danger.

Areawide flooding causes many more problems than simply getting things wet. The force of the water in a river at flood stage can move vehicles and destroy buildings and bridges. It can isolate areas from fire and police response and sever communications lines. Floods can, and often do, spread disease and contaminate drinking water.

In spite of all the water, fires can be a big problem during floods. Underground storage tanks containing hazardous or flammable liquids can be forced to the surface. Equipment can be damaged or destroyed by water and mud, which is often deposited everywhere. Finished product can be contaminated and vital records damaged or destroyed. The foundations of buildings can be undermined by the erosive effect of rapidly moving water. The growth of certain molds can be deadly, and the odor is difficult to remove.

Prevention and Preparedness

1. Know your flood risk and the risk of flooding to your location's access and escape routes.
2. Keep creeks and culverts free from debris that could restrict drainage or cause a creek to dam.
3. Be prepared for erosion or landslides.
4. Keep roof and parking lot drainage systems free of leaves and other debris or obstructions.
5. Inspect roofs for water stains, ponding, plant growth, or other signs of potential weakness.
6. Remove any yard storage from drainage or other low-lying areas. Coat exposed metal with grease if it cannot be moved to higher ground.
7. Anchor any items or equipment that may float away. (Large tanks of flammable or hazardous materials can and do float away.) Consider off-loading storage tanks of hazardous materials and separating chemicals that can react if mixed together. Also consider filling emptied tanks with water to add weight, if this will not contaminate, or cause an adverse reaction with, its contents when refilled.
8. Install check-valves in sewer traps to prevent flood water from backing up into the building.
9. Maintain an adequate supply of sandbags, if located in an area susceptible to flooding.
10. Maintain a supply of water proofing materials to protect equipment in the case of water leaks.
11. If located in an area prone to flash flooding, consider erecting diversion walls.
12. Park vehicles on the escape side of bridges in case they are weakened by rushing water. Keep vehicles fueled.
13. Monitor conditions via AM/FM radio, TV, or NOAA weather radio broadcasts (156.40 and 156.55 MHz are the main frequencies). Some amateur television radio clubs have rented helicopters to transmit live video of flood conditions.
14. Stockpile other materials in a secure, accessible location. This should include:
    - Clean-up and salvage equipment
    - Emergency food and water

- Flashlights and lightsticks
- Portable water pumps and hoses
- Portable generator and fuel
- First aid supplies and snake-bite kits
- Shovels and tools (including chain saw and crow bars)
- Rubber boots and gloves.

15. Inspect fire protection equipment. Test fire pump and ensure that it has sufficient fuel.
16. Sandbag protection equipment and backup generators if they are susceptible to flooding.
17. Move equipment and documents to upper levels or to higher ground.
18. Back-up data systems, and transfer operations to an alternate location.

Response

1. Immediately deenergize equipment if the flood is isolated to your facility due to sprinkler system activation, broken pipes, and the like. Cover equipment and product with waterproof sheeting.
2. Monitor conditions and escape routes.
3. Shut off electrical power and utilities if flooding is imminent.
4. Immediately evacuate to higher ground — flood waters often rise rapidly.
5. Watch for and avoid low-lying areas. Don't drive through flooded areas. If your car stalls, abandon it immediately. Six inches of rushing water can knock people off of their feet. Almost half of all flash flood fatalities involve the occupants of vehicles.
6. Don't attempt to cross flowing streams.
7. Beware of snakes and other animals.

Recovery

1. Ensure that facilities and equipment are cleaned, dehumidified, sanitized, and deodorized before allowing the reentry of employees and guests.
2. Do not turn on utilities until the structure, appliances, and utilities are dry and the building is checked for natural gas or propane leaks.
3. Be sure water supplies are safe to drink. Dispose of any food or consumables that may have been in contact with flood waters or mold.
4. Begin mitigation planning to avoid a repeat of the same problems in future flooding.

HURRICANES

The combined energy of the atmosphere and ocean can turn a tropical storm into a massive center of power and destruction. These cyclonic storms, intense low-pressure centers with swirling arms of clouds and winds over seventy-five miles per hour, cause billions of dollars in damage to the coastal areas of the Gulf of Mexico and Atlantic Ocean. Hurricanes are considered the most destructive type of weather condition, because they are capable of spawning tornadoes in addition to high winds and flooding.

While the center, or "eye," of these storms is clear and calm, the winds across the rest of their fifty-to-five-hundred-mile diameters can range from seventy-five to 150 miles per hour or more. In spite of the power of a hurricane, the storm itself usually progresses at a speed of only up to thirty miles per hour, at times stopping entirely. Although the strong winds account for many of the problems associated with hurricanes, high seas and flooding cause the most damage and loss of life. During storms of this magnitude, the level of the sea may rise many feet higher than normal (a phenomenon known as storm surge).

An average of seven storms per season form during the months of June through November and last for a week or more. This life span allows forecasters to spot and track a storm and predict its landfall. The loss of life in hurricanes in the United States is decreasing.[8] More accurate forecasting and a likelihood of people to take the warnings seriously account for this improvement. A *hurricane watch* means that hurricane conditions may occur; a *hurricane warning* means that a storm is expected within twenty-four hours.

Prevention and Preparedness

1. See the section on flooding and heavy rain for additional guidelines.
2. Check flood insurance policies for adequacy of coverage and exclusions.
3. Prior to the storm season, stockpile such extra supplies as food, water, battery-powered weather radio, cash, plywood and nails, ropes, sandbags, emergency lighting and power. These items can be in short supply when a storm is forecast.

---

[8] As of this writing, figures for the death and destruction caused by Hurricane Mitch, which devastated Central America on October 22, 1998, have yet to be totaled. "Hurricane 'Mitch,' a category 5 storm, with 180 mph sustained winds which reportedly killed over 10,000 people in Central America will serve for generations to show what hurricanes can do. These deaths are not just numbers, they were children, moms, dads, and friends." Jerry Jarrell, Director, National Hurricane Center.

4. Determine where to relocate business operations and employees if ordered to evacuate.
5. Develop equipment and manufacturing shutdown procedures.
6. Inspect the integrity of roof edging strips, drains, pipe racks, sign and stack supports.
7. Clean drains and catch basins.
8. Cover sensitive equipment and finished goods with waterproof covers.
9. Keep trees in good health and trim branches that may fall into the building or onto equipment.
10. Train employees to prepack clothes, medications, pictures, cash, extra glasses, and baby supplies, in case they are required to evacuate from their homes.
11. Prequalify restoration and building contractors for the business and employees.

Response

1. Monitor the progress of the storm and estimate the amount of time required to perform all essential tasks.
2. If ordered to evacuate, do so immediately.
3. Move valuables out of the area or to upper floors if located in a flood or storm surge zone.
4. Secure or store furniture, planters, or other objects outside the building.
5. Board up windows with plywood (taping does not work).
6. Turn off utilities.
7. Arrange for extra security if necessary.
8. If required to remain, stay inside and away from windows, doors, and outside walls. (Employees should never remain alone. Do as much as possible to ensure their safety.)

Recovery

1. Wait until the storm has passed before beginning repairs and restoration.
2. Evaluate the structural integrity of the building and utilities.
3. Ensure that the site is safe for cleanup, salvage, and reoccupation.
4. Account for employees as they return from evacuation.
5. Begin relocation and reconstruction.

TORNADOES

A tornado is a violently rotating column of air that makes contact with the ground. (A tornado that does not touch the ground is referred to as a *funnel cloud*; a tornado over water is a *waterspout*.) Tornadoes usually develop from severe thunderstorms. They originate in the right-rear quadrant of the storm cell or at the leading edge of a line of thunderstorms. Their paths are unpredictable, cutting straight lines of destruction, or zigzagging back and forth, or hopping and skipping around, even reversing general direction. They usually travel from the southwest to the northeast at an average speed of thirty miles per hour, but they have been known to remain stationary.

Although most tornadoes occur between 3:00 and 7:00 P.M. during the months of April, May, and June, they can occur any time of the day and anywhere in the world. The Texas Panhandle, Oklahoma, Kansas, Nebraska, Iowa, Missouri, parts of Arkansas, Illinois, and Indiana have the most tornadoes, although they form in every state, and at greater frequencies than previously thought. Southern Ontario accounts for a third of Canada's total tornadoes, with seven of the nine strongest occurring in this region.

Most (about 62 percent) fall into the "weak" category, with rotational wind speeds of one hundred miles per hour or less. Only 1.5 percent of tornadoes are classified as "violent," with wind speeds reaching three hundred miles per hour or more. These violent tornadoes account for almost 70 percent of the fatalities. It is the wind speed that accounts for most of the destruction, not the sudden drop in air pressure. Wind speed is greatest at the upper portions of the tornado. Flying debris is the cause of most injuries.

Although the practice is discouraged by some experts (Lopes), initial research by Kent State University (Schmidlin et al.), suggests that mobile home occupants may be safer in their automobiles during low to mid-intensity storms if they cannot get to a shelter or a sturdy building in one minute or less. The National Weather Service warns against attempts to outrun a tornado in a vehicle, as some tornadoes can travel at nearly seventy miles per hour.

A *tornado watch* is issued when severe thunderstorms or tornadoes are most likely to occur and when conditions are favorable for their formation. A *warning* is issued when a tornado is detected on radar or reported by observers. Warnings and firsthand reports are received over:

- NOAA Weather Radio broadcasts
- The Internet
- Real-time Doppler radar
- CCTV
- Citizens Band, Amateur Radio, and police communications frequencies
- Local television and commercial radio channels.

Prevention and Preparedness

1. Monitor weather broadcast stations and conditions. Learn what tornado conditions look and sound like (often described as the sound of a freight train or airplane). Know the meaning of watches and warnings.
2. Identify a shelter room. A storm cellar or basement is best, but an interior room without windows on the lowest floor is the next-best alternative (excluding mobile homes). Occupants of a high-rise building should go to an interior room, hallway, or interior stairwell on a lower floor.
3. Instruct employees in the meanings of local warning systems (sirens, a red bar on a television screen, and the like).
4. Construct storm shelters if none are close by.

Response

1. Seek shelter in a storm cellar, basement, or interior room without windows. Get under something sturdy, such as a desk or table.
2. Stay clear of windows (do not open them), doors, and outside walls.
3. If outside, seek a safe place in a sturdy nearby building. As a last resort, take cover in a ditch or low-lying area; lie flat with hands covering your head.
4. If in a vehicle, seek shelter in a ditch or under an overpass.
5. Leave mobile homes for a storm shelter or a safe place in a sturdy nearby building.

Recovery

1. Begin search and rescue operations only if properly trained and equipped.
2. Treat injuries.
3. Avoid the use of open flames.
4. Begin relocation and reconstruction.

HAZARDOUS MATERIALS INCIDENTS

Responses to a hazardous materials incident are regulated by federal law. Each state has its own set of regulations, and some more stringent than others. The following are basic procedures the firm can use to prepare and respond to chemical spills, toxic releases, and other hazardous materials emergencies. The reader should check with local regulations and match or exceed the level of response and training they required for the hazard present.

Prevention and Preparedness

1. Identify the hazardous materials used on site and maintain material data safety sheets (MSDS) in strategic locations (EOC, spill carts, and the like). Include a list of their quantities and their locations. Be aware of hazardous materials located at nearby facilities or transportation systems.
2. Determine what federal, state, and local regulations the company must follow. Train staff to the highest level appropriate to the level of response and clean up that may be required.
3. Work with local officials, such as the fire department, to coordinate pre-emergency plans.
4. Place spill kits, safety showers, and equipment at strategic locations.
5. Maintain the proper equipment for the first aid, cleanup, and decontamination of materials used in your operations.
6. Construct dikes and secondary containment around storage areas.
7. Install panic alarms and CCTV in hazardous areas.
8. Install wind socks and weather stations if appropriate.
9. Conduct joint training drills with city or county services.
10. Investigate the need to install a community warning system.
11. Inspect containers and piping for damage or leaks.
12. Separate incompatible materials that may react if mixed.

Response

1. Evacuate the immediate area (upwind if possible). If required, prepare for shelter-in-place (see below).
2. Isolate the area and deny access to any unauthorized personnel.
3. Decide if outside assistance is required; if it is, dial 911.
4. Wear the highest level of protective equipment available.
5. Remove injured victims or personnel overcome by fumes if you can do so safely.
6. Apply first aid appropriate to the injuries.
7. Identify the materials, their properties and hazards, cleanup procedures, and toxicologies. Assume the substance is hazardous until you know otherwise. Look for identification on containers (don't walk into the secured area), placards, or MSDS. Smell is not always a reliable way to identify chemicals. Never taste an unidentified

substance (during the early days of the semiconductor industry, a Ph.D. engineer could not speak for several weeks because of an acid burn on his tongue caused by an unsuccessful attempt to identify a spilled substance).

8. Eliminate ignition sources if a flammable liquid or explosive gas is involved. Stage fire control equipment at appropriate locations.
9. If it is safe to do so, mitigate or eliminate the source of the spill — that is, close valves, cap bottles, patch leaks.
10. Determine the size of the area affected and whether additional evacuations are warranted.
11. If properly trained and equipped, contain the spill. Do not let material go down a drain, into a waterway, basement, or confined space.
12. Use only properly trained, equipped, and certified personnel to clean up the hazard. Never work alone.
13. Make notifications to regulatory agencies as required.
14. Shelter-in-place procedures:
    - Turn off HVAC systems
    - Close all doors, windows, shades, blinds, and transoms
    - Place wet towels in spaces under doors
    - Block air vents with plastic, and place tape around doors and windows
    - Cover your body with clothing as much as possible
    - Avoid eating anything uncovered that may be contaminated
    - Listen to informational broadcasts.

Recovery

1. Activate the crisis management plan if not done earlier.
2. Decontaminate responders, facilities, and equipment.
3. Repair damage.
4. File any required reports with regulatory agencies.
5. Monitor health and environmental problems caused by the incident.
6. Investigate the cause and take actions to prevent a recurrence.

BOMB THREATS

Terrorist bombings are expected to increase in the coming years, causing greater loss of life, damage, and disruption to business operations. Domestically, the chance of finding a bomb after a threat is very low. While most security professionals no longer recommend the evacuation of a facility after most threats, a search should be conducted in all cases.

Prevention and Preparedness

1. Audit the physical security, incoming inspection, access, and internal controls of the facility. Analyze the firms exposure to bombings.
2. If warranted, develop an intelligence program and maintain continuous contact with law enforcement.
3. Place bomb threat questionnaires and brief instructions at all security, switchboard, and reception stations.
4. Provide specific training to all security officers, switchboard operators, and receptionists who could receive bomb threats.
5. Establish who will evaluate threats. Train this person or an evaluation committee to assess the credibility of threats.
6. Decide what procedures will be followed when a threat is received, if a device is discovered, and what methods will be used to search.
7. Decide what conditions (if any) should trigger an immediate evacuation of the building and list these conditions in a procedure for Security or for an emergency response team commander. Companies may decide to identify certain elements as justifying evacuation of employees without approval from the threat assessment committee. Depending on the company's bomb-risk profile, these elements may include disclosure of the location of the bomb, the time of detonation, a motive, or an apparent familiarity of the facility.
8. Identify search methods and searchers prior to the incident. Train searchers on technique, bomb recognition, and safety. Most police departments will *not* search for you!
9. Identify and prioritize search areas prior to the incident.
10. Consider delaying a search to protect the safety of the searchers if the threat is credible and a short time limit is given.
11. Establish a procedure to track the progress of the search. Develop sectionalized maps and checklists.
12. Test all procedures.
13. Review plans, procedures, and contact phone numbers regularly.

Response

1. Write down the *exact* time of the call. Find out whether the call originated from within the site or outside.
2. Record the caller's exact words. Permit the caller to say as much as possible, without interruption.
3. Ask the caller the following, and record the answers to these questions:

- When will it explode?
- Where is it located?
- What does it look like?
- Why was it placed?
- Who is calling?

4. Attempt to transfer the call to the head of security or to a member of the threat assessment team.
5. Initiate a search for a bomb. Use a checklist to ensure that all prioritized areas are searched in the most expedient and thorough manner possible. If the caller tells you where the bomb is located, obviously check that area first (myself, I check under my chair first).
6. Make other notifications as appropriate (to management, security, and the police).
7. If you find an object you suspect may be a bomb:
   - Evacuate people at least three hundred yards away and out of the line of sight or blast effect.
   - Dial 911.
   - Identify/evaluate the object.
   - Do not attempt to touch, move, dismantle, or pour water on any suspicious object.
   - If it is safe, open doors and windows around the area to reduce blast effect.
   - Isolate (secure) the area from entry.
   - Consider shutting down utilities and hazardous processes.
   - If it is safe, continue the search for additional bombs.
   - Relocate vital records and back-up computer systems if time permits.
   - Contact the public relations spokesperson or activate the crisis management plan.
   - Stage emergency response equipment and strategic resources.
   - Restrict access to the area.
8. If a bomb explodes, and persons are injured, some experts suggest removing the victims immediately and securing the area, not treating them where they are found. Their rationale is based on the practice of some terrorists to place in the same area additional bombs set to explode later to kill and injure rescue workers and police.

Recovery

1. Care for the injured.
2. Begin rescue operations only if properly trained and equipped, and if there are no other devices in the area.

3. Assess damage, including the structural integrity of the buildings.
4. Begin salvage and cleanup.
5. Test electronic and other sensitive equipment for blast damage.
6. Provide posttraumatic stress counseling for employees and rescue crews.
7. Begin relocation and reconstruction.
8. Investigate and prosecute every incident.

WORKPLACE VIOLENCE/CIVIL DISTURBANCE

Violence is the leading cause of death for women and the second-leading cause of death for men in the workplace. In 1994, robbery-homicide represented 9 percent of total crime but accounted for 75 percent of workplace homicide. With over two million workers physically attacked, over six million threatened, and over sixteen million workers harassed, it is not surprising that two-thirds of workers do not feel safe at work.[9] The 1995 cost of workplace violence was $36 billion. Direct legal and medical costs totaled $250,000 per incident, and jury awards exceed five million dollars. Firms that suffer an incident of workplace violence experience an 80 percent loss of productivity in the subsequent week. One San Francisco law firm went out of business because a former client, with no warning, using automatic weapons, killed and injured a number of attorneys and clients in what was regarded as a random act of violence.

Workplace violence is classified by the relationship of the perpetrator to the workplace:

- Type I — No legitimate relationship to workplace, usually robbery or other criminal act
- Type II — Customer or client, that is, a patient or passenger
- Type III — Employment-related involvement — employee, ex-employee, domestic violence "spillover."

Prevention and Preparedness

1. Observe good hiring practices, conducting criminal background verification and investigation where appropriate.
2. Establish policy strictly forbidding any form of workplace violence or possession of weapons and requiring employees to report threats

---

[9] National Institute of Safety and Health, Bulletin 57 (Washington, D.C., June 1996); 1994 figures.

and potential problems to management. Communicate this policy to all employees. Consistently enforce sanctions for noncompliance.

3. Train supervisory and management personnel to:
   - Recognize potentially aggressive behavior
   - Recognize signs of domestic violence
   - Diffuse aggressive behavior
   - Recognize the importance of an immediate response to complaints.
4. Foster a good working environment, with consistent discipline, a problem-solving rather than a blaming attitude, open communication, respect, and a nonauthoritarian management style.
5. Never terminate an employee in a manner that is degrading or does not allow him or her the full use of social services available.
6. Audit and improve physical security and access control.
7. Protect potential victims. Obtain corporate and personal restraining orders, provide special parking and escort privileges, change their shift or work location, and consider providing the employees with personal protection devices.
8. Form a committee to evaluate and manage threats or acts of violence. The committee should include the employee's manager, human resources, legal, security, medical (employee assistance program representative, staff or contract psychologist).
9. Remove objects, such as decorative rocks, that can be used by demonstrators, activists, or rioters to break windows, injure employees, or damage other property.
10. Train security officers to understand arrest policies, and *not* to:
    - Be provoked by name calling or derogatory remarks
    - Discuss or argue the merits or issues of the dispute with protesters or picketers
    - Antagonize demonstrators or picketers
    - Throw back objects thrown at them
    - Attempt to take anything from a protester unless in self-defense
    - Make physical contact unless blocking a doorway (in this instance, they should not place their hands on a protester).

Response (Type III)

1. Assess the situation (if safe to do so), but do not delay calling 911. In the case of a demonstration, determine the number of protesters, the purpose of the demonstration, and the affiliation of the groups involved.
2. If possible:
   - Isolate potential victims
   - Lock all doors

- Close blinds
- Take cover.
3. Summon help:
   - Dial 911
   - Activate panic alarm if available
   - Pull fire alarm. (Except in the case of protesters or if you don't want to place employees outside of the building.)
4. Warn other employees.
5. Notify appropriate managers.
6. Account for employees and guests when able.
7. Do not interact with participants in a disturbance.

Recovery

1. Activate the crisis management plan.
2. Immediately clean up biohazards and physical damage.
3. Provide stress counseling for employees, victims, and families.
4. Review security and response procedures.

SERIOUS INJURY OR ILLNESS

All employers have a legal and moral responsibility to protect the safety and health of their employees. Injury and illness are probably the most common emergencies found in the workplace. Businesses lose billions of dollars annually in lost productivity, recruiting, and other ways due to injuries. The firm's response to an injury is very visible and if handled incorrectly may become an issue, producing poor employee morale, a labor dispute, or negative publicity.

Prevention and Preparedness

1. Implement effective injury and illness prevention plans.
2. Inoculate employees at risk, if necessary.
3. Know any special conditions or needs of employees.
4. Train employees in first aid and cardiopulmonary resuscitation. Match or exceed the level of training required by regulations or to compensate for any extended response times of emergency medical personnel.
5. Maintain first aid supplies at strategic locations. First aid and medical (hospital) services may not be readily available after a disaster.

Most first aid kits are not designed for the type of injures or delay in care possible after a disaster. At least one kit should contain disaster first aid supplies.

6. Control traffic and parking so emergency vehicles have access to the facility.

Response

1. Dial, or request someone to dial, 911 and report:
   - Your name
   - A description of the illness or injury
   - Your location
2. Stay on the line until the dispatcher hangs up.
3. Determine the extent of the injuries.
4. Provide first aid if qualified:
   - Control bleeding
   - Check breathing
   - Check circulation
   - Treat for shock
5. Remain with the victim:
   - Ensure that the victim is not moved (unless to protect from further hazard)
   - Obtain as much information about the victim's condition, history, and needs as required
6. Keep those not involved in the emergency away form the area.
7. Send persons to meet the fire department, paramedics, or ambulance at the driveway and front door of the building to escort them to the victim.

Recovery

1. Follow biohazard procedures and regulations when cleaning up body fluids.
2. Notify regulatory agencies (OSHA), legal, and insurance carrier if required.
3. Completely investigate the cause of all injuries and take steps to prevent their recurrence.
4. Retrain injured employees on safety procedures.
5. Activate the crisis management plan if injuries are major, if illness is widespread or controversial, or if fatalities are involved.
6. Provide posttraumatic stress counseling if necessary.

EARTHQUAKE

The release of energy caused by resistance to the continual shifting of large segments of the earth's crust (tectonic plates) is responsible for most of the world's earthquakes. The boundaries of these plates are *fault zones*. Major earthquakes occur even many thousands of miles away from these boundaries; they are thought to be related to interplate crustal weakness. Such was the case for the largest earthquakes in the United States, along the New Madrid (Missouri) fault in 1811 and 1812. No portion of the United States or southern Canada is immune from the effects of earthquakes. The entire West Coast (including Canada, Alaska, Nevada, and Utah), the Midwest near the Mississippi River, and the East Coast north of Florida up to southeastern Canada and New England are susceptible to significant ground movement.

Damage from earthquakes is related to the amount of energy released, length of the fault rupture, the depth and type of fault, velocity and acceleration, distance from the fault, soil types and conditions, and the type of building construction. Various methods are used to measure earthquakes. The *Richter Scale* indirectly measures the energy released from an earthquake by recording needle deflections on a seismograph. An earthquake with a Richter magnitude of three is barely felt unless you are very close to it. A magnitude 6 earthquake can cause major damage. The Richter Scale uses a logarithmic progression. That is, the energy released from a magnitude 6 is not twice as big as in a magnitude 3: it is approximately *a hundred times* greater. The *Modified Mercalli Scale* is used to map areas of intensity, based on personal reports by victims and by inspection of the damage. It uses a scale from I through XII, based on the type of damage observed.

Certain soil conditions amplify or attenuate seismic forces. Soil and bedrock in the eastern United States tends to transmit this energy over a wider area than that in the West. An earthquake in Bolivia was actually felt in Minneapolis. Sand and silt near unstable bay and river areas can cause liquefaction and soil failure.

Most modern structures are designed to withstand earthquakes. They may sustain heavy damage, but they should not collapse. The greatest danger is from objects such as parapets, signs, bricks, and glass falling off the buildings. Older buildings, nonretrofitted buildings of concrete tilt-up or nonreinforced masonry construction, can partially or completely collapse. The Uniform Building Code in the United States and the National Building Code in Canada contain maps that assign a seismic risk (based on expected ground movement, not probability) to various parts of the countries and define building codes to balance the known level of risk in these areas.

Earthquakes can cause a complete collapse of transportation systems: highways, overpasses, bridges, shipping ports, and airport runways can be damaged or destroyed. Infrastructure can fail: expect to be without water, sewer, and utilities for three days or more; police, fire, and hospital services can be destroyed or overloaded. Thousands can be made homeless or refuse to return to their homes, even if damage is minor. Dam and levee failures, train derailments, landslides, hazardous material releases and spills, uncontrolled fires, avalanches, persons trapped in buildings, and persons injured in falls could all result from an earthquake.

Scientists may soon gain the ability to predict the location and specific time when an earthquake is likely — hours to weeks in advance. Presently, forecasting is based on known fault locations and the historic recurrence rate of earthquakes on these faults. In California, public agencies respond only to predictions endorsed by established scientific panels.

Prevention and Preparedness

1. Ensure that automatic fire-sprinkler systems are supported with earthquake sway bracing (see National Fire Protection Association [NFPA] Standard 13, Standard for the Installation of Sprinkler Systems). Pipes can break during an earthquake, causing water damage or inability to extinguish a fire.
2. Bolt bookcases, file cabinets, display racks, work stations, flammable liquid storage cabinets, wire or equipment racks, and other tall, heavy objects to the floor or wall. These objects can topple over during an earthquake, causing injuries to employees, blocking escape routes, damaging equipment, and delaying the cleanup and recovery process.
3. Strap sensitive, critical, or expensive equipment (including computers and servers) to desk, workbenches or equipment racks. Place equipment that cannot be strapped or that must be moved often on seismic damping mats. Base-isolate (prevent the base from moving, or attach devices that allow the base move independently) large equipment such as boilers, pumps, chillers, and backup electrical generators.
4. Stockpile supplies of food, water, lighting, and disaster first aid supplies. Employees may need to remain on site temporarily while transportation systems are being restored. Encourage employees to keep emergency supplies in their desk or car. At a minimum this should include:
   - First aid supplies and prescription medications
   - High-energy, low-salt packaged, dried or canned food
   - Nonelectric can opener
   - Portable radio with batteries

- Flashlight or light sticks
- Extra cash
- Tennis shoes
- Blanket
- Pocket knife
- Safety whistle (this should remain in the employee's pocket or purse
- Picture of kids, family
- Out-of-town contact phone numbers
- Change of underwear and socks
- Toiletries and personal hygiene items
- Proof of residence, such as a water bill
- Drinking water — at least one gallon per person per day. Water supplies may not be available for three to five days after the earthquake.

5. Identify and mitigate other nonstructural hazards, including light fixtures, storage racks, hanging objects, mirrors, and fireplaces.
6. Encourage individual and family preparedness. Employees who know that their families and loved ones are safe at home are more willing to remain at work or to return to work soon. Conduct earthquake-safety workshops and obtain information from the American Red Cross and the Federal Emergency Management Agency to distribute to employees.
7. Consult with a structural engineer to ensure that your buildings meet seismic safety standards. Arrange to have these engineers inspect the buildings after an earthquake.
8. Train personnel in the location of emergency shutoff valves for gas, electrical, water, and hazardous gas or chemical lines. Install flow valves on hazardous material lines to prevent uncontrolled discharge if the pipes are broken.
9. Strap water heaters to the wall and install flexible connections to the gas line. Water heaters can topple over during an earthquake, causing fires and the loss of a potential source of drinking water.
10. Train employees in first aid and cardiopulmonary resuscitation.
11. Maintain an adequate supply of cash.

Response

If you are inside — DUCK, COVER, and HOLD:

- Take cover under a desk or table, or sit or stand against an inside wall (not inside a doorway).
- Hold tightly to the desk or table until the shaking stops.

- Move away from windows or objects that may fall on you.
- Do not run outside during the shaking.
- After the shaking has stopped, evacuate the building if structural damage is apparent.
- Avoid use of the telephone. Replace telephone handsets shaken off the hook.
- Do not use open flames.

If you are outside:

- Do not enter any building.
- Move clear of buildings, falling glass, utility poles, wires, and large trees.
- Get on the ground — DUCK, COVER, HOLD.
- After the shaking stops, watch for falling glass, electrical wires, poles, and other debris.

If you are driving:

- Drive away from overpasses and underpasses.
- Stop in a safe place.
- Set the parking brake.
- Stay in the vehicle. If wires fall onto the vehicle, stay inside until rescued.

Recovery

1. Check for injuries.
2. Rescue victims, if trained and equipped to do so.
3. Check the structural integrity of the building.
4. Check for fires and other damage. Turn off gas only if a leak is detected.
5. Clean up hazardous material spills.
6. Turn off noncritical electrical equipment if power is out. When power is restored, turn equipment back on gradually.
7. Avoid the use of open flames. Do not use camp stoves or charcoal in an enclosed area, such as a tent.
8. Use caution when reentering damaged buildings; aftershocks can cause further damage.
9. Check that vents and exhaust pipes have not separated from water heaters or other machinery.
10. Listen to radio and TV stations for official information.
11. Begin relocation and reconstruction.

BIBLIOGRAPHY

Natural Hazards Observer 22, no. 2, November 1997 (University of Colorado at Boulder).

Fischer, Henry W., III. *Response to Disaster*. University Press of America, 1994.

Uniform Building Code. International Conference of Building Officials, Whittier, CA.

Cote, Arthur E., ed. in chief. *Fire Protection Handbook*. 17th ed. Quincy, MA: National Fire Protection Association, 1991.

Chemical Emergency Response/Hazardous Waste Resource Manual. The Center for Workplace Health and Safety Education, Washington, D.C., 1997.

Standard for Professional Competence of Responders to Hazardous Materials Incidents, ANSI/NFPA 472. National Fire Protection Association, 1992.

15

CRISIS MANAGEMENT PLANNING FOR KIDNAP, EXTORTION, OR RANSOM

The most functional philosophy of risk control consulting has as a basic tenet making the client as self-sufficient as possible in all matters pertaining to security. This includes crisis management programs.

J. F. Broder, CFE, CPP, FACFE
Security Consultant

The odds of any business organization being the victim of a kidnap, extortion, or ransom demand are slim. Nevertheless, we outline here the steps to be taken by a crisis management team (CMT), because a kidnapping could nonetheless occur at any time. More important, however, the CMT approach can be used to resolve *any* crisis of magnitude sufficient to threaten the financial existence of a corporation. We go into specific details regarding the threat of kidnap and extortion, because we have worked with organizations that, not having plans, had to develop them on an ad hoc basis to deal with these problems. We use this real-world experience as an example to the reader of how to develop, before it occurs and not after, a planned approach for dealing with such a crisis.

PLANNING FOR THE THREAT OF KIDNAP, EXTORTION, OR RANSOM AGAINST CORPORATIONS

Government officials and business executives have been attractive targets for kidnappers and extortionists since long before the 1960s. Domestic terrorist activity directed against executives, corporations, and political leaders in Asia, Europe, South America, and recently in Mexico and the United States has made the general populace justifiably apprehensive. As in the case of the Hearst family, corporations, their executives, and members of the executive's families have been, and are expected to continue to be, victims of kidnappings and extortion, which could inflict heavy losses on corporations or on the personal well-being and wealth of the victims' families.

There are two basic reasons for executive kidnappings — personal gain and political objectives. These kidnap (extortion) victims generally possess one or more of the common elements of money, power, or high public visibility. Individual chances of being kidnapped are extremely low, but the odds increase rapidly if the potential victim is wealthy; controls large amounts of money; is associated with such cash-driven industries as banking, savings and loans, gambling casinos, or food marketing; or works in industries such as airlines or public utilities. An executive's chances of being kidnapped are further increased if his industry is often victimized by terrorists or extortionists, or if his company has a history of paying ransom demands.

In order to mount a successful response to kidnappings and other forms of extortion, a plan to deal with such crises must be formulated in advance. The major responsibility for advance planning belongs to the organization. Organizational planning is more effective than individual effort, and it is more likely to be implemented, and thus successful. Therefore, organizations must develop crisis management skills that are adaptable to any extortionate demand made on them.

PRINCIPLES OF CRISIS MANAGEMENT

Crisis management can be addressed most advantageously by a crisis management team (CMT). The CMT should consist of a group of senior management personnel who have the authority to make decisions for the entire corporation during a crisis. Because a small unit is generally capable of reaching decisions more quickly, the CMT should consist of the least number of individuals possible. Because extortionists can often inflict heavy losses on organizations, it is imperative that the CMT prepare a readiness plan that will minimize these losses. This plan must fix corporate objectives and limitations, and it must be designed to be effective when the CMT is operating under the emotional strain of responsibility for human life, often with limited data and time for making decisions.

The plan must resolve the fixed elements of a crisis, so as to require the CMT to make only those decisions during a crisis that are affected by immediate variables. Also, it must have sufficient flexibility to enable the CMT to develop alternative strategies after gathering information and analyzing threats under rapidly changing crisis conditions.

The CMT is not a substitute for law enforcement or the organization's security department; rather, it is a complementary support organization. Decisions that affect the company directly and require corporate decisions or responses should be handled by the CMT in partnership with law enforcement. For example, a trained hostage negotiator working in conjunction with law enforcement personnel should be designated to act as the intermediary between the extortionist and the victim company. The extortionist must clearly understand that the negotiator has neither the authority nor the capacity to make decisions or commitments on behalf of the company. Used in the proper context, the trained negotiator often provides time for the CMT decision process to work effectively.

Most firms have capable, qualified, and responsible persons in their employ who can and should conduct all negotiations in these situations. These people, many of whom are schooled and experienced in industrial relations or similar types of business negotiations, need only receive training in how to negotiate in criminal situations in order to become effective.

The use of outside consultant resources for negotiations is impractical, for several reasons. Most extortion situations are resolved rather quickly. The one exception is a protracted terrorist kidnap, where publicity is a key ingredient of the case. By the time outside consultants could arrive at the scene and receive an update on the progress of the case, local law enforcement combined with company executives would probably have the situation stabilized and in some cases resolved. Coming on the scene six to twelve hours after a kidnap/extortion situation begins, the outside consultant will likely have no impact whatsoever. In addition, remember that the basic tenet of risk-control consulting is to make the client as self-sufficient as possible in matters pertaining to security; this includes crisis management programs. The best use of consultants is to have them help the corporation to develop the CMT, then to have them available for telephone consultation during the crisis.

There are several basic areas of concern to be addressed by the CMT as it provides corporate leadership during a crisis. The protection of assets, which in this case includes personnel, is of primary concern. Experience with a systems approach to assets protection, as well as a knowledge of the types of adversaries encountered, should be provided to the CMT by the organization's security director (consultant), who can also assist by acting as liaison with law enforcement agencies.

The CMT will require the assistance of its legal counsel to examine such issues as employee and stockholder rights vis-à-vis the legal standing of the company regarding various strategies and monetary payments to extortionists. Information from the financial arm of the corporation is needed to develop the monetary base for CMT operations, and its assistance is needed to set the corporate strategy and limitations regarding ransom of any particular corporate employee.

Provisions for gathering personal data, such as employee and family biographical sketches, as well as medical and other requirements of the employee and his family, must be incorporated into the CMT's plan along with methods to make this data readily available during the crisis period. The CMT must also consider the long-term effect of crisis decisions on employees of the company. A media relations expert should be available to the CMT for a positive, controlled response to media inquiries during the crisis — since one asset to be protected is the public image of the corporation. (See Box 15-1.) In this regard, it is imperative that responses to the media be coordinated with law enforcement officials to avoid premature release of information, which may jeopardize a victim's life.

The CMT must be given autonomous control over decisions the corporation must make during a crisis, consistent with an advance plan approved by the board of directors. Every action to be taken by the company not dependent on the specific nature of the crisis should be rehearsed, much like a fire drill; only the variable decisions will then have to be handled. Even those decisions will be addressed from a perspective of preset goals, limitations, and strategies.

A corporate crisis-management capability will enable professional law enforcement personnel to respond to the crisis with better initial information and a clear-cut base from which to operate. Also, this capability will lessen considerably the probability of loss through matters growing out of the original crisis, such as stockholders suits, employee negligence suits, wrongful-death suits, insurance cancellations, and expropriations of assets by foreign governments irritated by the way in which a corporation handled a problem.

A highly trained CMT is capable of handling not only those crises of an extortionate nature but also natural disasters, civil disturbances, domestic terrorism, and workplace violence, to name a few other problems facing businesses today.

HANDLING THE INITIAL CONTACT

When an extortionate demand is received, the CMT, the organization's security department, and law enforcement should be advised immediately and the crisis management program put into action. The actions taken during the first crucial moments after an extortionate demand is received may well determine the eventual outcome. Since most threats are transmitted by telephone, recording devices and tracing capabilities should be discussed with the local telephone company. Recording an extortionate call will not only preserve its details for later analysis in decision making but also may provide investigators with background noise and voice-print characteristics leading to the place of origin of the call and the identity of the extortionist.

Box 15-1. Communicating with the Media

Most crisis-management public relations disasters result more from firms' inability to communicate effectively with the media rather than from the incident that propelled them to public scrutiny. The following is a basic list of media interview dos and don'ts:

- Do establish a warm, friendly, businesslike attitude.
- Do prepare a brief three-to-five-sentence introduction.
- Do say Who, What, When, Where, Why, How.
- Do prepare to respond openly to criticism.
- Do anticipate questions and develop answers.
- Do speak slowly after silent moments.
- Do keep answers short—use silence effectively.
- Do ask questions that test understanding and acceptance.
- Do be sensitive to time constraints and deadlines.
- Do speak candidly, but accurately.
- Do repeat or rephrase questions for an audience before answering.
- Do use your own words when answering questions.
- Do use "communications bridging" tactics to change the focus of a question to an issue you wish to make and away from the topic a reporter wishes to make.
- Do lead the media "conversation."
- Do commit to follow-up with answers.
- Don't frustrate a reporters need for basic answers.
- Don't use highly technical jargon.
- Don't talk to or at reporters—talk *with* them.
- Don't cite competitors by name if your statement is derogatory.
- Don't make financial or product projections.
- Don't expect every media person to be well prepared or friendly.
- Don't be afraid to say you can't answer a question.
- Don't say "no comment." The public equates this phrase with dishonesty and deception. If the media does not get a comment from you or from the company spokesperson, they will seek out someone who will give one. Most often this person, such as an employee of the firm, will have nothing to offer but speculation. Rephrasing your response in a manner that simply avoids "no comment" is acceptable, but phrasing it in a positive manner gets better results. Instead of answering "We can't make a statement until we have read the legal documents," try "We will be happy to make a statement after we read the legal documents."
- Don't use trigger words from a question in your answer.
- Don't attempt to influence editorial reporting by promising or referring to advertising.

Persons who may receive initial extortionate communications are, in many respects, vital sources of information for the CMT. As such, a training program should be developed to ensure proper implementation of the procedure regarding handling this type of call. Individuals handling such calls should be instructed to remain calm, record or write down all data given by the extortionist, express cooperation, and ask questions to lengthen the time of the call. An attempt should be made to calm the extortionist and secure proof that the hostage is being held, and unharmed. The recipient of the call should attempt to talk with the hostage and to give the hostage the opportunity to relay critical information through a prearranged code. Above all, persons receiving the initial call should bargain for time; if possible, they should end the conversation in such a manner that additional contacts with the extortionist will be necessary before a ransom is paid. This allows for the opportunity to trace and record a second call from the extortionist, as well as providing time to implement the crisis management program and set the stage for a controlled negotiation response.

Many extortion demands are transmitted in the form of a written threat. The letter and its envelope should be protected from unnecessary handling and preserved for fingerprints, handwriting, and printing and typewriting examinations, as appropriate. Following receipt of a written threat, steps should be taken to identify the source of the document if it was not mailed. It may be necessary to interview all employees immediately in order to develop information leading to the identity of the person who delivered the communication.

During the initial phase of the crisis, it is imperative to determine whether the demand is a hoax. In a kidnap case, the whereabouts of the alleged victim must be established immediately. Employee-family biographical fact sheets can be of critical importance at this time. Several notable kidnap hoaxes have involved calls to the executive's family in which the caller pretended to be a telephone company representative. The caller would state that the family telephone was being serviced and request cooperation in not answering the telephone for the next hour. The executive would then be called at work and told his family has been kidnapped. Naturally, when he called home and got no answer, he would panic and comply with the extortion demands, believing that his family has been taken hostage. A family fact-sheet containing the telephone number of friends and neighbors who can confirm the whereabouts of the family can be one means of thwarting such a scheme.

RANSOM CONSIDERATIONS

Payment of ransom is a decision to be made solely by the corporation or the victim's family. Law enforcement officials will discuss the pros and cons of ransom payment with the top officials of the organization and with the family of the victim. They will not, however, make the final decision as to paying or not.

Policy and the limitations on payment of ransom should be developed by the corporation and approved by the board of directors. This way, directors or executives insulate themselves from civil liability. For example, a shareholder could allege that the executive approving or making the ransom payment had not acted legally, did not have corporate authorization, and therefore was personally liable to the corporation for the amount diverted. If the payment of ransom or any other action taken in response to the extortion demands was itself a violation of local criminal law, the civil liability position could be aggravated. Finally, if the executive approving or making the payment failed to consult other executives or directors but was nonetheless able to obtain the cash or other assets and complete the transaction, shareholders could allege that the other executives and the directors were negligent in failing to consider the possibility of such an extortion and in failing to require appropriate controls. In such a case, liability might be alleged against all involved.

Inadequate action or improper action by the corporation leading to death or injury of an employee might result in claims against the corporation for damages by the employee or his family. This is particularly true if there were no contingency plans and the injured employee was exposed chiefly because of his corporate employment.

The above examples are not all inclusive, and corporate counsel should be consulted in all such matters. This is not to suggest that no action be taken to free a kidnap victim merely because of the potential of civil liability. Instead, it emphasizes that the way to minimize or avoid such liability involves preplanning and prior authority.

It is not possible to fix any categorical limits on the amount that should be paid for the release of a kidnap victim. In most companies, the only likely financial gauge of the impact of the death of an executive or official is the amount of "key man" life insurance contracted by the company. This type of insurance is intended to cover the cost to the firm of replacing a deceased official and the interim expenses or losses likely to result from his sudden absence, and it does not address the sensitive area of public and employee attitude toward the company; nonetheless, the amount of such insurance is at least a rough standard that can be used as a first step in considering ransom payment amounts.

Another alternative in this situation is to refuse to pay ransom altogether. It has been suggested that paying a ransom of any type may induce others to try again, that the possible individual loss of life is a necessary cost. This is the position taken by many governments in regard to the kidnap and ransom of government officials, but it may be untenable when applied to private business enterprises. At least within the United States and Canada, the business community and the general public may not accept the position and its potential cost.

If a decision is made to pay a ransom, the net impact on the enterprise may ultimately be much smaller than the amount paid, for two reasons. First, active cooperation with law enforcement from the very beginning will improve the chances of capturing the kidnappers and recovering all or part of the money. Second, commercial insurance can be purchased to cover a portion of the ransom payment actually made.

If the decision has been made to meet ransom demands, law enforcement authorities will assist in preparing the ransom package. Plans must be made for availability of funds in appropriate denominations. It takes considerable time and effort to record currencies used in ransom payments, and this step should be completed as much in advance of the payoff as possible. Large amounts of money, in small denominations, produce surprisingly heavy, bulky packages; one million dollars in ten-dollar bills weighs approximately 225 pounds, for example. This should be kept in mind during negotiations.

Where nonmonetary demands are made, such as supplies, publicity, or chartered aircraft, the responsibility must be the result of thoughtful decision on the part of the CMT. In formulating a policy, the possibilities for ransom should not be limited to money. However, political demands, such as the release of prisoners and the provision of arms, generally cannot be influenced by officials of the kidnapped victim's enterprise.

PREVENTIVE SECURITY

Unfortunately, experience has shown that a dedicated group of terrorists (extortionists) can penetrate all but the most sophisticated personal and corporate security systems. However, a company's demonstrated crisis-response capability and an awareness by executives of personal and corporate security practices will likely decrease the chances that a corporation or its executives will become victims of a kidnap or extortion attempt. The key is to alert the corporation and its executives to the level of danger where the particular executives reside, the need to avoid patterns or routines in personal behavior, and the increased vulnerability of wives and children. All of the above are important factors in forming an appropriate preventive security plan.

Some of the more obvious suggestions include steps toward ensuring the physical security of executive residences, instructing children on appropriate precautions, limiting the dissemination of personal information to only those deemed in need of such information, and securing automobiles. Additional and more detailed security precautions can be developed through consultation and internal planning.

SUGGESTIONS FOR KIDNAPPED INDIVIDUALS

Based on information developed in past cases, it is clear that kidnapped individuals should control their fear and realize that professionals are working for their safe release. Problems should be analyzed and decisions made based on the individual's present condition; a display of anxiety could be contagious and counterproductive. In many instances, a victim can actually control an abductor's actions, through his or her dominating personality, leadership qualities, and calm approach to the situation.

If the victim is troublesome or appears to jeopardize the abductors' plan, serious harm to the victim may result. The victim should attempt to convince his captors that his or her well-being is essential to their success. Those working for release will be simultaneously making every effort to convince the abductors that their goals will not succeed under any circumstances unless the victim is set free, alive and unharmed. An attempt should also be made to develop a relationship with the abductors so as to change their perception of the victim from that of an "object" to that of a "person," similar to them. Attempts to cooperate with the abductors should be made with this in mind.

If given a chance to communicate with persons working for their release, victims should attempt to give maximum information through pre-arranged code words, phrases, or verbal mannerisms that have been developed by the CMT. If the victim recognizes his captors or any detail of the kidnapping, it is imperative that this knowledge be kept from his captors, because it may cost the victim his or her life.

There are almost no circumstances in which an escape attempt is recommended. The key word, however, is "almost." The possibility of escape should not be considered if the victim is goaded by impatience. Escape attempts should be viewed as a last resort, not a time-saving device. By considering the abduction a long-term venture, the victim will be less tempted by impatience. Escaped victims could find themselves lost in a remote, inaccessible, alien region, without transportation, money, food, water, or shelter, and perhaps unable to speak the local language. If recaptured (and not killed or seriously injured in the process), the victim will likely be treated more harshly. Thus, escape should only be considered as a lifesaving effort when success is reasonably certain and the likely alternative is death.

CONCLUSION

In order to prevent or minimize the harm that might result from executive kidnappings and other forms of extortion, the business community should recognize the need for, and take the necessary steps to develop, crisis management plans. The responsibility for developing such plans lies with the corporation itself. It is only through such planning, both internal and in consultation with experts, that the tragedies inherent in such crises may be avoided or minimized.

For more detailed information, see Appendix E, "Sample Kidnap and Ransom Contingency Plan."

BIBLIOGRAPHY

Max Ckonjevic, FBIC, CGCP, presentation to the "Survive" Conference, San Francisco, 1997.

Lawrence Barton. *Crisis in Organizations: Managing and Communicating in the Heat of Chaos.* Southwestern, 1993.

Peter Schwartz. *The Art of the Long View.* Doubleday, New York, 1991.

16

MONITORING
SAFEGUARDS

In God we trust, everyone else we monitor.
Anonymous FBI inspector

The security professional may be called upon to do design engineering. If a facility has a security system in place, the security professional may be asked to review it. The system, upon review, will prove to be either adequate or inadequate in meeting the client's objective, which is the *protection of assets*.

MONITORING OR TESTING THE EXISTING SYSTEM

One technique for making an adequacy determination is to monitor or test the existing system periodically to determine if it is still doing the job for which it was designed or installed.

The author was once assigned the task of evaluating the security system for a research and development (R&D) division of a large computer manufacturing firm. The R&D division, in existence at the same location for five years, had taken over facilities previously occupied by the consumer products division, which had been dissolved during a reorganization.

All of the administrative support systems, including security and safety, already at the facility had remained in place to serve the newly expanded R&D effort. In fact, the only significant change at the facility was that instead of manufacturing digital wristwatches and calculators, the facility was now developing artificial intelligence data and advanced computer-aided design information. Five years later, however, at the time of our survey, the security system was still protecting digital wrist watches and calculators!

I was asked simply to design a test to answer the question, "How well is the R&D facility protected against industrial espionage?" The answer was obvious even without testing: the R&D programs were totally unprotected! In five years of existence at this location, no one had bothered to test the security systems to see if they were still adequate to meet the client's objectives. The client was spending in excess of three-quarters of a million dollars a year to protect a product it had quit producing at this location five years earlier!

One might question why a multinational corporation with vast financial resources at its command would ever allow a situation such as that to exist. The answer, sad though it may be, is that such situations are not the exception; they are generally the rule. Such situations are seen over and over again, at many locations. Absent serious security problems, productivity is the only issue upon which management remains focused.

From the standpoint of achieving a totally functional security system, one that can be counted on to work when it is needed, testing of safeguards (countermeasures) in a production environment is probably the critical area that is most likely to be overlooked. This is in sharp contrast to the scientific and engineering fields, where testing is usually taken as an article of faith.

THE SCIENTIFIC METHOD

Most students have had an introduction to the "scientific method," the basis for all modern science and technology. The scientific method is, simply stated, a very basic problem-solving approach, namely, the gathering of data to be used to confirm or reject a developed hypothesis.

Few of us will object to the statement, "People and procedures must be tested in a number of scenarios, and testing, to be effective, must be an ongoing process." This same principle, however, is seldom accomplished in the real world of security. Yet in no other way than periodic, programmed testing can the integrity of any system or procedure be proven or, conversely, system flaws be detected before catastrophe strikes.

Depending on the type of security in question (procedures, hardware, electronics, or manpower) testing can take many forms and have many objectives. Here I am mostly concerned with tests that will evaluate performance and reveal weakness, failures, or potential flaws in the design or the system: testing that will uncover problems that otherwise might remain undetected. These tests, from a security perspective, are invaluable and should be included in every designed security system, no matter how large or small.

FIVE BASIC TYPES OF TESTING

There are five basic types of testing, which can be summarized as follows:

- Functional testing: a test to determine if a procedure, CCTV, or electronics access control system will do what it was designed to do.

- Safety testing: a test to determine if the object or procedure can be used without causing injury, loss, or harm.
- Performance testing: normally concerned with conformance to timing, resource usage, or environmental constraints (a good example is an anti-intrusion alarm).
- Stress testing: checks a person's or object's tolerance to abuse or misuse under deliberately introduced stress.
- Regression testing: usually applies to an object, system, or procedure that has been altered to perform a new function and must still perform some of the functions for which it was originally designed.

It is well to remember that testing can apply equally to persons, systems, procedures, methodologies, and objects. Also, regardless of the application, testing must have a specified objective. From a security viewpoint it is wise to question, prior to initiation, what the test objective is and why a particular test is deemed to be important. Other questions that should be answered are: Are the tests adequate? Are the results valid? Can this type of test uncover a weakness or flaw that might otherwise remain hidden?

The best time to prepare a hardware or electronics equipment test is during design, or at the latest, installation (prior to the acceptance stage). This facilitates changes, additions and deletions. Efforts should be made to facilitate testing. Electronic circuits can be designed to include self-test circuits, diagnostic lights, fault detectors, and other test aids.

Tests can be broken down into component segments. This makes it possible to test various sections at different times. It is sometimes more desirable to conduct functional tests this way. Performance testing is another area where it might be desirable to test only parts or segments of the whole system. The more complex the system is, the more difficult and expensive it is to test the complete system at one time. The modular or segment approach can be designed to be reliable, less time consuming, and, from management's standpoint, less expensive.

Depending on the facility involved, tests can be relatively easy, such as verifying and updating biographical data; they can range up to actual "tiger team" penetrations into a complex security environment, such as a nuclear energy facility. Most tests fall somewhere between the simplest testing and complex penetration efforts, but each is valuable and should be scheduled. The results should be studied thoroughly and subjected to interpretation by expert analysis.

AVOID PREDICTABLE FAILURE

It is also desirable to reduce one's identified risk by testing. Murphy's Law states, "Anything that can go wrong, will." A relevant corollary could be,

"Any system that is not periodically tested will eventually fail." Systems that are tested also occasionally fail! The idea however, is to avoid predictable failure. The testing concept is consistent with the objective of reducing risk by diminishing uncertainty — after all, one of the fundamental principles of an effective security system.

With all of the obvious benefits to be gained by testing, one might logically inquire, "Why don't security professionals do more of it?" The answer is simple — time and money! While routine testing is both time consuming and costly, testing complex systems can be enormously expensive in terms of time and money. A routine fire evacuation drill in a manufacturing plant, for example, can cause thousands of man-hours lost to production.

SOME AUDIT GUIDELINES

In some cases, test expense can be reduced by use of some basic audit techniques, such as

- Statistical sampling: limiting the number of test cases to a statistical (representative) sample of the universe being tested.
- Restricting the value of input parameters or limiting the scope or field of inquiry.
- Scheduled testing: breaking the audit or test into halves, quarters, or eighths and scheduling it over a period of months or even years, instead of doing the entire audit or test at one time.

A word of caution: every test shortcut has its price in terms of potential risk. Management is seldom concerned about potential (not actual) risks, as against actual cost. This is particularly true if the potential risk is insured, that is, perceived to be someone else's problem should anything drastic happen.

There is much that one can learn from testing techniques used by other disciplines, such as safety. As an example, Herbert H. Jacobs lists the attributes of an effective measurement (test) system:[1]

- Administratively feasible
- Adaptable to the range of characteristics to be evaluated
- Constant

---

[1] H. H. Jacobs, "Toward More Effective Safety Measurement Systems," in Measurement of Safety Performance, ed. W. Tarrants (New York: Garland, 1980).

- Quantifiable
- Sensitive to change
- Valid in relation to what it is supposed to represent
- Capable of duplication with the same results from the same items measured
- Objective, efficient, and free from error

In my research I have been especially shocked at the almost total absence of a general, accepted set of practices for testing security systems. This being the case, it becomes obvious that the security field must selectively borrow from related disciplines and adapt their principles or practices to solving security problems. One such field — auditing — sets forth the following guidelines, which can be borrowed and used with little or no modification:

- An audit is part of management control.
- Management is the planning, organization, direction, and control of activities to achieve desired goals.
- It is necessary in a successful business process to set policy, establish procedure, assign responsibility, institute an accountability system, and *measure performance*.
- Exceptionally good levels of security performance are achieved when risk control is perceived as an important and integral part of planning, organization, direction, and control.
- Risk-control management systems must be integrated into the mainstream of all management functions.
- There is usually a noticeable difference between issued policy and procedure and what actually occurs.
- Seldom is an activity as effectively managed as those responsible for it say it is.

Auditing risk control (security) programs can also serve as an appraisal of management's performance in relation to established company policy and procedure. The basic objective of the audit (test) is, however, the qualitative analysis of the existing security system(s) to determine whether performance is effective and acceptable.

As stated by a senior executive of M & M Protection Consultants, "It has been our experience in conducting audits of the effectiveness of hazard (risk) control programs that there are usually two such programs in place at every location — the one management thinks it has and the one it really has!" He concluded that a high degree of failure is implicit if the hazard (risk) control program that management really has is a great deal less effective than the one management thinks it has.

DEVELOP A PLAN OF ACTION

It is no longer acceptable conduct for security practitioners to ask themselves, "Are we testing the right things, or are we testing things right?" What is necessary is to develop a plan of action for submission to management. Some suggestions are:

- Review the existing test procedures, if any.
- What kinds of tests are being conducted, by whom, when, and where?
- Are tests cost-effective and proven to reduce (eliminate) risks?
- Are records of past tests conducted being maintained for future use?
- Are there better, less expensive tests available that can be adapted for use at your facility?
- Are tests being conducted that can be eliminated as no longer functional or effective?
- Can you identify high-risk areas within the organization that are not being tested (audited)? Can you develop a suggested test program for management's review and approval?
- For complicated tests (audits and surveys), would it be in the best interest of the company to invite an outside expert or consultant in to conduct a review? To give a second opinion?
- Is it within your capability to develop and implement formal testing policy and guidelines, in those areas where you have operational responsibility?

Risk control specialists must seek out existing testing systems and promote development of new ones through which the effectiveness of security programs can be measured. Performance examination is a necessary element of the security professional's job description. One should always strive to do the best job possible, recognizing that under the best of circumstances any measurement or test that one may develop, adopt, or adapt will have shortcomings. Any test is better than none, and following the axiom "test it, don't trust it," is a much safer course than ignoring a problem in hopes that a catastrophe will never occur.

17

THE SECURITY CONSULTANT

And so the time for the security consultant finally has come. We are few but we are of good quality and we follow the highest [ethical] standards. To live up to our worthy goal and new opportunities we must at all times be responsible professionals.

Chuck Sennewald, CPP
Founder, International Association
of Professional Security
Consultants (IAPSC)
September 20, 1972

IN-HOUSE VERSUS OUTSIDE ADVICE

Many companies call on outside consultants to perform studies, make evaluations, and offer recommendations for implementing or improving their security programs. Some companies have benefited from the experience and knowledge that consultants can bring to bear on problems encountered during surveys. Other companies have not benefited. Disappointments are a result of a number of factors. For one thing, employees sometimes regard an outsider as an interloper, a stranger, one who has no real feeling for the company or its employees. Rank-and-file employees as well as supervisors and line managers may be resentful and secretive, thus preventing the "outsider" from obtaining a full understanding of problems as they presently exist within the company. No matter how experienced the consultant may be, his first task, and it is often a difficult and time-consuming one, is to learn the intricacies of the company, its ingrained processes, procedures, and methods of operation. Also, the consultant's recommendations, usually seen first by line managers in the form of a written report, may produce a negative reaction. Some line managers may spend more time in defending the status quo than in implementing what may be valid recommendations for improving the operation. Among employees it is generally known that outside consultants charge large fees for work that might well be done, at substantially less cost, using inside resources. Lastly, some so-called "security consultants" represent manpower or hardware firms and are salesmen first and consultants second. As such, these people run the risk of reprimand if their proposals to prospective clients do not maximize the use of their companies' wares. The end result is that the client often finds he is paying for more "security" then he needs.

One example encountered by the author during a survey will suffice to make this point. A financial corporation dealing in wholesaling precious metals — gold, silver, and platinum — was found to be utilizing sixteen closed-circuit television cameras (CCTV) in a three-thousand-square-foot office area. One fixed CCTV camera was mounted on the ceiling of an interior corridor located about twenty-five feet from the security console. This CCTV camera was targeted on the display console area, which, among other things, contained sixteen monitors. Thus the security officer at the console was monitoring one CCTV screen that presented him with a camera image of himself at work! This can hardly be considered a cost-effective use of CCTV for building security.

Another technique that the author likes to cite is the oversubscribed-contract-guard service. Recommending the elimination of one guard post (coverage twenty-four hours per day, seven days per week) can save a client about eighty thousand dollars per year, more than the usual cost of hiring a consultant. Thus, the client receives all other conclusions and recommendations of the consultant virtually for free.

Security consultants can and do provide valuable services to their clients, provided the client does a reasonably good job of selecting the right consultant in the first place. As a onetime professional security consultant, one who earned his living by plying this trade, I would caution prospective users of consulting services to use the same solid business judgment and standards in selecting a security consultant that they would in selecting any other type of consultant. In order to do that, perhaps a brief look into the historical development of security consultancy would be worthwhile.

The field of protection consulting is relatively new, perhaps not more than thirty years old. Protection consulting has its origins in the insurance industry, principally with regard to property (fire) protection. The field then grew, as a natural extension, into accident prevention (casualty) and safety consulting. Last, but certainly not least, came security (crime prevention) consulting.

Security consulting probably got its start just before the United States entered World War II, with the development of the defense industry and its secret and top secret projects. Originally the emphasis was on perimeter protection, access control, and document classification as the principal means to protect defense secrets. The requirements for security were contractual in nature; that is to say, adequate security was necessary before the facility would be considered safe for secret or top secret defense projects. It was only when an obvious flaw or hole in the security was detected that anyone came in and analyzed the situation and made recommendations to improve the security sufficiently for the facility to remain "Cleared for Secret and Top Secret" production.

It is probably safe to say that most security consulting assignments then were based on problems that had already occurred. It has only been recently (during the 1970s) that professional security consulting experienced its greatest growth. It was at about this time that enlightened developers, owners, and managers began to recognize that to increase efficiency and reduce cost, security had to be built into facility design and not tacked on as an afterthought. Today, it is not uncommon for architects to seek the services of qualified protection consultants to ensure that their final designs take into account the security requirements for the buildings or projects under consideration. As such, security consultants are getting more and more involved in the business of design engineering.

Working with architects and engineers on complex design and construction projects is not a task to be assigned to an apprentice security consultant. Clearly a combination of education and experience leading to professional maturity is needed here. It is said that a wise man knows his limitations. In the consulting field, mistakes can be costly. One's professional reputation can suffer if one takes on a project for which one is not fully qualified, and fails. Huge industrial complexes, such as nuclear-power generating facilities or large hospital complexes, will probably require the services of a team of consultants, because of the multifaceted and varied disciplines required to survey such complicated environments. In the team approach, consultants are selected because of their expertise in the particular fields for which their talents will be utilized, recognizing that no one consultant can be expert in all fields of endeavor having to do with security or any other discipline.

Using the team approach to consulting assignments can reduce time and expenses for most large projects. Often it is the only way some large projects can be adequately handled, because of the many specialty areas encountered in these environments. No one security consultant should be expected to be an expert in all phases of security management, procedure, hardware, and electronics — though most, by necessity, have a general idea of the proper application of the various security systems that may be used under specific conditions.

WHY USE OUTSIDE SECURITY CONSULTANTS?

The author recalls a telephone conversation with a security professional who asked to be referred to a text or written guide to help him design an electronic access control system for a newly developed computer facility. At that time I knew of no such textbook (there have since been a number of excellent texts on the subject published) and told him so. I then asked him, "Why don't you contract the job out to a qualified security consultant?" He stated, "I can't do that! My corporation expects me to be able to handle every security problem that comes up, regardless of how complicated. I would be putting my professional reputation on the line if I ever admitted I didn't have the skills necessary to design an access control system for the computer center." The simple answer to this situation is — nonsense! No professional from any discipline should be expected to be able to solve every problem that arises. This situation would be analogous to a general practitioner (GP) in the field of medicine calling a surgeon, stating that he had a patient who needed brain surgery for the removal of a tumor, then asking the surgeon to recommend a textbook so the GP could read up on the subject prior to performing the operation himself.

The above example is by no means uncommon. The question concerning when to use the services of an outside consultant does frequently arise. Some of the more common questions regarding the use of outside versus inside resources to do a security survey or consulting job are as follows.

"Why Do I Need Outside Advice?"

An independent consultant can furnish objective opinions without prejudice and without regard to internal pressures or politics. The consultant can, in effect, "let the chips fall where they may."

More often than not, a competent security director or manager knows what the problem is and has even defined the solution. In these cases the outside consultant furnishes a "second opinion" that reinforces the initial opinion, especially regarding cost-effective solutions to complicated problems.

When one seeks outside advice and assistance, one will surely seek help from a professional with a high degree of experience in dealing with the topic at hand. As mentioned above, the "second opinion" technique is common practice among other professions and disciplines. Yet in the security field we find a great reluctance on the part of some professionals to admit to their obvious limitations.

Unlike manpower or hardware salesmen, the truly independent security professional has only one loyalty — the best interest of his client.

Manpower and hardware consultants (read *salesmen*) are limited in scope and understandably biased toward their own products or services. Their first loyalty is to the company that employs them, and rightfully so. Nevertheless, security professionals have little reluctance in accepting proposals for service from contract security salesmen. The very same security professional will agonize over the prospect of hiring a security consultant to do a comprehensive security survey of his entire operation, including procedures, manpower, and hardware. So the question often asked is,

"How Can I Justify the Cost of a
Consultant on a Limited Budget?"

One must not lose sight of the fact that most security surveys are full-time propositions. Assuming that the in-house professionals are fully employed at their day-to-day occupations (and who in our business will admit that they are not?) where will they find the time to conduct a meaningful audit or survey?

Professional consultants usually have available to them library and research assistance unavailable to the average security practitioner. The library resources have been collected, catalogued, and indexed over a period of many years. Admittedly, with the advent of the Internet this is less true today than in the past.

Few security professionals, however, have developed the depth of knowledge necessary to do risk assessment in a multidisciplined environment. Most professionals tend to become specialists in certain fields — government, finance utilities, hospitals, and retail, to name a few. It is not that most professionals are not capable of broadening their scope, it is just a fact of life that few of us do, preferring the "comfort" of our own field of expertise or practice.

An outside consultant can also discern the financial aspects of the necessary manpower and hardware solutions and then negotiate these cost factors with management. Not every in-house security professional is schooled in the financial and negotiating techniques necessary to sell program changes. Most consultants are.

"Will an Outside Consultant Provide Assistance
in Setting Up the Recommended Program?"

This touches on a very common fear — that the consultant will make broad-brush recommendations and then walk off into the sunset, counting his excessive fee, leaving a difficult job for those who must implement his recommendations. In actuality, consultants can continue to be employed to the extent that they and management feel is necessary to achieve the level of protection necessary to solve the problems identified during the survey. Risk assessment is at best a matter of opinion, with much uncertainty. The continued presence of the consultant with input at the implementation or installation stages can materially contribute to the final success of the project.

Most consultants do not provide contract services. Instead, they usually recommend several reliable firms in the immediate geographical vicinity that have reputations for providing quality service. The consultant then assists the client by drawing up minimum specifications and requirements that the client furnishes to several firms, requesting that each submit a bid. After the bids are returned to the client, the consultant can assist the client in reviewing the bids and selecting the service that meets the client's requirements at the best (not necessarily the lowest) cost. Once the service is accepted, the consultant can inspect, guide, provide administrative oversight, and critique the implementation or installation of the service.

This same procedure is applicable whether the product is security manpower, hardware, or electronics. But, as with all other phases of the survey, the consultant's key role is to function as the client's representative. Successful consultants function in the best interest of their clients at all times.

SECURITY PROPOSALS (WRITING AND COSTING)

A security survey can range from a simple telephone call to a one-day on-site review with verbal conclusions and recommendations, to a full field study. The latter would encompass a comprehensive review of all risks, complete with a fully documented report outlining the entire security effort. Consulting assignments may also include plan development and review of blueprints and purchase specifications for access-control and anti-intrusion alarm systems and other sophisticated security hardware and equipment.

To avoid misunderstanding the parameters of the task to be performed, both client and consultant should establish at the outset, the specifications of the tasks to be performed. Probably the best way to accomplish this is a written proposal.

Before a client asks for, or a consultant begins to prepare, a proposal, it is important that each have a basic understanding as to the problem or problems in need of being solved. This can be tricky. Often clients have only a limited idea of their problems and may not be able to articulate their needs. Some clients have not made a realistic appraisal of their problem and thus may not have realistic expectations regarding the solution or solutions. The only way to ensure that both parties understand exactly what is to be accomplished is by outlining the issues in a written proposal.

Written proposals can take many forms, but five basic elements are common to most. They are the *introduction, proposal, management, cost,* and *summary* sections.

Introduction

This section identifies the client and the problem in very broad terms. It also identifies the consultants and the firm that is submitting the proposal.

Proposal

This section must clearly state the need to be fulfilled, most often expressing it as a statement of work or scope. It sets forth in very specific terms both the problem and the proposed review or study that will be undertaken to gather the data necessary to solve the problem and meet the client's needs. It will also later serve as a general planning outline for the consultant doing the work.

Outlined below are some basic subject areas that may be considered in developing this part of the proposal. These areas are not all-inclusive and must be tailored or modified to fit the specifics of the task involved. They are presented here as examples only.

Security Objectives.   There are four prime objectives that will be developed during the evaluation of a facility: the *risk assessment, vulnerability assessment, criticality assessment,* and the *security function.*

Losses.   An in-depth assessment will be made into the trend of losses at the site, crime experience in the local area, investigation of existing shortages, and the incidence of fire, malicious damage, and vandalism.

Security Organization.   A review will be made of the security structure as it pertains to vested authority, policy, assignment of responsibility, and cost effectiveness.

Security Regulations and Procedures.   A total review will be made of the security program in effect. This would include access control, personnel identification, package inspection, after-hours security procedures, liaison with police and other law enforcement agencies, and security indoctrination of employees.

Guard Force.   A review of the present guard force or protective section will be made to cover organization, cost effectiveness, training, report writing, and the effective utilization of manpower.

Personnel Security.   This phase will include a review of background screening of employees, use of badges and passes, and termination procedures.

Physical Security Conditions.   The survey team will evaluate the physical conditions, including all aspects of peripheral and interior security and security of objects that are protected or may need protection. This evaluation will consider the present facility, temporary conditions during construction, and proposed expansion plans.

Utilities.   A security examination and evaluation will be conducted of critical utility points, for example, gas, telephone, computer, sewerage, water, and electricity. Storage practices and related security provisions will also be included.

Construction of Security Facilities.   Detailed advisory information will be provided to the architect and engineer concerning the methods of construction and the installation of equipment that impacts security. Examples are guardhouses, vaults, computer rooms, anti-intrusion devices, electronic card-access systems, and CCTV.

Security Hardware.   A locksmith will evaluate the existing security hardware, such as physical deterrents, locks, key scheduling, associated hardware, and installations. Recommendations will cover repair and replacement of existing equipment and suggested material for new construction.

Alarm Systems.   Evaluation will be made of the existing system and subsystems, to include expansion and improvements that may require substantial systems additions or complete replacement. State-of-the-art system conformity and performance will be considered. Interior and exterior intrusion-detection systems, fire-detection and fire-suppression systems, and building evacuation plans will be part of this task.

Communications.   A security evaluation will be made of the existing and proposed communications networks. These will include wired interior systems, telephone and computer systems, radio facilities, and networks.

Surveillance.   Security monitoring on CCTV and still and motion camera photography will be evaluated as applied or considered for future applications.

Security and Fire Safety Hardware.   Security containers, security hardware, locks, and products employed for life safety, fire control, and fire extinguishment will be evaluated.

Procurement.   Methodology for procurement, including sourcing, cost estimates, and scheduling, will be provided. Successful implementation of any security program hinges largely on a well defined and executed procurement contract.

Management

This section of the proposal will identify and fully describe the consulting organization, its experience, its personnel, and if necessary, a sampling of client companies that may be used as references. In any event, management, administration resources, and capabilities should be spelled out in some detail and should fully qualify the consultant and firm for the task at hand. Usually included in this part of the proposal are biographical sketches of the consultants who will actually be performing the survey.

Cost

Cost figures are the best-guess estimate of the consultant doing the job. They are only a yardstick and are subject to change if the scope of the inquiry changes when the job is under way. Nevertheless, the client is entitled to a reasonably accurate estimate of the cost and to prompt notification when the job is under way if the scope (and thus the cost) is going to change. Some clients specifically outline the task to be accomplished and send the outline out for several firms to bid on, and then accept the return bid with the lowest figure. This technique, found most often in government entities, is called an "RFP" (request for proposal). It is also used by large multinational corporations with well-structured purchasing departments. The cost proposal will generally include the following factors:

1. Direct labor (manpower) cost
2. Travel and expenses
3. Miscellaneous cost, if any
4. Overhead rate (usually in percentage)
5. General and administration (includes reports)
6. Total estimated cost
7. Profit
8. Total proposal cost

The wise consultant will also program a 10 percent contingency fee, based on the total cost figure, to take care of such unforeseen problems as

- Potential delays on site
- Meetings before, during, and after the on-site work commences
- Responding to follow-up inquiries after the final report is submitted
- Other unanticipated cost connected with the project

Summary

The summary is used to highlight the details of the proposal, as set forth in the previous four sections. It also contains the total cost of the proposed project, as obtained from section four. This section should identify the benefits the survey hopes to accomplish in terms that even the most recalcitrant, bottom line–oriented, bean-counting executive can understand. It must leave the reader with the positive feeling of having just read a proposal prepared in a timely, efficient, and professional manner. A late, poorly prepared, and disjointed proposal is a reflection of what the future holds regarding the primary task. Don't expect more or less from a consultant's proposal than you would expect to receive for the principal task.

A proposal pricing worksheet (Figure 17-1) is included to assist both consultants and clients in developing cost figures for submission with proposals.

EVALUATING PROPOSALS AND REPORTS

Charles Hayden, CPP, retired, formerly of the San Francisco office of Marsh & McLennan Protection Consultants, developed a list of criteria to be applied in evaluating proposals and reports prepared by consultants. The following criteria were submitted to and adopted by the client. They are reproduced here with the approval and permission of Mr. Hayden.

The report (proposal) should fully satisfy the purpose for which the evaluation was made.

The objective(s) of the evaluation should be identified and achieved.

The scope of the evaluation must be consistent with the purpose and objective(s).

The methodology used must be stated and must ensure that all significant information is collected, collated, and analyzed.

The documented qualifications of the consultant must be adequate to perform the task.

Figure 17-1. Proposal Pricing Worksheet

Name & Title of Contact: _____

PROSPECT NAME AND ADDRESS _____

    Street _____ Phone No. _____

    City & State _____ Zip Code _____

DESCRIBE SPECIFIC SERVICE TO BE PROVIDED:

_____
_____
_____
_____
_____

BILLING INSTRUCTIONS: _____

    Describe– _____

_____
_____
_____
_____

    Type Report Desired– _____
    Date Report Desired– _____

QUOTATION GOOD UNTIL _____

TIME	TRAVEL & EXPENSES (T&E)
No. Locations Involved: _____	Travel Hours: _____
On-Site Hours*: (Add 25-50%	Travel Costs: _____
for Foreign) _____	Air _____ Cabs _____
Report Preparation Hours*: _____	Rail _____ Car Rental _____
Ratio Guide for Report Prep.	Bus _____ Personal Car _____
to On-Site	Lodging: _____
Simple Reviews 1:1	Food: _____
Complex Reviews 2:1	Misc.: _____
*Above Hrs. Converted to Cost: _____	Note: Normal domestic travel will range $100
Support (typist, etc.) Cost: _____	to $130/day
TOTAL TIME COST: _____	TOTAL T&E: _____

INCIDENTALS

Films _____ Printing _____   Slides _____ Binders _____

Projector _____ Pictures _____   Tapes _____ Other _____

                                      TOTAL: _____

TIME COST _____   Estimated by: _____

T&E COST _____

INCIDENTALS COST _____   DATE: _____

10% CONTINGENCY _____

    GRAND TOTAL _____   APPROVED BY: _____

Conclusions drawn in the report must include
    a. Application of appropriate standards acceptable practice and/or experience.
    b. Credible estimates of comparative risk (probability/time) and potential damage/loss.
Recommendations for abatement of risk must be appropriate and effective in regard to
    a. Priority.
    b. Cost.
Estimated reduction of risk and potential damage.

The proposal should set forth a reporting procedure. Will the reports be periodic or final? When (date) can the client expect the report to be submitted, how, by whom, and in what form? Remember, keep the language and the format of reports simple.

Appendix A
Security Survey Work Sheets

This is a basic guide that may be used to assist personnel in performing physical surveys in most industrial settings. Questions have been prepared for the purpose of reducing the possibility of neglecting to review certain areas of importance and to assist in the gathering of material for the survey. While the list is comprehensive, it is not all inclusive. Individual adaptation will almost always be necessary to fit specific environments.

Also, attached as Annex A and B are some specific questions that pertain to hospitals, universities, and colleges.

General Questions before Starting Survey

- Date of survey.
- Interview with [name of decision maker].
- Number of copies of survey desired by client, to be forwarded to:
- Obtain plot plan. Plot the production flow on plot plan and establish direction of north.
- Position and title of persons interviewed.
- Correct name and address of plant.
- Type of business or manufacture.
- Square footage of production or manufacturing space.
- Property other than main facility to be surveyed is located at:
- Property known as:
- Property consists of:
- What activity is in progress here?
- Is there other local property that will not be surveyed? Why?
- If plot plan is not complete, sketch remainder of property to be surveyed.

Number of Employees

- Administrative—total number all shifts
- Skilled and unskilled—total number on each shift:
  1st shift
  2d shift
  3d shift

Maintenance/clean-up crew
Normal shift schedule and break times
- Salaried
1st shift
2d shift
3d shift
Maintenance/clean-up crew
- What days of the week is manufacturing in process?
- Are employees authorized to leave plant during breaks?
- Are hourly employees union or not?
- Are company guards in union bargaining unit?

Cafeteria

- Where is cafeteria located?
- What are hours of operation?
- Is it company or concession operated?
- What is security of proceeds from sales?
- What is security of foodstuffs?
- What is method of supply of foodstuffs?
- How are garbage and trash removed?
- Where is location of vending machines?
- Where is change maker, if any?

Credit Union

- Where is credit union located?
- How is money secured?
- How are records secured?
- How is office secured?
- What are hours of operation?
- How much money is kept during day and overnight?

Custodial Service

- Is it outside contract or company employees?
- What hours do they actually start and complete work?
- Do they have keys in their possession?

- How is trash removed by them?
- Who, if anyone, controls removal?
- Who controls their entrance and exit?
- Are they supervised by any company employee?

Company Store

- Where is company store located?
- What are hours of operation?
- What method is used to control stock?
- How is stock supplied from plant?
- Number of clerks working in store?
- How is cash handled?
- When are and who performs inventories?
- How are proceeds from sales secured?
- How is the store secured?

Petty Cash or Funds on Hand

- In what office are funds kept?
- What is the normal amount?
- How are these funds secured?
- What is the control and security of containers?
- Who has general knowledge of amount normally on hand?

Classified Operations

- Is government classified work performed?
- What is the degree of classification?
- How are classified documents secured?
- What is security during manufacture?
- What is classification of finished product?
- Are government cognizant officers on premises?
- Is company classified R&D performed?
- Is company classified work sensitive to industry?
- What degree of security is it given?
- What degree of security does it require?
- What are the locations of the various processing areas and containers?

Theft Experience

- Office machines or records.
- Locker room incidents.
- Pilferage of employees' autos.
- Pilferage of vending machines.
- Pilferage from money changer.
- Thefts of company-owned safety equipment.
- Theft of tools.
- Theft of raw material and finished product.
- Are thefts systematic or casual?
- Have any definite patterns been established?
- Are background investigations conducted prior to employment of any personnel?
- What category of personnel is investigated?
- What is the extent of investigations?

The foregoing questions, answered properly, will assist you in developing the degree of control required for various areas, information that can be secured only through an interview—the more probing the better. You should now also have a working knowledge of the general operational plan. Before starting your detailed examination and study, you must take a guided orientation tour of the facility to acquaint yourself with the physical setting. Make notes on your plot plan and pad during this tour.

I. Physical Description of the Facility

- Is the facility subject to natural-disaster phenomena?
- Describe in detail the above if applicable.
- What major vehicular and railroad arteries serve this facility?
- How many wood-frame buildings? Describe and identify them.
- How many load-bearing brick buildings? Describe and identify them.
- How many light or heavy steel-frame buildings? Describe and identify them.
- How many reinforced concrete buildings? Describe and identify them.
- Are all buildings within one perimeter? If not, describe.

II. Perimeter Security

- Describe type of fence, walls, buildings, and physical perimeter barriers.
- Is fencing of acceptable height, design, and construction?
- What is present condition of all fencing?

- Is material stored near fencing?
- Are poles or trees near fencing? If so, is height of fence increased?
- Are there any small buildings near fencing? If so, is the height of fence increased?
- Does undergrowth exist along the fencing?
- Is there an adequate clear zone on both sides along fencing?
- Can vehicles drive up to fencing?
- Are windows of buildings on the perimeter properly secured?
- Is wire mesh on windows adequate for its purpose?
- Are there any sidewalk elevators at this facility? If so, are they properly secured when not in operation?
- How are sidewalk elevators secured during operation?
- Do storm sewers or utility tunnels breach the barrier?
- Are these sewers or tunnels adequately secured?
- Is the perimeter barrier regularly maintained and inspected?
- How many gates and doors are there on the perimeter?
- Number used by personnel (visitors, employees)?
- Number used by vehicles?
- Number used by railroad?
- How is each gate controlled?
- Are all gates adequately secured and operating properly?
- Are railroad gates supervised by the guard force during operations?
- How are the railroad gates controlled?
- Do swinging gates close without leaving a gap?
- Are gates not used secured and sealed properly?
- What is security control of opened gates?
- Are chains and locks of adequate construction used to secure gates?
- Are any alarm devices used at the gates?
- Is CCTV used to observe gates or any part of the perimeter?
- How many doors from buildings open onto the perimeter?
- What type are they—personnel or vehicular?
- How are they secured when not in use?
- What is security control when in use?
- How many emergency doors breach the perimeter barrier?
- How are the emergency doors secured to prevent unauthorized use?
- Are there any unprotected areas on the perimeter?
- What portion of the fence do guards observe while making rounds?

III. Building Security

A. Offices
   - Where are the various administrative offices located generally?
   - When are offices locked?

- Who is responsible to check security at end of day?
- How and where are company records stored?
- How are they secured?
- Are vaults equipped with temperature thermostats? (rate-of-rise, Pyro-Larm)
- Are offices equipped with sprinklers? Fire extinguishers?
- Are any central station or local alarms installed to protect safes, cabinets, etc?
- Are various file cabinets locked?
- Are individual offices locked?
- Does the company have IBM computer rooms?
- What type of fire protection are they given?

B. Plant
- When and how are exterior doors locked?
- When and how are dock doors locked?
- Are individual plant offices locked?
- Are warehouses apart from production area secured?
- Are certain critical and vulnerable areas protected by alarms? What type?
- What are these areas? What do they contain?
- Are locker room windows covered by screening?

C. Tool Room
- Is one or more established?
- Departmental or central tool room?
- What is the method of control and receipt?
- How is tool room secured?

D. Locker Rooms
- What is basis of issue to individual?
- What is type of locker—wall or elevated-basket type?
- How are individual lockers secured?
- Does company furnish keys/locks?
- Who or what department controls keys/locks?
- What control methods are used?
- How and when are keys and locks issued and returned?
- Are issued uniforms kept in lockers?
- Are unannounced locker inspections made?
- Who conducts inspections and how often?

E. Special Areas That May Require Additional Attention (If the facility houses the following types of activities, they may require special individual inspection. Base recommendations on any or all of the applicable portions of the checklist. You will, after the initial inspection tour, design a checklist applicable to these special areas.)

- Research and development areas
- Laboratories
- Storage areas for valuable, critical, or sensitive items
- Finished-product test areas
- Finished-product display areas
- Vehicle parking garages apart from the facility
- Vacant or used lofts, attics, etc.
- Mezzanines or subbasements
- Aircraft hangars, maintenance shops, and crew quarters.

IV. Security of Shipping and Receiving Areas

- How many shipping docks, vehicle and railroad?
- What are the hours of operation of docks?
- What is the method of transportation?
- What is the method of inventory control at docks?
- What is the method of control of classified items?
- What is the security of classified or "hot" items?
- What supervision is exercised at the docks?
- Are loaded and unloaded trucks sealed?
- Who is responsible for sealing vehicles?
- What type of seals are being used?
- How are truck drivers controlled?
- Is there a designed waiting room for truck drivers?
- Is it separated from company employees?
- Are areas open to other than dock employees?
- Do guards presently supervise these areas? Is this necessary?
- What is the method of accounting for material received?
- Is shipping done by parcel post?
- What is the control at point of packaging?
- Who controls stamps or stamp machines?
- Who transports packages to post office?
- What is the method of transport to post office?
- Where is pick-up point at plant?
- What controls are exercised over the transport vehicle?
- Are inspections of operations made presently?
- Who conducts these inspections and how often?
- Does the facility have ship-loading wharves or docks?
- Are contract longshoremen used?

- How do longshoremen get to and from the docks?
- If they pass through the facility, how are they controlled?
- How are ships' company personnel controlled when given liberty?
- Are any specific routes through the facility designated for long-shoremen and ship personnel?
- If so, how is it marked and is it used?
- Are these personnel escorted?
- If they are not escorted what measures are taken to escort them?
- Is there any way in which these personnel could be kept from passing through the facility?

V. Area Security

- Can guards observe outside areas from their patrol routes?
- Do guards expose themselves to attack?
- Are patrols staggered so no pattern is established?
- What products are stored in outside areas?
- Is parking allowed inside the perimeter?
- If so, are controls established and enforced?
- Where do employees, visitors, and officials park?
- What security and control is provided?
- Are parking lots adequately secured?
- Is there a trash dump on the premises?
- How is it secured from the public?
- Is it manned by company employees?
- Is its approach directly from the manufacturing facility?
- Do roads within the perimeter present a traffic problem?
- Do rivers, canals, public thoroughfares, or railroads pass through the plant?
- Are loaded trucks left parked within the perimeter?
- If so, what protection is given them?
- Do the roads outside the facility present a traffic problem?
- What are these problems and how can they be remedied?
- Is there any recreational activity within the perimeter, such as baseball?
- Are these areas fenced off from the remainder of the property?
- Could they logically be fenced off?

VI. Protective Lighting

- Is protective lighting adequate on perimeter?
- What type of lighting is it?

- Is lighting of open areas within perimeter adequate?
- Do shadowed areas exist?
- Are outside storage areas adequately lighted?
- Are inside areas adequately lighted?
- Is the guard protected or exposed by the lighting?
- Are gates adequately lighted?
- Do lights at gate illuminate interior of vehicles?
- Are critical and vulnerable areas well illuminated?
- Is protective lighting operated manually or automatically?
- Do cones of light on perimeter overlap?
- Are perimeter lights wired in series?
- Is the lighting at shipping and receiving docks or piers adequate?
- Is lighting in the parking lots adequate?
- Is there an auxiliary power source available?
- Is the interior of buildings adequately lighted?
- Are top secret and secret activities adequately lighted?
- Are guards equipped with powerful flashlights?
- How many more and what type of lights are needed to provide adequate illumination? In what locations?
- Do security personnel report light outages?
- How soon are burned-out lights replaced?

VII. Key Control, Locking Devices, and Containers

- Is there a grandmaster, master, and submaster system? Describe it.
- Are locks used throughout the facility of the same manufacture?
- Is there a record of issuance of locks?
- Is there a record of issuance and inspection of keys?
- How many grandmaster and master keys are there in existence?
- What is the security of grandmaster and master keys?
- What is the security of the key cabinet or box?
- Who is charged with handling key control? Is the system adequate? Describe the control system.
- What is the frequency of record and key inspections?
- Are keys made at the plant?
- Do key gows have a special design?
- What is the type of lock used in facility? Are all adequate in construction?
- Would keys be difficult to duplicate?
- Are locks changed periodically at critical locations?
- Are any "sesame" padlocks used for classified material storage areas or containers?
- If a key cutting machine is used, is it properly secured?

- Are key blanks adequately secured?
- Are investigations made when master keys are lost?
- Are locks immediately replaced when keys are lost?
- Do locks have interchangeable cores?
- Are extra cores properly safeguarded?
- Are combination locks three-position type?
- Are safes located where the guard can observe them on rounds?
- How many people possess combinations to safes and containers?
- How often are combinations changed?
- What type of security containers are used for the protection of: Money? Securities? High value metals? Company proprietary material? Government classified information?
- Are lazy-man combinations used?
- Are birth dates, marriage dates, etc., used as combinations?
- Are combinations recorded anywhere in the facility where they might be accessible to an intruder?
- Are the combinations recorded and properly secured so that authorized persons can get them in emergencies?
- Is the same or greater security afforded recorded combinations as that provided by the lock?
- Where government classified information is concerned, does each person in possession of a combination have the proper clearance and the "need to know"?
- Have all faces of the container locked with a combination lock been examined to see if combination is recorded?
- Are padlocks used on containers containing classified material chained to containers?

VIII. Control of Personnel and Vehicles

- Are passes or badges used? By whom?
- Type used? Describe in detail?
- Is color coding used?
- Are badges uniformly worn on outer clothing?
- Are special passes issued? To whom? When?
- Who is responsible for issue and receipt of passes and badges?
- Are badges and passes in stock adequately secured?
- How are outside contractors controlled?
- How are visitors controlled?
- How are vendors controlled?
- How many employee entrances are there?
- What type of physical control is there at each entrance and exit?

- Where are the time clocks located?
- Is it possible to consolidate clock locations to one or two main clock alleys?
- Is there any control at time clock locations?
- Are there special entrances for people other than employees?
- How are the special entrances controlled?
- Are fire stairwells used for operational purposes?
- Does the facility use elevators to various floors?
- What control is exercised over their use?
- Are elevators used by operating employees?
- Do the elevators connect operational floors and strictly office floors?
- Does this present a problem in personnel control?
- Are the elevators automatic or attended?
- If automatic, are floor directories posted in them?
- Do avenues within the buildings used for emergency egress present a problem of personnel control?
- Examine pedestrian flow from entrance, to locker room, and to work area.
- Can changes be made to shorten routes or improve control of personnel in transit?
- Are personnel using unauthorized entrances and exits?
- If government classified work is being performed, do controls in use comply with the Defense Department pamphlet for safeguarding classified information?
- Are groups authorized to visit and observe operations?
- How are these groups controlled?
- Do registers used to register visitors, vendors, etc. contain adequate information?
- Are these registers regularly inspected? By whom?
- Are employees issued uniforms?
- Are different colors used for different departments?
- What control is exercised over employees during lunch and coffee breaks?
- Do guards or watchmen ever accompany trash trucks or vending machine servicemen?
- Is parking authorized on premises within the perimeter?
- Are parking lots fenced off from the production areas?
- What method of control of personnel and vehicles is there in the parking lots?
- Is vehicle identification used?
- What type of vehicle stickers or identification is used?
- How are issue and receipt of stickers controlled?

- If executives park within the perimeter, are their autos exposed to employees?
- If nurses and doctors park within the perimeter, are their autos exposed to employees?
- Where do vendor servicemen park?
- Do vendor servicemen use plant vehicles to make the service tours? Are small vehicles available?
- How are outside-contractor vehicles controlled?
- What method is used to control shipping and receiving trucks?
- Are the parking facilities adequate at the docks?
- Does parking present a problem in vehicle or personnel control?
- What is the problem encountered?
- During what hour does switching of railroad cars occur?
- Is it possible for persons to enter the premises during switching?
- Are there adequate directional signs to direct persons to specific activities?
- Are the various buildings and activities adequately marked to preclude persons from becoming lost?
- Are safety helmets required?
- Are safety shoes required?
- Are safety glasses required?
- Are safety gloves required?
- Are safety aprons required?
- Are full-time nurses or doctors available?
- Is there a vehicle available for emergency evacuation? What type is it?

IX.   Safety for Personnel

- How far away is the nearest hospital in time and distance?
- Are any company employees or guards trained in first aid?
- Is a safety director appointed?
- Is there a safety program? What does it consist of?
- How often does the safety committee meet?
- Is a first aid or medical room available?
- How are medicine cabinets secured?
- Who controls these keys?
- How is the first aid room secured?
- Are any narcotics on hand?
- If so, has narcotics security been established?
- Are the required safety equipment items worn? By visitors?
- What is the safety record of this facility?

- How does it compare with the national record?
- Are areas around machinery well policed?
- Does machinery have installed guards where needed? Are they used?
- Are mirrors used where needed to allow forklift operators to observe "blind" turns?
- Could or would mechanical devices used for forklift control improve safety?
- What type of device could be used? Pneumatic alarm system? Signal light?

X.   Organization for Emergency

- Are doors adequate in number for speedy evacuation?
- Are they kept clear of obstructions and well marked?
- Are exit aisles clear of obstructions and well marked?
- Are emergency shutdown procedures developed, and is the evacuation plan in writing?
- Do employees understand the plans?
- Are emergency evacuation drills conducted?
- Do guards have specific emergency duties? Do they know these duties?
- Are local police available to assist in emergencies?
- Are any areas of the building in this facility designated as public disaster shelters?
- If so, what control is established to isolate the area from the rest of the facility?
- Do the emergency plans provide for a designated repair crew? Is the crew adequately equipped and trained?
- Are shelters available and marked for use of employees?
- If the plant is subject to natural disaster phenomena, what are they? Floods? Tornadoes?
- What emergency plans have been formulated to cope with these hazards?
- When and what was the latest incident involving a natural disaster?
- Did it result in loss of life or loss of time?
- Attach a copy of the emergency procedures.

XI.   Theft Control

- Are lunchbox inspections conducted?
- Is a package-pass control system being used? Describe it.

- Is a company-employed supervisor assigned to check the package-pass system regularly?
- Is a company official occasionally present during lunchbox inspections?
- Are package passes serially numbered or otherwise containing control numbers?
- Is security of package passes in stock adequate?
- Are comparison signatures available for comparison?
- Is the list of signatures kept up to date?
- What action is taken when anyone is caught stealing?
- What controls are established on tools loaned to employees?
- What controls are established on laundry being removed?
- What is the method of removal of scrap and salvage?
- What controls are exercised over removal of useable scrap?
- Is control of this removal adequate?
- Are vending and service vehicle inspections being conducted?
- Do employees carry lunch boxes to their work areas?
- Are railroad cars inspected entering and leaving the plant?
- Are company-owned delivery or passenger vehicles authorized to park inside buildings of the plant?
- Does this parking constitute a possible theft problem?
- Do guards check outside the perimeter area for property thrown over fences?
- Do guards occasionally inspect trash pick-up? Does anyone?

XII. Security Guard Forces

- What is present guard coverage—hours per day and total hours per week?
- Describe in detail guard organization and composition.
- Number and times of shifts each twenty-four-hour period during weekdays and weekends?
- Number of stationary posts? When are they manned?
- Number of patrol routes? When and where are they, and when are patrols made?
- Are tours supervised by ADT or DETEX stations or both?
- How many stations? Locate them on your plot plan (use different colors or shapes or symbols for different floors and routes).
- What is length of time of each patrol?
- Is there additional coverage on Saturdays, Sundays, or holidays?
- Do the patrol routes furnish adequate protection as presently established?

- Are the guards required to be deputized?
- Are armed guards required?
- How do guards communicate while on patrol?
- Are written guard instructions available? If so, secure a copy.
- If no written instructions are available, generally describe duties of each shift and post.
- What equipment does the guard force have issued? Need?
- Do they require security clearances? What degree?
- Do they require special training?
- Is there a training program in force?
- What communications are available to the guard force to call outside the facility?
- Is the number of guards, posts, and patrol routes adequate?
- Are mechanical or electrical devices used in conjunction with the guard force?
- Do the guards know how to operate, reset, and monitor the devices properly?
- Do the guards know how to respond when the alarms are activated?
- Are guards included in emergency plans?
- Do guards know their duties? Emergency duties?
- Do guards make written reports of incidents?
- Are adequate records of incidents maintained?
- Are the guards familiar with the use of fire-fighting equipment?

Recommendations for changes must indicate each post, patrol, and so forth, by number of hours for weekdays, weekends, and holidays, as well as a brief description of the guard's duties. List the total present coverage, total after recommendations, and the difference in hours. If your recommendations increase coverage, you should justify the hours and the cost.

REFERENCE MATERIALS

- DOD Industrial Security Manual—Classified Information
- American Standard Practices for Protection Lighting
- General Electric brochure, How to Select and Apply Floodlights
- Factory Mutual, Organizing Your Plant for Fire Safety
- Security Equipment Brochure Catalogue
- Alarm Installation Estimate Work Sheets
- NFPA—Quarterly Reports
- National Safety Council—Previous and Current Reports.

ANNEX A: HOSPITAL SURVEYS

(Use applicable portions of the Industrial Security Survey Checklist.)

A. Pharmacy

- Where is the pharmacy located?
- What are operating hours of pharmacy?
- Is pharmacist registered and licensed?
- Is license displayed in pharmacy?
- How many pharmacists are employed?
- How are narcotics received and recorded?
- How are narcotics issued and recorded?
- How are narcotics secured in pharmacy?
- How are narcotics secured by nurses on wards?
- How are narcotics secured in emergency room?
- Are medicines issued on prescription only?
- What type of inventory control is used for accounting?
- What type personnel control is used at the pharmacy?
- Can entrance be gained, or is "dutch door" used?
- How are keys to pharmacy secured?
- Are keys carried away from hospital by pharmacists?
- Are "reach through" storage cupboards used?
- Are "reach through" refrigerators used? If so, how are outside doors secured? Who possesses the keys?

B. Morgue

- Where is the morgue located?
- Does morgue remain locked when not in use?
- Who is responsible for morgue security?
- Who inventories items found on cadavers DOA?
- How are they inventoried and secured?
- Who is authorized to release cadavers to undertakers?
- Are local police escorted when they enter morgue?

C. Linen Department

- Where is the linen department located?
- What type of inventory control is used?
- Is linen laundered on property?
- Where is the laundry located?
- How are various items marked for identification?

- Is soiled linen accounted for upon receipt?
- Is clean linen issued by receipt?
- Are both the laundry and linen departments adequately secured?

D. Security of Receipts

- Where are daily receipts paid and stored?
- How are receipts secured?
- How much is normally accrued on one business day?
- How often and how is it deposited?
- Are containers furnished to secure patients' valuables?
- How are these valuables inventoried and secured?

E. Emergency Room

- Are security guards present?
- Do local police remain with patients they bring in?
- How are patients under the influence of alcohol or narcotics controlled?
- Are emergency medicines and narcotics properly secured?
- Who inventories items of patients arriving unconscious?
- How is this inventory done and when?
- Is a female nurse assigned or on call?
- Is emergency entrance clear of obstruction?
- Is emergency vehicular approach kept clear?
- Are emergency phone numbers posted at or near phone?

F. Security Furnished to Nurses

- Where are the nurses' quarters located?
- Are nurses escorted to their quarters?
- Are nurses escorted to local transportation? If so, what time does this occur, and who escorts them?
- Are nurses' quarters included in patrol system?

G. Security of Resident Doctors' Quarters

- Do doctors live in the hospital?
- What is location of their quarters?
- How are keys to quarters issued?
- Are visitors allowed in quarters?
- Are doctors' quarters included in patrol system?
- What is theft experience at quarters, if any?

- Are visiting doctors furnished a check room?
- What security is furnished the check room?
- Do doctors normally leave their medical bags in the cloak room?
- What is theft experience at the cloak room, if any?
- What security is exercised over doctors' parking area?
- Are signs displayed reminding them to lock their cars?

H. Dietary Department

- Where is the dietary department (kitchen) located?
- What type of inventory system is used?
- When are "dry" or canned goods received?
- When are fresh meats received?
- Who inventories food received?
- How is food issued for preparation?
- What are hours of preparation?
- How is food for breakfast meal issued?
- What are the hours of operation of the cafeteria?
- How are personnel authorized to use cafeteria identified?
- What is percentage of turnover of dietary employees?
- Are these employees' backgrounds investigated?
- What system is used to issue food to bed patients?
- Do any floors have individual kitchens? If so, what system is used to issue food from stock?
- How are stock rooms secured?
- Who has possession of keys? Who controls keys?
- How is garbage removed?
- Is garbage ever inspected upon removal?
- How is combustible trash removed?
- Is this trash inspected upon removal?
- Are employees allowed to bring parcels, packages, or briefcases to work?

I. Identification and Control of Visitors

- What are the authorized visiting hours?
- How many and what entrances are used?
- Are visitors issued passes? Do they register?
- Who issues passes or registers visitors?
- Are passes required to be returned?
- Are passes color-coded by location within the hospital?
- How many visitors are authorized per patient at one time?

- Are visitors policed by the hospital staff?
- What system is used to prompt visitors to leave?
- What are the areas or locations where visitors are not authorized to go?

J. Emergency Evacuation Plan for Patients

- Have emergency evacuation plans been formulated?
- Are emergency evacuation drills conducted?
- Are staff members familiar with the plans?
- Are the procedures posted in strategic locations?
- Are emergency exits plainly marked?
- How are ambulatory patients evacuated?
- How are bed patients evacuated?
- Does the guard force participate in actual evacuation of bed patients?
- Where are patients housed after they are evacuated?
- Are nurses, hourly employees, and staff members trained in emergency removal of bed patients?
- Are all hospital employees included in the emergency evacuation plan?
- Are local police and fire department personnel included in removal operations?
- Does the emergency evacuation plan include specific routes for specific cases?
- Do the routes used for evacuation of bed patients conflict with the routes used by ambulatory patients?
- What system is used to sound the alert for fire?
- Is the method coded or disguised so as not to cause panic?

K. Parking Facilities

- Are the parking lots for doctors, staff, employees, and visitors separated or plainly posted?
- Are employees parking adjacent to the linen or dietary departments?
- If so, are fences erected so employees cannot gain entrance to their automobiles at will?
- Does the problem exist of visitors and/or doctors parking in fire and emergency lanes?
- Is emergency parking available for doctors?
- Does the administrator have a parking violation ticket system established? Describe it.

- Could visitors entering the hospital from the parking lot be canalized to pass a guard?
- Could this be accomplished for visitors entering from the street?
- Examine closely the traffic flow plan. Is it possible to organize the flow pattern and obtain a more efficient flow using one-way arteries or other devices?
- Is it possible to change the designation of the various parking areas (for instance, doctors' parking where visitors now park, and vice versa)?

ANNEX B: UNIVERSITY AND COLLEGE SURVEYS

A.   Locking, Key Control, and Security Containers

Note: All questions included in the basic industrial security survey work sheet will apply to universities and colleges, but the locking problems of such institutions are more complex and need additional scrutiny.

- Is there a system used for issuing keys to lockers to students at registration time?
- Is there a deposit charge made on the key?
- How much is the deposit?
- What type of locks are used on student lockers?
- How much difficulty is encountered if a lock must be changed when the student fails to return a key?
- Does the institution keep a record of keys issued to lockers?
- Are keys issued to students to any classrooms?
- Who keeps a record of such issue?
- Is there a deposit charge made on these keys?
- How much?
- Are locks changed between terms when such keys are not returned?
- Is any method provided to deny entrance to classrooms during hours when no one has authority to be in them?
- What protection is provided over examinations to be given?
- Is this material kept in combination or key locked containers?
- If key locks are used, how securely is the room locked?
- Are windows to such rooms locked with key locks?
- Are windows to such rooms accessible from the ground or fire escapes?

- Is any special locking protection provided in areas where damage could be done to important experiments?
- What type of lock is used to protect areas where college funds are kept, book stores, food storage areas, cafeteria offices, supply and equipment rooms, libraries, museum areas, valuable collections, dispensary narcotics, cabinets, and so forth?
- Are they adequate?
- How are doors to girls' dormitories locked and controlled?
- How are windows at first floor level, basements, and those accessible by use of fire escapes protected?

B. Protective Lighting

- Are open areas of the campus sufficiently lighted to discourage illegal or criminal acts against pedestrians?
- Is the campus equipped with emergency call stations placed at strategic locations in open areas?
- Are there any areas that are covered with high growing shrubs or woods where the light is not sufficient?
- Are the outsides of buildings holding valuable or critical activities or materials lighted?
- Are interiors of hallways and entrances lighted when buildings are open at night?
- Are areas surrounding women's dormitories well lighted?
- Are lighting fixtures used for this purpose placed in a position to shine out from the building into the eyes of persons approaching?
- Are halls and entrances of dormitories well lighted?
- Are campus parking lots lighted sufficiently to discourage tampering with parked cars or other illegal activities?
- Are areas where materials of high value are stored well lighted? Safes, libraries, book stores, food storage areas, and the like?

Appendix B

Danger Signs of Fraud, Embezzlement, and Theft

I. Situational Pressures   Yes   No   N/A

  A. Individuals against the Company
    1. Do any of the key employees have unusually high personal debts or financial losses (i.e., high enough that they probably could not meet them with their own level of income)?
    2. Do any of the key employees appear to be receiving incomes that are inadequate to cover normal personal and family expenses?
    3. Do any of the key employees appear to be living beyond their means?
    4. Are any of the key employees involved in extensive stock market or other speculation (i.e., extensive enough so that a downturn would cause them severe financial difficulty)?
    5. Are any of the key employees involved in excessive or habitual gambling?
    6. Do any of the key employees have unusually high expenses resulting from personal involvement with other people (e.g., maintenance of separate apartments)?

        From the book How to Detect and Prevent Business Fraud by W. Steve Albrecht, Ph.D., C.P.A., Marshall B. Romney, Ph.D., C.P.A., David J. Cherrington, D.B.A., I. Reed Payne, Ph.D., Allan J. Roe, Ph.D. © 1982 by Prentice-Hall, Inc. Published by Prentice-Hall, Inc., Englewood Cliffs, N.J. 07632.

    7. Do any of the key employees feel undue family, community, or social expectations or pressures?
    8. Do any of the key employees use alcohol or drugs excessively?

Yes   No   N/A

9. Do any of the key employees strongly believe that they are being treated unfairly (e.g., underpaid, poor job assignments)?
10. Do any of the key employees appear to resent their superiors?
11. Are any of the key employees unduly frustrated with their jobs?
12. Is there an undue amount of peer pressure to achieve in this company, so much so that success is more important than ethics?
13. Do any of the key employees appear to exhibit extreme greed or an overwhelming desire to self-enrichment or personal gain?

B. Individuals on Behalf of the Company
   1. Has the company recently experienced severe losses from any major investments or ventures?
   2. Is the company attempting to operate with insufficient working capital?
   3. Does the company have unusually high debts, so high that either interest payments or balances due impose a threat to the stability of the company?
   4. Have tight credit or high interest rates reduced the company's ability to acquire credit? Is there undue pressure to finance expansion through current earnings rather than through debt or equity?
   5. Is the company caught in a profit squeeze (i.e., are costs and expenses rising higher and faster than sales and revenues)?
   6. Do existing loan agreements provide little available tolerance on debt restrictions?
   7. Has the company's quality of earnings been progressively deteriorating (e.g., adopting straight-line depreciation to replace an accelerated depreciation without good reason, or reporting good profits but experiencing cash shortage)?

Yes   No   N/A

8. Is the company experiencing an urgent need to report favorable earnings (e.g., to support a high stock price or to meet forecasted earnings)?

9. Does company management believe there is a need to gloss over a "temporarily bad situation" in order to maintain management position and prestige?

10. Does the company have a significant amount of unmarketable collateral?

11. Does the company depend heavily on only one or two products, customers, or transactions?

12. Does the company have an excess of idle productive capacity?

13. Does the company suffer from severe obsolescence (i.e., is a significant amount of inventory or physical facilities obsolete)?

14. Does the company have an unusually long business cycle, long enough so that profits or cash flows are threatened?

15. Does the company have any revocable or possibly imperiled licenses that are necessary for the firm's existence or continued operation?

16. Has the company expanded rapidly through new business or product lines? If so, has expansion been orderly or has it been done in an attempt to salvage profitability?

17. Are there currently, or have there recently been, unfavorable economic conditions within this company's industry, or is the company's performance running counter to industry trends?

18. Is the company experiencing undue difficulty in collecting receivables (i.e., is the receivable turnover slowing down)?

19. Does the company face unusually heavy competition, heavy enough that its existence appears threatened?

Yes   No   N/A

20. Is the company experiencing a significant reduction in sales backlog indicating a future decline in sales?
21. Is the company being pressured to either sell out or merge with another company?
22. Is the company experiencing sizable inventory increases without comparable sales increases?
23. Has the company recently experienced any significant adverse tax adjustments or changes?
24. Is the company experiencing significant litigation, especially between stockholders and management?
25. Has the company recently been suspended or delisted from a stock exchange?

II. Opportunities

A. Individuals against the Company
   1. Do any of the key employees have close associations with suppliers or key individuals who might have motives inconsistent with the company's welfare?
   2. Does the company fail to inform employees about rules of personal conduct and the discipline of fraud perpetrators?
   3. Is the company experiencing a rapid turnover of key employees, either through their quitting or being fired?
   4. Have any of the key employees recently failed to take annual vacations of more than one or two days, or has the company failed periodically to rotate or transfer key personnel?
   5. Does the company have inadequate personnel screening policies when hiring new employees to fill positions of trust (e.g., check on secondary references, etc.)?
   6. Does the company lack explicit and uniform personnel policies?

Yes   No   N/A

7. Does the company fail to maintain accurate personnel records of dishonest acts or disciplinary actions?

8. Does the company fail to require executive disclosures and examinations (e.g., personal investments or incomes)?

9. Does the company appear to have dishonest or unethical management?

10. Is the company dominated by only one or two individuals?

11. Does the company appear to operate continually on a crisis basis?

12. Does the company fail to pay attention to details? (e.g., are accurate accounting records unimportant?)

13. Does the company place too much trust in key employees and overlook traditional controls?

14. Is there a lack of good interpersonal relationships among the key executives in the company?

15. Does the company have unrealistic productivity measurements or expectations?

16. Does the company have poor compensation practices? Is pay commensurate with the level of responsibility?

17. Does the company lack a good system of internal security (e.g., locks, safes, fences, gates, and guards)?

18. Does the company have adequate training programs?

19. Does the company have an inadequate internal control system, or does it fail to enforce the existing controls?

B. Individuals on Behalf of the Company
1. Has the company recently had any significant related-party transactions?

2. Does the company retain different auditing firms for major subsidiaries, or does it change auditors often?

Yes   No   N/A

3. Is the company reluctant to provide the auditors with data needed to complete the audit
   examination?
4. Does the company retain several different
   legal counsels, or does it change legal counsels often?
5. Does the company use several different
   banks, none of which can see the company's
   entire financial picture?
6. Does the company seem to have continuous
   problems with regulatory agencies?
7. Does the company possess an unduly complex business structure, so complex that
   many facets lack purpose or meaning?
8. Does the company seem to need but lack an
   effective internal auditing staff?
9. Is the company highly computerized? If so,
   are there insufficient controls over hardware,
   software, computer personnel, etc.?
10. Does the company have an inadequate
    internal control system, or does it fail to
    enforce the existing internal controls?
11. Is the company in a "hot" or high-risk
    industry (i.e., an industry which has experi-
    enced a large number of business failures or
    frauds)?
12. Does the company have a number of large
    year-end or unusual transactions?
13. Does the company have unduly liberal
    accounting practices?
14. Does the company have poor accounting
    records?
15. Does the accounting department of the com-
    pany appear to be inadequately staffed?
16. Does the company fail to disclose question-
    able or unusual accounting practices?

C. Personal Characteristics
   1. Do any of the key employees appear to have
      low moral character?

Yes   No   N/A

2. When confronted with difficulty, do any of the key employees appear consistently to rationalize contradictory behavior?

3. Do any of the key employees appear to lack a strong personal code of honesty?

4. Do any of the key employees appear to be "wheeler-dealer" individuals who enjoy feelings of power, influence, social status, and excitement associated with financial transactions involving large sums of money?

5. Do any of the key employees appear to be unstable (e.g., frequent job changes, frequent changes of residence, mental problems)?

6. Do any of the key employees appear to be intrigued by the personal challenge of subverting a system of controls (i.e., do they appear to have a desire to beat the system)?

7. Do any of the key employees have criminal or questionable backgrounds?

8. Do any of the key employees have poor credit ratings?

9. Do any of the key employees have poor past work records or references?

Appendix C
Professional Practices for Business Continuity Planners

April 1997

DRI International
1819 Craig Road, Suite 125
St. Louis, Missouri 63146
USA

The Business Continuity
Institute
PO Box 4474
London 5W18 3XB
England

ACKNOWLEDGMENTS

This document was initially developed through a cooperative effort of the Disaster Recovery Institute International and Business Continuity Institute (13CI). It represents a merger of two proprietary documents—the DRI International's "Common Body of Knowledge" published in September of 1993, and the Business Continuity Institute's "Certification Standards for Business Continuity Practitioners" published in December of 1994.

The following organizations and committees have been instrumental in developing, revising, editing, and producing this document.

DRI International	Board of Directors
	Certification Board
	Education and Testing Standards
	Committee of the Certification Board
BCI	Executive Board
	Advisory Board

COMMENTS

Organizations and individuals may submit comments and proposals for modification to this standard. All such comments must be submitted in writing on the modification proposal form and should be addressed to:

Education Standards Committee
DRI International
1819 Craig Road, Suite 125
St. Louis, Missouri 63146
USA

or

The Business Continuity Institute
PO Box 4474
London 5W18 3XB
England

INTRODUCTION

Professions are characterized, in part, by a body of knowledge shared by members of the profession and used in their work. This body of knowledge is usually abstract, stable, and technology-independent. It is independent of necessary skills, tasks, or activities. Rather, the specific skills, tasks, or activities for the profession emerge and evolve from *a set of subject areas of a common body of knowledge that characterize a profession*. To certify professionals where work is related to specific industries or activities, institutions such as DRI International and BCI must define, share, and continually refine a common body of knowledge essential for members of the profession.

The existence of such a common body of knowledge is necessary, but not sufficient evidence of the existence of the profession. Proper application and periodic update of the common body of knowledge are also required for success in the profession. Therefore, continued education and on-going professional development are essential to maintain and enhance membership status in the profession.

For certification purposes, minimum continuing involvement and experience in the profession must be demonstrated in addition to satisfactory completion of an oral or written examination based on the common body of knowledge. Demonstrated experience must be related to the content of the common body of knowledge.

This document defines the boundaries of the business continuity planning profession and knowledge that must be considered for DRI International's designation as an Associate Business Continuity Planner (ABCP), Certified Business Continuity Professional (CBCP), or Master Business Continuity Professional (MBCP). BCI also uses this document as the basis for their examination procedures for Membership of the Business

Continuity Institute (MBCI) and the Fellowship of the Business Continuity Institute (FBCI).

Each subject area in this document provides

- a description of the area.
- the role of the professional.
- an outline of the knowledge the professional should demonstrate within that subject area.

Illustrative examples and references are also provided where appropriate.

SUBJECT AREA OVERVIEW

Subject Area	Title and Description
1	**Project Initiation and Management** Establish the need for a Business Continuity Plan (13CP), including obtaining management support and organizing and managing the project to completion within agreed upon time and budget limits.
2	**Risk Evaluation and Control** Determine the events and environmental surroundings that can adversely affect the organization and its facilities with disruption as well as disaster, the damage such events can cause, and the controls needed to prevent or minimize the effects of potential loss. Provide cost-benefit analysis to justify investment in controls to mitigate risks.
3	**Business Impact Analysis** Identify the impacts resulting from disruptions and disaster scenarios that can affect the organization and techniques that can be used to quantify and qualify such impacts. Establish critical functions, their recovery priorities, and inter-dependencies so that recovery time objective can be set.
4	**Developing Business Continuity Strategies** Determine and guide the selection of alternative business recovery operating strategies for recovery of business and information technologies within the recovery time objective, while maintaining the organization's critical functions.

Subject Area	Title and Description
5	**Emergency Response and Operations** Develop and implement procedures for response and stabilizing the situation following an incident or event, including establishing and managing an Emergency Operations Center to be used as a command center during the emergency.
6	**Developing and Implementing Business Continuity Plans** Design, develop, and implement the Business Continuity Plan that provides recovery within the recovery time objective.
7	**Awareness and Training Programs** Prepare a program to create corporate awareness and enhance the skills required to develop, implement, maintain, and execute the Business Continuity Plan.
8	**Maintaining and Exercising Business Continuity Plans** Pre-plan and coordinate plan exercises, and evaluate and document plan exercise results. Develop processes to maintain the currency of continuity capabilities and the plan document in accordance with the organization's strategic direction. Verify that the Plan will prove effective by comparison with a suitable standard, and report results in a clear and concise manner.
9	**Public Relations and Crisis Communication** Develop, coordinate, evaluate, and exercise plans to handle media during crisis situations. Develop, coordinate, evaluate, and exercise plans to communicate with and, as appropriate, provide trauma counseling for employees and their families, key customers, critical suppliers, owners/stockholders, and corporate management during crisis. Ensure all stakeholders are kept informed on an as-needed basis.
10	**Coordination with Public Authorities** Establish applicable procedures and policies for coordinating response, continuity, and restoration activities with local authorities while ensuring compliance with applicable statutes or regulations

Subject Area 1 — Project Initiation and Management

Establish the need for a Business Continuity Plan (BCP), including obtaining management support and organizing and managing the project to completion within agreed upon time and budget limits.

The professional's role is to

1. **Lead Sponsors in Defining Objectives, Policies, and Critical Success Factors**
   - Scope and objectives
   - Legal and requirements reasons
   - Case histories

2. **Coordinate and Organize/Manage the BCP Project** using a steering committee and project task force. Understand the difference between disaster recovery, response, mitigation/avoidance, contingency planning, business continuity, and crisis management.

3. **Oversee the BCP Project Through Effective Control Methods and Change Management**

4. **Present (Sell) the Project to Management and Staff**

5. **Develop Project Plan and Budget**

6. **Define and Recommend Project Structure and Management**

7. **Manage the Process**

The professional should demonstrate a working knowledge in the following areas.

1. **Establish the Need for Business Continuity**
   a. Reference relevant legal/regulatory/statutory/contractual requirements and restrictions
   b. Reference relevant regulations of industry trade bodies or associations, where appropriate
   c. Reference current recommendations of relevant authorities (define these)
   d. Relate legislation, regulations, and recommendations to organizational policy
   e. Identify any conflicts between organizational policies and relevant external requirements
   f. Identify any audit records
   g. Propose methods, which may include a BCP, to resolve any conflicts between organizational policies and relevant external requirements

      h. Identify business practices (e.g., just in-time inventory) that may adversely impact the organization's ability to recover following a disaster event

2. **Communicate the Need for a Business Continuity Plan**
   a. Develop awareness by means of formal reports and presentations
   b. State the benefits of the BCP and relate the benefits to organizational mission, objectives, and operations
   c. Gain organizational commitment to the BCP project
   d. Develop a mission statement/charter for the BCP project

3. **Involve Executive Management in the BCP Project**
   a. Explain executive management's role in the BCP project
   b. Explain and communicate management's accountability and liability

4. **Establish a Planning/Steering Committee: Roles and Responsibilities, Types of Organization, Control and Development, and Membership**
   a. Select appropriate personnel
   b. Define their roles and responsibilities
   c. Develop an overall project plan with realistic time estimates and schedule
   d. Develop a suitable set of objectives for the BCP

5. **Develop Budget Requirements**
   a. Clearly define resource requirements
   b. Obtain estimates of financial requirement
   c. Verify the validity of resources requirements
   d. Validate the estimates of financial requirements
   e. Negotiate resource and financial requirements with management

6. **Identify Planning Team(s) and Responsibilities**
   a. Emergency management/crisis response/crisis management team
   b. Business continuity planning teams (multi-location, multi-divisions, etc.)
   C. Recovery/response and restoration teams

7. **Develop and Coordinate Action Plans**

8. **Develop Project Management and Documentation Requirements**

9. **Report to Senior Management and Obtain Senior Management Approval Commitment**
   a. Set up a schedule to report the progress of the BCP project to senior managers
   b. Develop regular status reports for senior management that contain concise, pertinent, accurate, and timely information on key parameters of interest or information of which senior management should be made aware

10. **Project Management**
    a. Identify and develop business continuity plan phases similar to classical project plan phases: problem investigation, problem definition, feasibility study, systems description, implementation, installation, and review
    b. Establish business continuity plan project characteristics: goals, tasks, resources, time schedules, and critical success factors
    c. Execute generally accepted responsibilities of a business continuity planning project manager:
       1. Define the business continuity planning project
       2. Assess the business continuity planning project risk
       3. Organize the business continuity planning project
       4. Plan the business continuity planning project in detail, including time management and project scheduling (milestone, Gantt, and/or PERT/CPM charts, use of computer-based software for scheduling)
       5. Monitor and manage the business continuity planning project activities
       6. Track and report the business continuity planning project progress
       7. Manage change associated with the business continuity planning project

Subject Area 2 — Risk Evaluation and Control

Determine the events and environmental surroundings that can adversely affect the organization and its facilities with disruption as well as disaster, the damage such events can cause, and the controls needed to prevent or minimize the effects of potential loss. Provide cost-benefit analysis to justify investment in controls to mitigate risks.

The professional's role is to

1. **Understand the Function of Probabilities and Risk Reduction/ Mitigation Within the Organization**

2. **Identify Potential Risks to the Organization**
   - Probability
   - Consequences

3. **Identify Outside Expertise Required**

4. **Identify Vulnerabilities/Threats/Exposures**

5. **Identify Risk Reduction/Mitigation Alternatives**

6. **Identify Credible Information Sources**

7. **Interface with Management to Determine Acceptable Risk Levels**

8. **Document and Present Findings**

The professional should demonstrate a working knowledge in the following areas.

1. **Understand Loss Potentials**
   a. Identify threats from both internal and external sources. These should include, but not be limited to, the following:
      1. Natural, man-made, technological, or political disasters
      2. Accidental versus intentional
      3. Internal versus external
      4. Controllable risks versus those beyond the organization's control
      5. Events with prior warnings versus those with no prior warnings
   b. Determine the probability of events
      1. Information sources
      2. Credibility
   c. Create methods of information gathering
   d. Develop a suitable method to evaluate probability versus severity
   e. Establish ongoing support of evaluation process
   f. Identify the relevant key security and legislative issues
   g. Establish cost benefit analysis to be associated with the identified loss potential

2. **Determine the Organization's Vulnerability to Loss Potentials**
   a. Identify primary threats the organization may face, and secondary/collateral events that could materialize because of such threats (e.g., hurricane threat could result in several events including high winds, flood, fire, building and roof collapse, etc.)
   b. Select vulnerabilities most likely to occur and with greatest impact

3. **Identify Controls and Safeguards to Prevent or Minimize the Effect of the Loss Potential**
   a. Location(s) and security considerations. The actions taken and facilities installed to reduce the probability of occurrence of incidents that would impair the ability to conduct business.
      1. Physical protection
         (a) Understand the need to restrict access to buildings, rooms, and other enclosures where circumstances demand a "3-dimensional" consideration
         (b) Understand the need for barriers and strengthened structures to deter willful and accidental and/or unauthorized entry
      2. Physical presence
         (a) Understand the need for the use of specialist personnel to conduct checks at key entry points
         (b) Understand the need for manned and/or recorded surveillance equipment to control access points and areas of exclusion
      3. Logical protection
         (a) Understand the need for system-provided protection of data stored, in process, or in translation
      4. Location of assets
         (a) Understand the inherent protection afforded key assets by virtue of their location relative to sources of risk.
   b. Location: physical construction, geographic location, corporate neighbors, facilities infrastructure, community infrastructure
   c. Protection: detection, notification, suppression
   d. Security and access controls, tenant insurance, leasehold agreements
   e. Personnel procedures
   f. Procedural controls
   g. Information backup and protection
   h. Information security: hardware, software, data, network
   i. Preventive maintenance and equipment preplanning
   j. Utilities: duplication of utilities, redundancies in utilities
   k. Interface with outside agencies
   l. Services: electricity, air conditioning, water, communications, maintenance, equipment replacement and spares, documentation

4. **Evaluate, Select, and Use Appropriate Risk Analysis Methodologies and Tools**
   a. Identify alternative risk analysis methodologies and tools
      1. Qualitative and quantitative methodologies
      2. Advantages and disadvantages
      3. Reliability/confidence factor
      4. Basis of mathematical formulas used
   b. Select appropriate methodology and tool(s) for company-wide implementation

5. **Identify and Implement Information Gathering Activities**
   a. Develop a strategy consistent with business issues and organizational policy
   b. Develop a strategy that can be managed across business divisions and organizational locations
   c. Employ credible information sources
   d. Create organization-wide methods of information collection and distribution
      1. Forms and questionnaires
      2. Interviews
      3. Meetings
      4. Documentation review
      5. Analysis
   e. Use software

6. **Evaluate the Effectiveness of Controls and Safeguards**
   a. Develop communications flow with other internal departments/divisions
   b. Establish business continuity service level agreements for both supplier and customer organizations and groups
   c. Develop preventive and pre-planning options
      1. Cost/benefit
      2. Implementation priorities, procedures, and control
      3. Testing
      4. Audit functions and responsibilities
   d. Understand options for risk management and selection of appropriate or cost-effective response, i.e. risk avoidance, transfer, or acceptance of risk
   e. Develop interface with suppliers and utilities
   f. Develop security practices
   g. Identify methods to minimize the effects of the loss potential
   h. Brief participants, ensuring they understand their objectives and reporting structure

7. **Risk Evaluation and Control**
   a. Establish disaster scenarios based on risks to which the organization is vulnerable. The disaster scenarios should be based on these types of criteria: severe in magnitude, occurring at the worst possible time, resulting in severe impairment to the organization's ability to conduct business.
   b. Evaluate risks and classify them according to relevant criteria, including: risks under the organization's control, risks beyond the organization's control, threats with prior warnings (such as tornadoes and hurricanes), and threats with no prior warnings (such as earthquakes).
   c. Evaluate impact of risks and threats on those factors essential for conducting business operations: availability of personnel, availability of information technology, availability of communications technology, status of infrastructure (including transportation), etc.
   d. Evaluate controls and recommend changes, if necessary, to reduce impact due to risks and threats
      1. Controls to inhibit impact threats: preventive controls (such as passwords, smoke detectors, and firewalls)
      2. Controls to compensate for impact of threats: reactive controls (such as hot Sites)

8. **Security**
   a. Identify the organization's possible security exposures, including the following specific categories of security risks
      1. Physical/plant security
      2. Information security — computer room and media Storage area security
      3. Communications security — voice and data communications security
      4. Network security — intranet security, Internet security
   b. Advise on feasible, cost-effective security measures required to prevent/reduce security-related risks and threats

9. **Backup and Restoration Procedures**
   a. Identify vital record needs in the organization, including paper and electronic records
   b. Evaluate existing backup and restoration procedures for vital records
   c. Advise on and implement feasible, cost-effective backup and restoration procedures for all forms of the organization's vital records

Subject Area 3 — Business Impact Analysis

Identify the impacts resulting from disruptions and disaster scenarios that can affect the organization and techniques that can be used to quantify and qualify such impacts. Establish critical functions, their recovery priorities, and inter-dependencies so that recovery time objective can be set.

The professional's role is to

1. **Identify Organization Functions**

2. **Identify Knowledgeable and Credible Functional Area Representatives**

3. **Identify and Define Criticality Criteria**

4. **Present Criteria to Management for Approval**

5. **Coordinate Analysis**

6. **Identify Interdependencies**

7. **Define Recovery Objectives and Timeframes,** including recovery times, expected losses, and priorities

8. **Identify Information Requirements**

9. **Identify Resource Requirements**

10. **Define Report Format**

11. **Prepare and Present**

The professional should demonstrate a working knowledge in the following areas.

1. **Establish the Project**
   a. Identify and obtain a project sponsor for the Business Impact Analysis (BIA) activity
   b. Define objectives and scope for the BIA project
   c. Choose an appropriate BIA project planning methodology/tool
   d. Identity and inform participants of the BIA project and its purpose
   e. Identify training requirements
   f. Establish a training schedule and undertake training
   g. Ensure the project leader has a sound understanding of the purposes of the organization

    h. Obtain agreement on final project time schedule and initiate the BIA project

2. **Assess Effects of Disruptions, Loss Exposure, and Business Impact**
   a. Effects of disruptions
      1. Loss of assets: key personnel, physical assets, information assets, intangible assets
      2. Disruption to the continuity of service and operations
      3. Violation of law/regulation
      4. Public perception
   b. Impact of disruptions on business
      1. Financial
      2. Customers and suppliers
      3. Public relations/credibility
      4. Legal
      5. Regulatory requirements/considerations
      6. Environmental
      7. Operational
      8. Personnel
      9. Other resources
   c. Determine Loss Exposure
      1. Quantitative
         (a) Property loss
         (b) Revenue loss
         (c) Fines
         (d) Cash flow
         (e) Accounts receivable
         (f) Accounts payable
         (g) Legal liability
         (h) Human resources
         (i) Additional expenses/increased cost of working
      2. Qualitative
         (a) Human resources
         (b) Morale
         (c) Confidence
         (d) Legal
         (d) Social and corporate image
         (e) Financial community credibility

3. **Business Impact Analysis (BIA) — A Suggested Methodology to Understand Assessment Techniques: Quantitative and Qualitative Methods**
   a. BIA data collection methodologies

    1. Finalize an appropriate data collection method (e.g., question-naires, interviews, workshop, or in agreed combination)
    2. Recommend and obtain agreement as to how potential financial and non-financial impact can be quantified and evaluated
    3. Identify and obtain agreement on requirements for non-quantifiable impact information and gain agreement
    4. Develop questionnaire (if used) and completion instructions
    5. Determine data analysis methods (manual or computer)
b. Data collection via questionnaires
    1. Understand the need for appropriate design and distribution of questionnaires, including explanation of purpose, to participating departmental managers and staff
    2. Understand the role of; and manage, project kick-off meetings to distribute and explain the questionnaire
    3. Understand the role of; and support respondents during completion of questionnaires
    4. Review completed questionnaires and identity those requiring follow-up interviews
    5. Conduct follow-up discussions when clarification and/or additional data is required
c. Data collection via interviews only
    1 Understand the need for consistency, with the structure of each interview predefined and following a common format
    2. Ensure the base data to be collected at each interview is predefined
    3. Understand the need for initial interview to be reviewed and verified by the interviewee
    4. Schedule follow-up interviews, if initial analysis shows a need to clarify and/or add to the data already provided
d. Data collection via a workshop
    1. Understand the need for, and set a clear agenda and set of objectives
    2. Identify the appropriate level of participating management and obtain agreement. Choose appropriate venue, evaluating location, facilities, and staff availability
    3. Act as facilitator and leader during discussions
    4. Ensure workshop objectives are met
    5. Ensure all issues outstanding at the end of the workshop are identified and responsibility for their resolution agreed upon
e. Business Impact Analysis report
    1. Prepare draft BIA report containing initial impact findings and issues
    2. Issue draft report to participating managers and request feedback

3. Review manager feedback and, where appropriate, revise findings accordingly or add to outstanding issues
4. Schedule a workshop or meeting with participating manager(s) to discuss initial findings, when necessary
5. Ensure original findings are updated to reflect changes arising from these meetings
6. Prepare final Business Impact Analysis report according to organization or house standards
7. Prepare and undertake formal presentation of Business Impact Analysis findings to peers and executive bodies

Note: No standards exist for the format or distribution of Business Impact Analysis reports, so these reports will vary between companies.

4. **Define Criticality of Business Functions and Records, and Prioritize**
   a. Establish definition of criticality, and negotiate with management single or multiple levels of criticality
   b. Identity critical functions
      1. Business functions
      2. Support functions
      3. Interdependencies
   c. Identify vital records to support business continuity and business restoration
   d. Prioritize critical business functions

5. **Determine Recovery Timeframes and Minimum Resource Requirements**
   a. Determine recovery windows for critical business functions based on level of criticality
   b. Determine the order of recovery for critical business functions, and support functions and systems based on parallel and interdependent activities
   c. Determine minimum resource requirements for recovery and resumption of critical functions and support systems
      1. Internal and external resources
      2. Owned versus non-owned resources
      3. Existing resources and additional resources required

6. **Identity Business Processes**
   a. Interrelationship between the business processes
   b. Process dependencies
      1. Intradepartment
      2. Interdepartment

3. Technology
4. Processes

7. **Determine Replacement Times**
    a. Equipment
    b. Key personnel
    c. Raw materials/sub-assemblies
    d. Other

Subject Area 4 — Developing Business Continuity Strategies

Determine and guide the selection of alternative business recovery operating strategies for recovery of business and information technologies within the recovery time objective, while maintaining the Organization's critical functions.

The professional's role is to

1. **Understand Available Alternatives and Their Advantages, Disadvantages, and Cost Ranges, Including Mitigation as a Recovery Strategy**

2. **Identify Viable Recovery Strategies with Business Functional Areas**

3. **Consolidate Strategies**

4. **Identify Off-Site Storage Requirements and Alternative Facilities**

5. **Develop Business Unit Consensus**

6. **Present Strategies to Management to Obtain Commitment**

The professional should demonstrate a working knowledge in the following areas.

1. **Identify Business Continuity Strategy Requirements**
    a. Review business recovery issues
        1. Timeframes
        2. Options
        3. Location
        4. Personnel
        5. Communications
    b. Review technology recovery issues for each support service
    c. Review non-technology recovery issues for each support service, including those support services not dependent upon technology

    d. Compare internal/external solutions
    e. Identify alternative recovery strategies
       1. Do nothing
       2. Defer action
       3. Manual procedures
       4. Reciprocal agreements
       5. Alternative site or business facility
       6. Alternate source of product
       7. Service bureau
       8. Consortium
       9. Distributed processing
       10. Alternative communications
       11. Mitigation
       12. Preplanning
    f. Compare internal and external solutions
    g. Assess risk associated with each optional recovery strategy

2. **Assess Suitability of Alternative Strategies Against the Results of a Business Impact Analysis**
    a. Effectively analyze business needs criteria
    b. Clearly define recovery planning objectives
    c. Develop a consistent method for evaluation
    d. Set baseline criteria for options

3. **Prepare Cost/Benefit Analysis or Recovery Strategies and Present Findings to Senior Management**
    a. Employ a practical, understandable methodology
    b. Set realistic time schedules for evaluation and report writing
    c. Deliver concise specific recommendations to senior management

4. **Select Alternate Site(s) and Off-Site Storage**
    a. Criteria
    b. Communications
    c. Agreement considerations
    d. Comparison techniques
    e. Acquisition
    f. Contractual consideration

5. **Understand Contractual Agreements for Business Continuity Services**
    a. Understand and prepare requirement statements for use in formal agreements for the provision of continuity services
    b. Formulate any necessary technical specifications for use in "invitation-to-tende" format

    c. Interpret external agreements proposed by suppliers in relation to the original requirements specified

    d. Identify specific requirements excluded from any standard agreements proposed

    e. Understand and advise on the inclusion of optional elements and those that are essential

6. **Enterprise-Wide**

    a. Develop, implement, and exercise enterprise-wide plans for business continuity to emphasize coordination of business unit continuity, information technology, and communications technology recovery and continuity

    b. Develop, implement, and exercise enterprise-level crisis management plans for media handling, crisis communications, etc.

7. **Business Unit Plans**

    a. Develop, implement, and exercise business unit response, recovery, resumption, restoration, and return plans

    b. Designate and obtain approval for recommended staff and access to essential equipment resources for work area recovery sites

8. **Emergency Telecommunications**

    To gain a thorough understanding of this area of professional practices, the business continuity professional is strongly urged to undergo formal education and training through telecommunications or communications technologies courses.

    a. Voice communications

        1. Develop strategies to recover/restore voice communications

        2. Make arrangements with local loop and long distance phone service providers for voice communications recovery (e.g., alternate exchanges, alternate routing, dial backup, foreign exchanges, etc.)

    b. Data communications

        1. Develop, implement, and exercise plans to recover/restore data communications

        2. Evaluate and select appropriate arrangements with local, long distance, and global telecommunications network service providers for data communications recovery strategies and action plans.

Subject Area 5 — Emergency Response and Operations

Develop and implement procedures for response and stabilizing the situation following an incident or event, including establishing and managing an

Emergency Operations Center to be used as a command center during the emergency.

The professional's role is to

1. **Identify Potential Types of Emergencies and the Responses Needed (e.g., fire, hazardous materials leak, medical)**

2. **Identify the Existence of Appropriate Emergency Response Procedures**

3. **Recommend the Development of Emergency Procedures Where None Exist**

4. **Integrate Disaster Recovery/Business Continuity Procedures with Emergency Response Procedures**

5. **Identify the Command and Control Requirements of Managing an Emergency**

6. **Recommend the Development of Command and Control Procedures to Define Roles, Authority, and Communications Processes for Managing an Emergency**

7. **Ensure Emergency Response Procedures are Integrated with Requirements of Public Authorities** (Refer also to Subject Area 10, Coordination With Public Authorities)

The professional should demonstrate a working knowledge in the following areas.

1. **Identify Components of Emergency Response Procedure**
   a. Reporting procedures
      1. Internal (escalation procedures)
         (a) Local
         (b) Organization (decision-making process)
      2. External (response procedures)
         (a) Public agencies and media
         (b) Suppliers of products and services
   b. Pre-incident preparation
      1. By types of disaster
         (a) acts of nature
         (b) accidental
         (c) intentional
      2. Management continuity and authority

      3. Roles of designated personnel
- c. Emergency actions
    1. Evacuation
    2. Medical care and personnel counseling
    3. Hazardous material response
    4. Firefighting
    5. Notification
    6. Other
- d. Facility stabilization
- e. Damage mitigation
- f. Testing procedures and responsibilities

2. **Develop Detailed Emergency Response Procedures**
   - a. Protection of personnel
       1. Recognize and understand the value of supplementing any relevant statutory precautions
       2. Identify options for immediate deployment and subsequent contract
       3. Provide for communication with staff; next-of-kin, and dependents
       4. Understand implications of statutory regulations
   - b. Containment of incident
       1. Understand the principles of salvage and loss containment
       2. Understand options available to supplement the efforts of the emergency services in limiting business impact
       3. Understand possibilities within business functions to limit the impact of a disaster, within statutory constraints
   - c. Assessment of effect
       1. Analyze the situation and provide effective assessment report
       2. Estimate the event's direct impact on the organization
       3. Communicate situation to employees at involved facility and any other organization locations
       4. Demonstrate awareness of the likely media interest and formulate a response in conjunction with any existing public relations and/or existing marketing unit
   - d. Decide optimum actions
       1. Understand the issues to be considered when recommending or making decisions on recovery options
       2. Understand the roles of the emergency services
       3. Maintain principles of security, especially in regard to the disposal of stored/archived materials or damaged materials with retained value

3. **Identify Command and Control Requirements**
   a. Designing and equipping the Emergency Operations Center
   b. Command and decide authority roles during the incident
   c. Communication vehicles (e.g., radio, messengers, and cellular telephones)
   d. Logging and documentation methods

4. **Command and Control Procedures**
   a. Opening the Emergency Operations Center
   b. Security for the Emergency Operations Center
   c. Scheduling the Emergency Operations Center teams
   d. Management and operations of the Emergency Operations Center
   e. Closing the Emergency Operations Center

5. **Emergency Response and Triage**
   a. Develop, implement, and exercise emergency response and triage procedures, including determination of priorities for actions in an emergency
   b. Develop, implement, and exercise triage procedures such as first aid and medical treatment; identify location and develop procedures for transportation to nearby hospitals

6. **Salvage and Restoration**
   a. Assemble reaction team
      1. Understand the need for effective diagnosis of incident by telephone
      2. Understand the need for effective assembly of relevant resources at the affected site
      3. Develop internal escalation procedures to provide required level of resources on-site as incident/response develops
   b. Define strategy for initial on-site activity
      1. Understand the need to identify immediate loss mitigation and salvage requirements
      2. Understand the need for and, if necessary, prepare an action plan for site safety, security, and stabilization
      3. Identify appropriate methods for protection of assets on-site, including equipment, premises, and documentation
      4. Recognize potential need to establish liaison with external agencies (e.g., statutory agencies, emergency services such as fire departments and police, insurers, loss adjusters, etc.), and specify type of information these agencies may require.

5. Understand business requirements and interpret them to aid physical asset recovery
6. Establish procedures with public authorities for facility access

Subject Area 6 — Developing and Implementing Business Continuity Plans

Design, develop, and implement the Business Continuity Plan that provides recovery within the recovery time objective.

The professional's role is to

1. **Identify the Components of the Planning Process**
   - Planning methodology
   - Plan organization
   - Direction of efforts
   - Staffing requirements

2. **Control the Planning Process and Produce the Plan**

3. **Implement the Plan**

4. **Test the Plan**

5. **Maintain the Plan**

The professional should demonstrate a working knowledge in the following areas.

1. **Determine Plan Development Requirements**
   a. Planning aids
   b. Tools
      1. Job descriptions
      2. Action plans
      3. Checklists
      4. Matrices and flowcharts
      5. Forms
      6. Information database
      7. Other supporting documentation

2. **Define Recovery Management and Control Requirements**
   a. Define disaster
      1. Differentiate between an interruption and a disaster
      2. Suggest severity criteria that may be used to create a definition

       3. Design escalation criteria
    b. Identify and agree on approach to key phases of recovery; document agreed approach
    c. Recovery team concept
       1. Team description
       2. Team organization
       3. Responsibilities
          (a) Recovery coordinator
          (b) Group coordinators
       4. Support staff
       5. Emergency Operations Center
    d. Establish procedure to transition from emergency response plan to business continuity plan.

3. **Identify and Define the Format and Structure of Major Plan Components. Develop Procedures to Ensure Business Continuity using a format suitable for use under emergency conditions**
    a. Plan design and structure
       1. Identify examples of alternative plans and structures
       2. Define how plan structure is tied to the organization.
       3. Document structure and design of departmental continuity plans
       4. Ensure built-in mechanisms to ease maintenance
       5. Plan and implement the gathering of data required for plan completion
    b. Allocate tasks and responsibilities
       1. Differentiate between recovery teams and departmental teams
       2. Identify tasks to be undertaken
       3. Identify necessary teams to perform required tasks
       4. Assign responsibilities to teams
       5. Identify and list key contacts, suppliers, and resources

4. **Draft the Plan**
    a. Select appropriate tools for plan development and maintenance
    b. Draft the Business Continuity Plan, ensuring adequate and appropriate involvement of personnel required to implement the Plan
    c. Continue gathering data as needed to ensure Plan is complete and accurate

5. **Define Business Continuity Procedures**
    a. Locate and catalogue organization information
       1. Identify and confirm information and documentation critical to the organization's key business
       2. Select or recommend appropriate methods of business backup

3. Determine which information should be duplicated
4. Establish duplication or replication methods
5. Set up regular schedules for duplication
6. Quantify storage requirements
7. Identify suitable storage facilities
8. Establish schedules for safe transfer of information to suitable storage facilities
9. Understand retention periods
10. Identify key suppliers

b. Protection and replication strategies
1. Define assumptions governing the choice of replication and storage strategies
2. Define program for replication and storage of specific classes and types of information
3. Understand the advantages and disadvantages of
(a) Duplication methods
(b) Replication methods
(c) Storage methods
4. Understand the advantages and disadvantages of available protection methods
5. Predict shelf-life of stored information
6. Understand suitable treatment that may be required during storage, according to the media used and environmental conditions

c. Information recovery
1. Recommend suitable procedures, taking into account:
(a) Most suitable sequence of recovery
(b) Compatibility of reading and writing equipment and storage media
(c) Timeframes determined by the business requirements
(d) Timeframes determined by the legislative requirements
(e) Requirements of daily or weekly routines, where applicable
2. Identify recovery or starting point for processing or handling information
3. Develop a reasonable set of assumptions, taking various realistic scenarios into account

d. Develop optional business methods
1. Recommend alternative ways to conduct business when normal resources are unavailable following a disaster or other disruptive event that will be effective until recovery procedures are successfully completed

    2. Recommend method/procedures to easily transfer business functions from any alternative, temporary, or emergency operation into the new/replaced/re-installed service

6. **Damage Assessment**
   a. Damage assessment
      1. Create an action plan for assessing damage
      2. Understand economics of repair versus replacement
      3. Understand the capabilities of salvage specialists in selecting and applying relevant methods of contamination analysis
      4. Understand the criteria for selecting appropriate sub-contractors for salvage operations
      5. Clearly relate damage assessment to business continuity of organization
   b. Define restoration strategy
      1. Employ a logical but relevant and practical approach to business recovery requirements
      2. Demonstrate ability to reduce consequential losses
      3. Agree upon restoration methods for business assets (e.g., equipment, electronics, documents, data, furnishings, premises, plant, computers, etc.)
      4. Understand the approval process for restoration and especially the implications of warranties
      5. Define a strategy for restoration

7. **Critical Resource Acquisition**

8. **Security**

9. **Human Resource and Personnel Considerations**

10. **Develop General Introduction or Overview**
    a. General information
       1. Introduction
       2. Scope
       3. Objectives
       4. Assumptions
       5. Responsibility overview
       6. Testing
       7. Maintenance
    b. Plan activation

    1. Notification
      (a) Primary
      (b) Secondary
    2. Disaster declaration procedures
    3. Mobilization procedures
    4. Damage assessment concepts
      (a) Initial
      (b) Detailed
      (c) Team members

c. Team organization
    1. Team description
    2. Team organization
    3. Team leader responsibilities

d. Policy statement

e. Emergency Operations Center

11. **Develop Administration Section**

a. Identify recovery functions for specific support functions
    1. Personnel/human resources
    2. Security
    3. Insurance/risk management
    4. Equipment/supplies purchasing
    5. Transportation
    6. Legal

b. Understand need for public relations/media communications coordinator
    1. Qualifications
    2. Responsibilities

c. Other specialist coordinator/team responsibilities
    1. Relations/liaison with regulatory bodies
    2. Investor relations
    3. Relations with other involved groups (e.g., customers and suppliers)

d. Identify components of vital records program

e. Action sections
    1. Recovery team
      (a) Personnel
      (b) Responsibilities
      (c) Resources

f. Action plans
    1. Department/individual plans
    2. Checklists
    3. Technical procedures

12. **Develop Business Operations Plan**
    a. Operating department plans
        1. Essential business functions
        2. Information protection and recovery
        3. Activation actions
        4. Disaster site recovery/restoration actions
        5. End-user computing needs
    b. Components of a vital records program
    c. Action sections
        1. Recovery team
            (a) Personnel
            (b) Responsibilities
            (c) Resources
    d. Action plans
        1. Specific department/individual plans
        2. Checklists
        3 Technical procedures

13. **Develop Information Technology Recovery Plan**
    a. Recovery site activation
        1. Management
        2. Administration/logistics
        3. New equipment
        4. Technical services
        5. Application support
        6. Network communications
        7. Network engineering
        8. Operations
        9. Inter-site logistics and communications
        10. Data preparation
        11. Production control
        12. End-user liaison
    b. End-user requirements
    c. Identify components of vital records program
    d. Action sections
        1. Recovery team
            (a) Personnel
            (b) Responsibilities
            (c) Resources
    e. Action plans
        1. Specific department/individual plans
        2. Checklists
        3. Technical procedures

14. **Develop Communication Systems Plan**
    a. Voice communications recovery plans
       1. Phone lines, including in-bound toll-free (1-800) lines and fax lines
       2. Voice mail, voice response units, and other voice-based services
       3. Alternate arrangement for automated voice response during a disaster
    b. Data communications recovery plans
       1. Data communications with mainframe-based information Systems
       2. Local area network (LAN) recovery for work area recovery
       3. Wide area network (WAN) recovery for restoring global connectivity
       4. E-mail, groupware, and other data communications-based work support
    c. Emphasize and ensure detailed and up-to-date documentation of voice and data communications networks throughout the enterprise

15. **Develop End-User Applications Plans**
    a. Plan design and structure
       1. Identify examples of alternative plans and structures
       2. Define how plan structure is tied to the organization
       3. Document structure and design of departmental continuity plans
       4. Ensure built-in mechanisms to ease maintenance
       5. Plan and implement the gathering of data required for plan completion
    b. Identify and agree on approach to key phases of recovery; document agreed approach
    c. Allocate tasks and responsibilities
       1. Differentiate between recovery teams and departmental teams
       2. Identify tasks to be undertaken
       3. Identify necessary teams to perform required tasks
       4. Assign responsibilities to teams
       5. Identify and list key contacts, suppliers, and resources

16. **Implement the Plan**
    a. Develop an education program
       1. Standard guidelines for developing and implementing continuity plans
       2. Employee roles and responsibilities defined in the continuity plans

        3. Procedures to be followed by employees throughout the organization
        4. Training and awareness presentations to management and employees
    b. Complete required tasks
        1. Acquiring additional equipment
        2. Contractual arrangements
        3. Preparing backup and off-site storage
    c. Develop test plans, schedules, and reporting procedures
    d. Develop maintenance, updating, and reporting procedures

17. **Continuity Actions and Procedures**

18. **Establish Plan Distribution and Control Procedures**
    a. Establish procedures for distribution and control of business continuity plans
    b. Establish procedures for distribution and control of results of plan exercises
    c. Establish procedures for distribution and control of plan changes and updates

Subject Area 7 — Awareness and Training Programs

Prepare a program to create corporate awareness and enhance the skills required to develop, implement, maintain, and execute the Business Continuity Plan.

    The professional's role is to

1. **Establish Objectives and Components of Training Program**

2. **Identify Functional Training Requirements**

3. **Develop Training Methodology**

4. **Develop Awareness Program**

5. **Acquire or Develop Training Aids**

6. **Identify External Training Opportunities**

7. **Identify Vehicles for Corporate Awareness**

The professional should demonstrate a working knowledge in the following areas.

1. **Define Training Objectives**

2. **Develop Various Types of Training Programs**
   a. Computer based
   b. Classroom
   c. Test based

3. **Develop Awareness Programs**
   a. Management
   b. Team members
   c. New employee orientation

4. **Identify Other Opportunities for Education**
   a. Professional business continuity planning conferences and seminars
   b. User groups
   c. Publications

Subject Area 8 — Maintaining and Exercising Business Continuity Plans

Pre-plan and coordinate plan exercises, and evaluate and document plan exercise results. Develop processes to maintain the currency of continuity capabilities and the Plan document in accordance with the organization's strategic direction. Verify that the Plan will prove effective by comparison with a suitable standard, and report results in a clear and concise manner.

The professional's role is to

1. **Pre-plan the Exercises**

2. **Coordinate the Exercises**

3. **Evaluate the Exercise Plans**

4. **Exercise the Plans**

5. **Document the Results**

6. **Evaluate the Results**

7. **Update the Plan**

8. **Report Results/Evaluation to Management**

9. **Understand Strategic Directions of the Business**

10. **Attend Strategic Planning Meetings**

11. **Coordinate Plan Maintenance**

12. **Assist in Establishing Audit Program for the Business Continuity Plan**

The professional should demonstrate a working knowledge in the following areas.

1. **Establish an Exercise Program**
    a. Effectively analyze complex issues
    b. Employ a logical, structured approach
    c. Develop an exercise strategy that
        - does not put the organization at risk
        - is practical, cost-effective, and appropriate to the organization
        - ensures a high level of confidence in recovery capability
    d. Create a suitable set of exercise guidelines

2. **Determine Exercise Requirements**
    a. Define exercise objectives and establish levels of success
    b. Identify types of exercises, and their advantages and disadvantages
        1. Simulations and walk-throughs
        2. Modular
        3. Functional
        4. Announced
        5. Unannounced
    c. Establish and document scope of the exercise
    d. Exercise growth or expansion
    e. Exercise frequency
    f. Logistics and preplanning

3. **Develop Realistic Scenarios**
    a. Create exercise scenarios to approximate the types of incidents the organization is likely to experience and the problems associated with these incidents

   b   Train team members in new roles and decision-making falling
       outside the normal requirements of their permanent positions
   c. Exercise opening and communications, as well as logging and doc-
       umentation requirements for the Emergency Operations Center
       1. Reconstruction
           (a) Damage assessment
           (b) Facility
           (c) Equipment
           (d) Environment
           (e) Salvage/restoration (specialist services)
           (f) Insurance

4. **Establish Exercise Evaluation Criteria and Document Findings**
    a. Observation
    b. Documentation
    c. Evaluation
        1. Expected versus actual results
    d. Plan update requirements

5. **Create an Exercise Schedule**
    a. Develop a progressive, incremental schedule
    b. Set realistic time scales
    c. Allocate appropriate and realistic resources

6. **Select Exercise Method**
    a. Understand different methods of exercising
    b. Identify advantages and disadvantages of alternate exercise
        methods
    c. Select a sound and appropriate exercise method
    d. Define controls and responsibilities
    e. Document exercise specifications and circulate to all parties

7. **Define Exercise Objectives**
    a. Clearly define exercise objectives and scope
    b. Ensure objectives do not put the organization at risk
    c. Brief participants, ensuring they understand the objectives and
        their roles

8. **Prepare Exercise Control Plan and Reports**
    a. Create realistic exercise scenarios appropriate to the organization
    b. Define assumptions and describe limitations
    c. Identify resources required to conduct the exercise
    d. Identity exercise adjudicators (umpires)

    e. Provide an inventory of items required for the exercise and specifications for the exercise environment
    f. Provide a timetable of events
    g. Provide an alternate exercise plan to ensure that value is gained from the exercise in the event of adverse circumstances

9. **Conduct and Manage Exercises**
   a. Conduct and manage each exercise
   b. Audit exercise actions

10. **Post-Exercise Reporting**
    a. Provide a summary of events for participants
    b. Provide a cogent, comprehensive summary with recommendations, commensurate with levels of confidentiality requested by exercise umpire/adjudicator or as specified by the subject organization

11. **Feedback and Monitor Actions Resulting from Exercise**
    a. Ensure that scheduled plan maintenance addresses all documented recommendations
    b. Identify actions and owners for recommendations; confirm owner acceptance
    c. Confirm time schedules for completing or reviewing agreed actions
    d. Monitor (and escalate where necessary) progress to completion of agreed actions
    e. Identify recommendations that require specific verification through exercising.

12. **Establish Review Criteria**
    a. Periodic review
    b. Key change events
    c. Exercise results

13. **Define Plan Maintenance Scheme and Schedule**
    a. Define ownership of plan data
    b. Analyze Sensitivity of particular elements to change
    c. Develop suitable timeframes for amendment and/or review
    d. Prepare maintenance schedules and review procedures

14. **Maintain the Plan**
    a. Select tools
    b. Monitor activities
    c. Establish update process
    d. Audit and control

15. **Formulate Change Control Procedures**
    a. Analyze business changes with business continuity planning implications
    b. Set guidelines for feedback of changes to planning function
    c. Develop change control procedures to monitor changes
    d. Create proper version control; develop plan re-issue, distribution, and circulation procedures
    e. Understand the potential implications of change on the Plan and, therefore, the requirement for exercising as required

16. **Establish Status Reporting Procedures**

17. **Establish Plan Distribution and Control Procedures**
    a. Select support tools for the maintenance process
       1. Understand the advantages and disadvantages of word processing plans
       2. Understand the advantages and disadvantages of software support tools
       3. Understand maintenance implications when selecting support tools (e.g., questionnaires, database based, or with combined features, etc.)
    b. Integration with organization awareness programs
       1. Identify and integrate the various factors that influence the orientation and effectiveness of the business continuity program
       2. Integrate and establish input to any existing organization orientation training programs
       3. Integrate and arrange liaison functions with key business users

18. **Set Audit Objectives and Scope**
    a. Understand the different audit options and methods
    b. Understand possible viable structures for a business continuity plan, and the methods of controlling such a plan
    c. Understand the essential characteristics of a viable business resumption plan
    d. Recommend and agree upon objectives and scope for the audit

19. **Assess and Select Audit Method**
    a. Determine whether to conduct a preliminary study and identify appropriate method (e.g., by use of questionnaires, interviews with key personnel)
    b. Develop a schedule of audit activities
    c. Assess resource requirements for the audit activities

     d. Prepare an audit plan

     e. Prioritize audit area

     f. Be aware of available techniques for auditing business continuity plans, and select appropriate techniques to achieve the audit objectives

20. **Audit the Administrative Aspects of the Business Recovery Program**

     a. Devise a schedule to audit any or all the following

        1. Awareness and training

        2. Documentation

        3. Organization

        4. Vital records

        5. Stand-by facilities

        6. Maintenance

        7. Contracts, SLAs or other commitments

        8. Backup regimes

        9. Suppliers

        10. Exercises

        11. Logistics

21. **Audit the Plan's Structure, Contents, and Action Sections**

     a. Determine if a section in the Plan addresses recovery considerations

     b. Evaluate the adequacy of emergency provisions and procedures

     c. Recommend improved positions if weaknesses exist

22. **Audit the Plan's Documentation Control Procedures**

     a. Determine whether the Plan is available to key personnel

     b. Review update procedures

     c. Demonstrate that update procedures are effective

     d. Examine the provision of secure backup copies of the Plan for emergency use

     e. List those individuals with copies of the Plan

     f. Ensure that plan copies are current

Subject Area 9 — Public Relations and Crisis Coordination

Note: Details of this subject area vary from country to country, and from industry to industry. The following basic components should be considered in addition to those specific to your country and/or industry.

Develop, coordinate, evaluate, and exercise plans to handle media during crisis situations. Develop, coordinate, evaluate, and exercise plans to communicate with and, as appropriate, provide trauma counseling for employees and their families, key customers, critical suppliers, owners/ stockholders, and corporate management during crisis. Ensure all stakeholders are kept informed on an as-needed basis.

The professional's role is to

1. **Establish Public Relations Programs for Proactive Crisis Management**

2. **Establish Necessary Crisis Coordination with External Agencies**

3. **Establish Essential Crisis Communications with Relevant Stakeholder Groups**

4. **Establish and Test Media Handling Plans for the Organization and its Business Units**

The professional should demonstrate a working knowledge in the following areas.

1. **Identify Components of Proactive Public Relations Program**
   a. Internal (corporate and business unit level) groups
   b. External groups
   c. External agencies

2. **Identify External Agencies with Which Liaison Is Required**
   a. Local/state/national emergency services
   b. Local/state/national civilian defense authorities
   c. Local/state/national weather bureaus
   d. Other governmental agencies as appropriate

3. **Identify Stakeholder Groups and Establish Essential Communications Plans**
   a. Owners/stockholders
   b. Employees and their families
   c. Key customers
   d. Key suppliers
   e. Corporate/headquarters management
   f. Other stakeholders

4. **Establish and Exercise Media Handling Plans**
   a. Policies and procedures for media handling
   b. Plans and preparations for media handling
   c. Implement and exercise media handling plans

Subject Area 10 — Coordination with Public Authorities

Note: Details of this subject area vary from country to country, and from industry to industry. The following basic components should be considered in addition to those specific to your country and/or industry.

Establish applicable procedures and policies for coordinating continuity and restoration activities with local authorities while ensuring compliance with applicable statutes or regulations.

The professional's role is to

1. **Coordinate Emergency Preparations, Response, Recovery, Resumption, and Restoration Procedures with Public Authorities**

2. **Establish Liaison Procedures for Emergency/Disaster Scenarios**

3. **Maintain Current Knowledge of Laws and Regulations Concerning Emergency Procedures**

The professional should demonstrate a working knowledge in the following areas.

1. **Identify Applicable Laws and Regulations Governing Emergency Response**
   a. Gather/identify sources of information on applicable laws and regulations
   b. Gather disaster recovery, environmental cleanup, and business resumption requirements

2. **Identify and Coordinate with Agencies Supporting Disaster Recovery and Business Continuity**
   a. Identify statutory requirements for the industry in which the organization participates
   b. Identify and coordinate with public agencies providing disaster assistance (financial and resources); establish liaison procedures
   c. Work with statutory agencies to conform to legal and regulatory requirements

3. **Develop, Implement, and Exercise Plans to Meet Statutory Requirements**
   a. Ensure that plans conform to statutory requirements
   b. Ensure that plan execution is coordinated with public authorities where necessary or required under law (e.g., during a disaster

due to terrorism, bombing, or other criminal activities that
require intervention by public authorities)

c. Periodically review liaison procedures

SUPPLEMENTAL INFORMATION

North America
Edition: North America
While the Professional Practices for Business Continuity Planners provides
an international standard, this Appendix varies from country to country.
Sources and references cited in this version of Appendix A are located in
North America.

Business Continuity Planning Informational Materials

1. *Blueprint for Community Emergency Management*, Emergency
   Response Institute Inc., Olympia, WA, 1989.

2. *Business Resumption Guidelines* 6/93, California Office of Emergency
   Services Earthquake Program.

3. *Capability and Hazard Identification Program for Local Governments*,
   Federal Emergency Management Agency, U.S. Government Printing
   Office, Washington, DC, 1992.

4. *Civil Preparedness Guides* 1-3, 1-5, 1-8, 1-20, Federal Emergency
   Management Agency, Washington, DC, 1985.

5. *Crisis Management*, Ian Mitroff & Christine M. Pearson, Jossey Bass
   Publishers, San Francisco, CA, ISBN 1-55542-563-1, 1993 (139 pages).

6. *Disaster Planning for Health Care Facilities*, Hanna, James AL, Ottawa,
   Ontario, 1988, CHA.

7. *Disaster Planning Guide for Business and Industry*, Federal Emergency
   Management Agency, FEMA 141, August 1987.

8. *Disaster Response Principles of Preparation and Coordination*, Erik Auf
   der Heide, CV Mosby Co., St. Louis, MO, ISBN 0-8016-03854, 1989
   (363 pages).

9. *Disaster Services Regulations and Procedures — Disaster Mental Health
   Services*, American Red Cross, ARC 33050M, Nov.1991.

10. *Emergency Broadcast System Plan: Greater Portland/Vancouver
    Operational Area*, Greater Portland/Vancouver Emergency
    Broadcast System Operational Area Committee, Portland, OR,
    October 1993.

11. *Emergency Management Principles and Practice for Local Government,* International City Management Association, 1991.

12. *Emergency Planning for Industry, A National Standard of Canada,* CAN/CSA-Z73 1-M9 1, Canadian Standards Association, Toronto, Ontario, 1991.

13. *The Emergency Program Manager,* Federal Emergency Management Agency, HS — 1, February 1989.

14. *Exercise Design Course: Guide to Emergency Management Exercises;* SM 170.2, Federal Emergency Management Agency, Emergency Management Institute, U.S. Government Printing Office, Washington, DC, 1989.

15. *Exercise Design Course: Instructor Guide,* SM 170, Federal Emergency Management Agency, Emergency Management Institute, U.S Government Printing Office, Washington, DC, 1989.

16. *Exercise Design Course: Student Workbook;* SM 170.1, Federal Emergency Management Agency, Emergency Management Institute, U.S. Government Printing Office, Washington, DC, 1989.

17. *The Federal Response Plan,* Federal Emergency Management Agency, Washington, DC, 1992.

18. *Guidelines/or Hazard Evaluation Procedures: Second Edition with Worked Examples;* American Institute of Chemical Engineers, New York, NY, 1992, "Overview of Hazard Evaluation Techniques," pp.51-722.

19. *Industrial Emergency Preparedness,* Robert B. Kelly, Van Nostrand Reinhold, NY, NY, ISBN 0422-20483-3, 1989 (297 pages).

20. *Major Transportation Disasters Improving Response and Coordination,* American Hospital Association, Chicago, IL, 1991, AHA.

21. *Model Ordinances for Post-Disaster Recovery Andrea-construction,* California Office of Emergency Services, Sacramento, CA.

22. *Multi-hazard Functional Planning Guidance,* State of California; Governor's Office of Emergency Services, 1989.

23. NCRP Report #111, *Developing Emergency Radiation Plans/or Academic, Medical, or Industrial Facilities.*

24. NEPA 99, *Standard for Health Care Facilities,* 1993 edition, National Fire Protection Association, Quincy, MA.

25. NFPA 130, *Standard/or Fixed Guide Way Transit Systems,* 1995 edition, National Fire Protection Association, Quincy, MA.

26. NRT- 1 *Criteria/or Review of Hazardous Materials Emergency Plans.*

27. NUREG-0654 *Criteria for Preparation and Evaluation of Radiological Emergency Response Plans and Preparedness in Support of Nuclear Power Plants.*

28. NUREG-0849 *Standard Review Plan/or the Review and Evaluation of Emergency Plans for Research and Test Reactors.*

29. *Planning for Emergencies,* American Insurance Services Group, Engineering and Safety Services, NY, NY, 1991(54 pages).

30. Post-Disaster Safety Assessment Plan Program Organization and Response Procedures: A Guide to the Professional Organizations, California Office of Emergency Services, Sacramento, CA, June 1992.

31. Post-Disaster safety Assessment Plan: Local Building Officials' Guide to the Activation and Utilization of Safety Assessment Volunteers, California Office of Emergency Services, Sacramento, CA, June 1992.

32. Pre-Emergency Planning, 2nd Ed., William F. Jenaway, ISFS1, Ashland, MA, ISBN 9615990-2-2, 1992 (204 pages).

33. Statement of Understanding Between the American Hospital Association and the American National Red Cross with Respect to Responsibility for Disaster Preparedness and Relief, American Red Cross, Washington, DC, 1985.

34. Statement of Understanding Between the American Psychological Association and the American National Red Cross, American Red Cross, ARC 4468, Dec.1991.

Disaster Management and Related Organizations

United States

American Public Works Association Agency (APWA)
City of Boulder Director of Public Works
POBox 791
Boulder, CO 80306
(303) 441-3320 / (303) 441-4210 (FAX)

NEWSLETTER: Yes (The APWA Reporter)

Federal Emergency Management (FEMA)
HQ FEMA
Federal Center Plaza
500 C Street SW, Room 512
Washington, DC 20472
(202) 646-3692

NEWSLETTER: Yes

American Society for Public Administration
Emergency Management Section
5580 La Jolla Boulevard
La Jolla, CA 92037
(619) 549-3581

NEWSLETTER: Yes

International Association of Chiefs of Police (IACP)
Center for Police Traffic Safety
1110 N. Glebe Road, Suite 200
Arlington, VA 22201
(703) 243-6500

NEWSLETTER: Yes (IACP News)

FEMA National Emergency Training Center (NETC)
Chief, Emergency Management
Division, EMI
National Emergency Training Center
(NETC)
116825 South Seton Avenue
Emmitsburg, MD 21727
(301)4 47-1164 / (301) 447-1081 (FAX)

NEWSLETTER: No

National Association of Counties (NACO)
P0 Box 1431
Safety
Conrad, MT 59425
(406)278-7681

NEWSLETTER: Yes

National Association of Emergency Medical Technicians
9140 Ward Parkway
Kansas City, MO 64114
(816) 444-3500 / (816) 444-0330 (FAX)

NEWSLETTER: Yes (NAEMT News)
National Association of SARA Title III Program Officials (NASTTPO)
c/o Right-to-Know
Kansas Dept. of Health and
Environment
Mills Bldg., Suite 501
Topeka,KS 66612
(913) 296-1690

NEWSLETTER: No

International Association of Fire Chiefs (IAFC)
50 Eaglesville Road
Eaglesville, PA 91403
(215) 631-6507/(215) 631-6536 (FAX)

NEWSLETTER: Yes (On-Scene)

International City Management Association (ICMA)
Director Program Development
1120 G Street NW
Washington, DC 20005
(202) 289-4262/(202) 626-4661 (FAX)

NEWSLETTER: Yes (ICMA
Newsletter)

National Governors Association
Committee Director, Justice and
Hall of the States
444 North Capitol Street
Washington, DC 20001-15722
(202) 624-5300

NEWSLETTER: Yes (The
Governor's Bulletin)

REACT International, Inc.
POBox998
Wichita, KS 67201
(316) 263-2100 /
(316) 263-2118 (FAX)

NEWSLETTER: Yes (The REACTer)

National Coordinating Council on Emergency Management (NCCEM)
72297 Lee Highway, Suite N
Falls Church, VA 22042
(703) 533-7672

NEWSLETTER: Yes (NCCEM Bulletin)

National Emergency Management Association (NEMA)
PO Box 11910
Lexington, KY 40578-1910
(606)231-1876 / (606)231-1928 (FAX)

NEWSLETTER: Yes (NEMA News)

State Guard Association of the United States
PO Box 206
Lothian, MD 20711

(301) 261-9099 (phone and FAX)

NEWSLETTER: Yes (The Militia Journal)

Emergency Management and Related Organizations

Canada

Canada Coast Guard
Tower "A" Room 1244
Place de Ville
Ottawa, Ontario
Canada K1A ON7

Canadian Association of Fire Chiefs
1-2425 Don Reid Drive
Ottawa, Ontario
Canada K1H 1A4

Emergency Preparedness Canada
122 Bank Street, 2nd Floor
Ottawa, Ontario
Canada K1A OW6

Major Industrial Accidents Council of Canada
600-265 Carling Ave.
Ottawa Ontario
Canada KIA 2EI

Transport Canada
Ottawa, Ontario
Canada K1A ON5

Canadian Transport Commission
Les Terrasses de la Chaudiere
Ottawa, Ontario
Canada K1A ON9

Environment Canada
3439 River Road South
Ottawa, Ontario
Canada KIA OH3

Academic Institutions Involved in Business Continuity and Disaster Recovery Planning/Management

United States

Colorado State University
Hazards Assessment Laboratory
202 Aylesworth Hall
3890 Central Avenue
Fort Collins, CO 80523
(303) 491-5951

Memphis State University
Center for Earthquake Research and
Information
Memphis, TN 38152
(901) 678-2007

Texas A&M University
Hazard Reduction and Recovery
Center
College of Architecture
College Station, TX 77843-3137
(409) 845-7813

The University of Texas at Arlington
Center for Information Technologies
Management
PO Box 19437
Arlington, TX 76019
(817) 273-3569 / (817) 273-3502

University of California at Berkeley
Business and Management Division
2223 Fulton Street
Berkeley, CA 94720
(510) 642-4231

University of Colorado — Boulder
Natural Hazards Research/
Applications Center
Floodplain Management
Resource Center
Campus Box 482
Boulder, CO 80309-0492
(303) 492-6818

University of Delaware
Disaster Research Center
Newark, DE
(302) 451-6618

University of Nebraska — Lincoln
International Drought
Information Center
Center for Agriculture and
Meteorology
Lincoln, NE 68583-0728
(402) 472-3679

University of North Texas
PO Box 13438
Denton, TX 76203-3438
(817) 565-4077

University of Tennessee
Institute for Public Service
Suite 105
Student Services Administration
Building
Knoxville, TN 37996-0213
(615) 974-6621

Washington University in SL Louis
Center for the Application of Information
Technology
Campus Box 1141
1 Brookings Drive
St. Louis, MO 63130-4899
(314) 935-7575

Internet: www.cait.wustl.edu

Non-Government Business Continuity Organizations

United States

American Public Works Association
Council on Emergency Management
1313 East 60th Street
Chicago, IL 60637
(312) 667-2200

Association of Contingency Planners
P0 Box 73-149
Long Beach, CA 90801
(213) 398-2277

**Association of State Dam
Safety Officials**
P0 Box 55270
Lexington, KY 40355
(606) 257-5140

**Association of State
Floodplain Managers**
P0 Box 7921
Madison, WI 53707
(608) 266-1926

**Central U.S. Earthquake
Consortium**
2630 East Holmes Road
Memphis, TN 38118
(901)398-9054

**Chemical Manufacturers
Association**
Chemical Awareness/ER
Program
2501 M Street, NW
Washington, DC 20037
(202) 887-1150

**Disaster Recovery Institute
International**
1810 Craig Road, Suite 125
St. Louis, MO 63146
(314)434-2272 / (314)434-1260 Fax

**National Coordinating Council
on Emergency Management**
7297 Lee Highway, Suite N
Falls Church, VA 22042
(703) 533-7672

Building Seismic Safety Council
1201 L Street NW, Suite 400
Washington, DC 20005
(202) 289-7800

**Business Emergency Preparedness
Council**
125 N. Mid-America Mall, Room 2B49
Memphis, TN 38103
(901) 528-2980

SURVIVE! USA
1201 Mt. Kemble Avenue
Morristown, NJ 07960-6628
1 -800-SURVIVE

Oak Ridge National Laboratory
Hazard Management Group
MS: 6206, PO Box 2008
Oak Ridge, TN 37831-6206
(615) 576-2716

**Science Applications
International Corporation**
Engineering and Tech
Services Group
PO Box 2501
301 Laboratory Road
Oak Ridge, TN 37831
(615) 481-2909

Global Business Continuity Organizations

Leadership Coalition for Global Business Protection
1801K Street NW, Suite 100~L
Washington, DC 20006
(202) 530-0400 / (202) 530-4500 (FAX)

Appendix D
Sample BIA Introduction Letter

January 1, 1999

Iva Bucks
Chief Financial Officer
XYZ Corporation
4100 Enterprise Drive
Palo Alto, CA 94025

Dear Mr. Bucks:

XYZ Corporation asked the security department to assist the company with the development of business continuity (disaster recovery) plans for its major facilities at Menlo Park and Dublin. This request was motivated by concerns over regulatory requirements, the potential for loss from an extended business interruption, and by the degree of similar planning by major competitors. Also, the financial auditors listed the lack of effective recovery plans as a deficiency on their report.

The basis or starting point for this process is the development of a "Business Impact Analysis." During our meeting scheduled for Tuesday, April 2, 1997, at 10:00 A.M., we will ask you to help us determine the financial impact to XYZ from the loss of individual critical business functions over time. We will use this information to:

- Demonstrate loss potential to senior management
- Form the basis for the planning process
- Evaluate or verify a function's "outage tolerance"
- Prioritize recovery actions and resources
- Focus our questions to other managers we may need to interview.

We will provide a questionnaire to help explain what information is needed and to assist you and your staff with the assembly of this information. All data and results are maintained according to our confidentiality agreements.

Sincerely,

Eugene Tucker, CFE, CPP
Assistant Vice President
Business Continuity Planning

Appendix E
Sample Kidnap and Ransom Contingency Plan

This plan was designed to fit the needs of a particular company with a unique K&R exposure. It is not a blueprint that can or should be followed by any other organization, though parts of it will apply to most K&R situations.

I. INTRODUCTION

Even the most carefully tailored security procedures sometimes are not enough. As evidenced by repeated bombings, kidnappings, extortion plots, and other acts of violence, security procedures are not infallible; they can be compromised or penetrated. For this reason, it is vitally important for this company to have a written contingency plan that outlines some of the steps to be taken in the event a kidnap or extortion plot against the company becomes an actuality. The threat/risk ratio for _____ has been assessed as low to medium. Therefore, some security precautions are deemed to be essential. Should the threat/risk ratio change, it will be necessary to review the existing security program to reassess the level of security and determine if it is adequate in view of the changing circumstances.

Note: The contents of this report are confidential. The details contained herein should receive limited distribution.

II. BASIC PLAN

A. Policy Regarding Ransom

Company policy is that a reasonable ransom or extortion will be paid in the event of a kidnap of one or more corporate officials or members of their immediate families. The same applies in the event of an extortionate plot against the company. The limitations of our insurance coverage are as follows:

1. Dollar limitations
2. Persons covered (general)

Note: A copy of the insurance policy covering kidnap and extortion should be attached hereto as an exhibit and remain a permanent part of this file. [The existence of this document is usually "confidential."]

B. Crisis Management Team Composition

Members of the crisis management team should include those few individuals having authority to implement and carry out the policy as dictated by the board of directors and the procedures contained in this plan. The presence of more than five people on this team could easily lead to confusion at a time when confusion is least desirable. In addition, the team should be aware that all the resources, in terms of manpower and material, of the company are available for their use on an ad hoc basis.

Members of the team should include:

1. The coordinator, chairman of the board or chief executive officer
2. President and chief operating officer
3. Executive vice president of finance
4. Executive vice president of operations
5. Executive vice president of administrative and technical services

Other members of the team may vary, depending on the nature of the threat or demand or whether the crisis occurs in [company's location], the United States, or a foreign country.

C. The Coordinator (and Alternate)

The coordinator's function is to implement the plan and procedures and to coordinate the crisis operation. He should also be the person with the top decision-making authority. In the event that _____ becomes a victim, the next person in line of succession in the crisis management team would be the alternate coordinator. In the event he or she is unavailable, the next in line of succession would be _____. [The line of succession must be worked out in advance. You may wish to reduce this succession policy to writing. A copy of this policy should then be attached to this document as an exhibit.]

The coordinator, _____ (code name "Mr./Ms. Adams," when dealing with a kidnaper or extortionist) will not act as the negotiator. It is vitally important that the task of negotiator be assigned to only one person—a person who has had training as a negotiator in criminal situations. In this case, we strongly recommend that _____ Vice President, Industrial

Relations, who has been trained in union negotiations, be trained for crim-
inal-type negotiations. In the event of a kidnap or ransom against the company [he/she] would become an ad hoc member of the team, serving in the
capacity as negotiator and advisor. Mr./Ms. _____ should also direct the
preparation of the list of names and related information, which will become
a permanent part of this plan (see Exhibit G-1).

In addition, the coordinator shall:

1. Formulate plans and procedures for handling crisis situations.
2. Gather an advisory staff (if deemed appropriate) to generate information and perform services to facilitate these procedures. Example:
   a member of the legal staff may be necessary to review the plans for
   compliance with established corporate policy.
3. Maintain in a secure place the current crisis management plan and
   procedures.
4. Communicate these plans and procedures to only authorized persons, and follow-up to ensure that these individuals are fully cognizant of any changes in plan or procedures.
5. Maintain current personal information and biographies of all corporate executives in a secure place. The personnel department maintains a very limited amount of biographical information pertaining
   to company executives. Enclosed with this document is a biographical inventory. We recommend all executives complete the document,
   to be placed in their individual personnel files where they can be
   quickly located in the event of an emergency.
6. Recruit and train the personnel necessary to carry out the crisis management program.
7. Exercise good judgment in determining the course of action in any
   crisis situation not covered by approved policy.
8. Implement plans and procedures according to the management plan.

D. The Crisis Management Center

The purpose of the crisis management center is to serve as the focal point for
directing a coordinated and planned response during a crisis situation. It
should be located within the organization's headquarters facility at or in the
executive conference room. It should be furnished with all documents, supplies, and communications that may be needed during a crisis. At the minimum, items such as tape recorders, office equipment, computers, and a log
to record all calls and actions taken will be necessary.

E. Crisis Management Plan (CMP) Implementation

When an executive, employee, or family member becomes the victim of a kidnap, or the company becomes the victim of an extortion or terrorist plot, the organization will respond by implementing the CMP. The authority to implement the plan must be clearly spelled out. Implementation criteria should be defined:

1. Who has the authority to implement the crisis management plan?
    a. Chairman of the board or chief executive officer.
    b. Alternatively, the president and chief operating officer.
2. What are the minimum circumstances that must exist for this authority to become effective (example: if a threat of kidnapping is received)?
    a. Time period of duration that this authority will remain in effect is: (example: until the crisis is satisfactorily resolved).
    b. Succession of this authority should the holder be removed or incapacitated: (names).

F. The Crisis Management Program

When an extortion demand or threat is received, it should be immediately reported to the decision-making authority, as outlined in the crisis management plan. The decision as to when this crisis management program should be implemented will depend on the following factors:

1. Threat verification (true/false)
2. Threat analysis:
    a. How valid is the threat?
    b. Who is doing the threatening?
        • Terrorists (political). Like their counterparts in other countries, these people are the most dangerous. One of their principal goals is publicity, which can be accomplished most effectively by shock tactics. A large multinational company or utility represents a prime target.
        • Criminals. Many criminals in foreign countries have turned to kidnapping, extortion, and other terrorist tactics for criminal gain. Since the goals of these people are identifiable, they are usually open to bargaining, and their demands can be negotiated.
        • The Mentally Ill. This is the fanatic whose sense of values is at odds with those of society. This person if often prepared to

die or go to jail for a cause. In this category fall the cunning, the clever, and the inept. They are always unpredictable and therefore hard to plan for and deal with. Also, as in the case of the "Unibomber," they are also difficult to identify, locate, and arrest.

Note: Most kidnappings are carried out by criminals or the mentally ill. Although kidnappers seeking publicity or nonmonetary rewards usually select large companies, those wanting money frequently select a prominent official of a medium-sized company. Most such organizations have considerable amounts of money available and do not have blanket policies against paying ransom money.

Note: Threat analysis in complicated cases is usually best left to trained security, risk management, or law enforcement personnel. The tools of threat analysis should be used only as aids in decision making. Total reliance on any one method or tool may cause serious error. In a situation as complicated and dangerous as a kidnapping, all factors must be weighed in order to arrive at effective resolutions.

G. Verification of the Validity of the Threat

1. Does a threat exist?
2. Is the threat as serious, more serious, or less serious than the creator of the threat would have us believe?
3. What is the present vulnerability of the intended victim of the threat? How will this vulnerability increase if we:
   a. Ignore the demands?
   b. Grant the demands?
   c. Engage in prolonged negotiations?

H. The Threateners

1. Can we identify the individual or group responsible for the threat?
2. Can we pinpoint the origin of the threat (physical location)?
3. What is the previous history or experience of this type of threat in this specific environment? (Law enforcement input here is usually necessary.)
4. What is the previous history of other organizations experiencing this type of threat in this specific environment? (In some foreign locations the police may not be privy to this data.)

5. What type of threat are we faced with?
   a. A simple extortion?
   b. A simple threat, no demands?
   c. A demand without a threat?
   d. What does the type of threat indicate about the demanders' view of the company?
   e. What does the type of threat indicate about the group or person making the threat?
6. How was the threat delivered?
   a. Verbally, telephone (see Exhibit G-2, ransom demand telephone checklist).
   b. By messenger:
      i. Delivered
      ii. Mailed
      iii. Found at crime scene in a protected area.
   c. What does the manner in which the threat was delivered indicate about:
      i. The individual or group making the threat?
      ii. The location of the individual or the group making the threat?
      iii. The nature of the group or individual making the threat?
7. What is the nature of the demand, if any?
   a. Who, or what is the precise victim?
   b. Who is or will become the victim(s) if the demand is not met?
   c. Are demands:
      i. Within the realm of possibility? (Release of political prisoners, for example, is something most corporations cannot influence, much less accomplish.)
      ii. Of propaganda value to the threatener? (Usually a tactic of terrorists.)
8. Who is making the demand?

Note: All the above information plus any other data available that may be helpful must be collected and analyzed in order to evaluate the validity of a threat. Time is a critical element in threat analysis. In situations where time is very short, it must not be wasted on deciding what categories of data are most necessary to be collected prior to analysis.

All genuine threats will be manifestations of careful preplanning. Only a preplanned response will suffice to meet such a threat. Such preplanning in threat analysis must begin from the very inception of the threat. Remember, time is of the essence. Few sophisticated kidnappers (extortionists) will allow you much time for decision making. Hence, as much contingency planning as possible must be accomplished prior to the actual receipt of a threat.

I. Resources of Verification

Listed below are some resources one might consider using to verify the genuineness of a threat, providing of course that there is sufficient time:

1. Corporation-processed pre-event data (may indicate a kidnapper has inside information).
2. Prearranged codes and procedures. For example, "Mr./Ms. Adams" (the coordinator) to "Mr./Ms. Able" (the kidnapper-extortionist). This will preclude an opportunist from taking advantage of publicity.
3. Local and national law enforcement liaison.
    a. The Federal Bureau of Investigation (FBI)
    b. The Department of Public Safety (State level).
4. The Office of Security, U.S. Department of State (if the victim is overseas).
5. Host government liaison (if overseas).
6. Propaganda analysis (for terrorists).
7. Psychological stress evaluator (PSE), if conversation tapes are available.
8. Psychiatric analysis.
9. Psycholinguistics (tapes only).
10. Graphology (document examination).
11. Forensic document examination.
12. Voice-print analysis (tapes only).
13. Electronic tracing.
14. Noise analysis.
15. Previous case histories.

Note: In most cases, the initial threat is communicated by telephone, so that demands can receive maximum attention with minimum delay. The information contained in the threat messages is of vital importance.

Ideally, the initial threat message should be recorded. In practice, this is seldom accomplished, although, with preplanning, any secondary, and beyond-threat messages can and should be recorded. (Usually the FBI or local law enforcement will arrange to do this.)

Alternatively, the threat call must be reduced to detailed notes. A form to assist in this task is attached and should be furnished to the central switchboard operator. It should be located at or near the telephone in an inconspicuous place, for ready reference (see Exhibit G-2, sample ransom demand telephone checklist).

All demands must be communicated to the crisis management team via oral or written message. Analysis of the communication itself can often reveal a great deal about the character of the individuals making the demand and may also reveal if the threat implicit in the demand is genuine or not.

J. Analysis

The purpose of threat analysis is to turn any form of threat into a manageable problem that can be analyzed and then neutralized or controlled by the crisis management team. A schematic of the crisis management process is as follows:

1. Preplanning.
   a. Resource identification.
   b. Crisis program operating on standby.
2. Threat reception: competent reception of threat and the circumstances of its receipt.
3. Threat verification: what must we know to be certain that the threat is real?
4. Threat analysis: what must we know to determine:
   a. Threat level?
   b. Identification of threateners?
   c. Safety of personnel/assets?
   d. Validity of negotiations?
   e. Origin of threat and location of our personnel?
   f. Real goal of the threatener?
   g. Creation of a risk matrix (if deemed necessary)?
5. Threat response: what steps must be taken to neutralize or control the threat and guarantee the safety of our personnel and assets?

K. Extortion Demands

The demands criminals, terrorists, and mentally ill persons make in these cases usually fall into one or more of the following categories:

1. The amount of ransom money for the safe return of a kidnapped executive or a member of his or her family depends upon:
   a. The wealth of the organization.
   b. The criminal's (terrorist's) needs.
   c. An intention to demand a "measured quota" from the organization.
   d. "Value" of the kidnap victim in the criminal's perception.
2. Medical supplies for hospitals, public works, and the like, in exchange for the hostage.
3. Public recognition of their cause (terrorists).

4. Release of fellow gang members jailed by authorities.
5. Protest against national politics and policies, or those of the victim organization.
6. To embarrass the organization, victim, or victim's family.

Note: Prenegotiation preparation and training should cover the possibility of more than one of the above demands being presented.

L. Presentation of Demands

Characteristics of the demands of some criminals and most terrorist organizations are:

1. The demands are nonnegotiable (at least in the beginning).
2. All demands (if more than one) must be met in full.
3. Time periods are usually short and are often established at the outset. The initial demands and time frames are rarely realistic.
4. The consequences may be the prompt carrying out of the threat if the demands are not met.

M. Response

The response of the organization to the demands will probably be determined by the policy of agreeing to negotiate for "reasonable" ransom demands, as set forth above (paragraph II.A).

N. Counterdemands and Proposals

Depending on the information available, the crisis management team may respond as follows:

1. By asking for (actually, demanding) proof that the executive (victim) is still alive and unharmed. (Captors can be required to supply any item of personal identification; however, a handwritten letter—containing a key phrase or code that we dictate—would be the preferred proof. The letter should contain the date and time it was written.)
2. By asking for the exact time and place of the executive's (victim's) release if the agreement on demands can be reached.
3. By asking for time to study the demands and raise the currency. (You may not get it, but ask for it anyway.)

Note: It is extremely important that the crisis management team signal that all reasonable demands can be negotiated and will be met, providing the safety of the executive (victim) can be assured. The reverse should also be stressed—that without a firm guarantee that the victim will be released unharmed, neither the money nor any other demand will be delivered. The remaining part of the plan can then be accomplished by negotiation. The best policy regarding negotiation is to play for time, total agreement, and guarantees.

O. Insurance

The insurance policy should be given close scrutiny at this point. Look closely at the coverage and restrictions to ensure that you are in full compliance. The following items should be reviewed:

1. Publicity regarding the policy.
2. Genuineness of the extortion demand.
3. The specific names or titles of the persons covered in the policy.
4. Coverage of executives in particular job categories.
5. Whether payment must be made under duress.
6. Cooperation by the insured with law enforcement.

Exhibit G-1. List of Executives and Personnel

---

1. Executives and Publicity Identified Personnel
    Name   Title

    _____   _____
    _____   _____
    _____   _____

2. Branch or Profit Center Executive Personnel
    Name   Title

    _____   _____
    _____   _____
    _____   _____

3. Personnel to Authorize Ransom Payment (2 needed)

    _____
    _____

Exhibit G-1. List of Executives and Personnel *(continued)*

---

4. Name of Financial Institution
   Contact: _____
   Telephone Number: _____

5. Personnel to Administer Payment and Plan/Draw Payment (1)

   _____

   _____

7. Personnel to Handle Police, Press Contact (1)
   Press: _____
   Police: _____
   Federal Bureau of Investigation: _____

   _____

8. Persons to Be Notified of Demand
   Name   Telephone (Office)   (Home)

   _____   _____   _____

   _____   _____   _____

   _____   _____   _____

Exhibit G-2. Ransom Demand Telephone Checklist

Time of Call _____

Make every attempt to gain as much information from the caller as he will furnish, but do not give the caller the impression you are reading questions from a checklist or are trying to keep him on the line so the call can be traced. Write down the responses of the caller *word for word.*

Would you please repeat your statement?

Who is making this demand?

How do I know this is not a joke? We get many pranks here.

Exhibit G-2. Ransom Demand Telephone Checklist *(continued)*

IF A KIDNAP:

What is (he, she) wearing? _____

May I talk to (him, her)? _____

Could you explain what you want? _____

I will have to give your demands to my superior. We will want you to include the word (key word)* and the number (key number)** in all future communications with us.

If the caller gets into specifics on payment, ask, "What do you want"?

If money: what currency and how do you want it? _____

Where and when should the ransom be delivered? _____

How should the payment be made? _____

End the call on a positive note, by assuring the caller his demand will be communicated to the proper person in the company as soon as possible. Leave the caller with the impression that his or her call has been understood and action will be taken. Make note of the following information.

Time call ended: _____

Background noises _____

Sex of caller _____

Approximate age _____

Any accent _____

Any voice peculiarity such as lisp or stutter _____

What was the caller's attitude? _____

Was the caller sober? _____

Did the caller sound educated? _____

What did you notice about the call that you find unusual? _____

If the caller seemed familiar with the building or operation indicate how _____

---

*Recognition code has been established as: Mr. Adams

**Private unlisted telephone number

Exhibit G-3. Negotiator with the Family

---

1. KEEP THE FAMILY AS CALM AND AS UNWORRIED AS POSSIBLE. Assure the family that the company is doing, and will do, everything possible for the safe release and return of the victim. Assist the family by doing small chores. Try to have the family resume normal activities as far as is possible. Act cheerful and confident.
2. If possible, the family members should not be interviewed by the news media. Younger family members, especially teenagers, might reveal detailed information that might jeopardize the success of your operation.
3. If necessary for its safety, comfort, and security, move the family to a safe haven—for instance, a motel in a secluded location, until the situation is resolved. The police will usually cooperate by assigning protection to the family. If not, hire a private bodyguard.
4. COOPERATE WITH OTHER NEGOTIATORS SO THAT EVERYONE CONCERNED IS AWARE OF THE SITUATION. Do not discuss the situation with anyone other than your fellow negotiators.

Exhibit G-4. Negotiator with Law Enforcement

---

1. AS SOON AS PRACTICAL, NOTIFY LAW ENFORCEMENT OF THE SITUATION. Most terrorist situations are under the joint jurisdiction of federal and local authorities. The Federal Bureau of Investigation (FBI) and the U.S. Postal Service are concerned with possible federal law violations; local police are concerned with possible local law violations.
2. BE HONEST AND FRANK WITH LAW ENFORCEMENT. In all situations, law enforcement will cooperate with you, and with each other, for the safe return of the victim. Law enforcement agencies will do nothing to jeopardize the safe return of the victim and will conduct investigations in a covert manner until the victim is returned.
3. HONESTLY ASSESS THE CAPABILITIES OF LAW ENFORCEMENT. In some communities, local police have limited capabilities and experience. In such cases, it will be better to notify the FBI first, for their primary investigative activity and to make sure that a capable investigation is conducted. Local law enforcement, in this case, would handle secondary investigation, upon notification by the FBI.

Exhibit G-4. Negotiator with Law Enforcement *(continued)*

---

4. COOPERATE WITH OTHER NEGOTIATORS. Cooperate so that everyone concerned is aware of the situation. Do not discuss the situation with anyone other than your fellow negotiators.
5. LOCAL POLICE ARE CLOSELY CONNECTED TO THE PRESS. A telephone call to the local police switchboard or emergency number will usually be monitored by the press and television news reporters. If you are to exercise any control over the press, let the FBI notify the local police in every instance.

Exhibit G-5. Negotiator with the Media

---

1. REMAIN IN CONTROL OF ALL INFORMATION RELEASED TO THE MEDIA. It is better for the safe return of the victim that as little detailed information as possible be released to the press, television, and radio. You can admit that a situation exists, but do not reveal any details about the family situation, the amount of ransom demanded, or the details of the ransom delivery. In a terrorist situation where the safety of personnel is at stake, it is better to release too little rather than too much information. Law enforcement advice should be sought about the release of specific details. Criminals and terrorists read the papers and listen to news broadcasts. If too many details are furnished:
   - Sick, antisocial, or greedy people may enter the picture and complicate things by fraudulent attempts to get money (this is why code names are necessary in all negotiations with the kidnappers);
   - Overly aggressive news reporters might complicate funds delivery by close surveillance;
   - The efforts of law enforcement to secure the return of the victim, to apprehend the kidnappers, or to recover the ransom funds might be jeopardized.
2. A SINGLE PERSON SHOULD HANDLE ALL CONTACTS WITH THE MEDIA. All other people should refer any contacts from the media to that one person. This will prevent the media from playing one official against another to obtain more information. It will also permit the controlled release of nonvital information. It is standard media procedure to induce a person, by feeding his or her self-importance, to release small details that are then used to confront a second person in an attempt to extract more substantial information.

Exhibit G-5. Negotiator with the Media *(continued)*

---

3. DO RELEASE TO THE MEDIA ALL DETAILS ABOUT SPECIAL MEDICATION OR TREATMENT NEEDED BY THE VICTIM.
4. REMEMBER AT ALL TIMES THAT YOU DO NOT HAVE TO ANSWER ANY QUESTIONS by the media or anyone else, except in a court under subpoena. Many people feel that they should, or have to, answer questions from the media or well-intentioned citizens. Learn to say, "I'll have to get back to you later with the answer to that question."
5. COOPERATE WITH OTHER NEGOTIATORS so that everyone concerned is aware of the situation. Do not discuss the situation with anyone other than your fellow negotiators.

Exhibit G-6. Negotiator with Terrorists

---

1. TRY TO MAKE SURE THE VICTIM IS ALIVE. If you can talk to the terrorist, tell him honestly:
   - That you will do everything for the release of the victim.
   - That you just want to make sure that the victim is unharmed.
   - That you would like the victim to write a note to you or say something to you so that you know positively that he is alive and unharmed. (Dictate a key phrase to be included in the note.)
2. ASK THE TERRORIST TO REFER TO HIM OR HERSELF BY A CODE NAME that you agree upon, so that you will know that you are talking to the same person each time. Do not reveal the code name to anybody until after the victim is released. It is common for several different people to try to collect a ransom in any publicized kidnapping. Give each person calling a different code name. Use a neutral or even a favorable code name, not a derogatory one— "Robin Hood," rather than "Dirty Tom."
3. OBTAIN AND REPEAT INSTRUCTIONS FOR FUNDS DELIVERY. If possible, work out alternate instructions in case you cannot comply fully with the original instructions.
4. ENDEAVOR TO LESSEN THE AMOUNT OF FUNDS BEING DELIVERED. Since the safety of the victim is most important, do not haggle over the amount of funds. However, if the opportunity arises, tell the terrorist that you can obtain one-half or one-third for immediate, same-day delivery to any spot he or she wants, but that delivery of the full amount might take longer since you need higher authorization. If the terrorist is intransigent, drop the subject immediately.

Exhibit G-6. Negotiator with Terrorists *(continued)*

---

5. ASSURE THE TERRORIST THAT THE TELEPHONE IS NOT BEING TAPPED, THAT LAW ENFORCEMENT HAS NOT BEEN INVOLVED, AND THAT THE NEWS MEDIA IS BEING KEPT OUT (but only if he or she brings up these subjects first).
6. COOPERATE WITH OTHER NEGOTIATORS so that everyone concerned is aware of the situation. Do not discuss the situation with anyone other than your fellow negotiators.

Exhibit G-7. Sample Notification of Company Policy

The personal safety and well-being of all of your employees and their families is very important to the company. This cannot be overemphasized. While your company does not believe that the company, or the employees, will be the object of any criminal actions, the following procedures for action are being set out for your guidance.

In any situation involving a hostage, ransom, or extortion, the only important consideration is the safety of our personnel, of their family members, and their safe return.

In any criminal situation or in any questionable situation, notify a company official as promptly and as completely as is possible. Do not delay action to investigate the matter fully just so you can give complete details to a company official.

The company official, and his alternate, are:
Notify _____

_____ Office Phone

_____ Home Phone

_____ Alternative

_____ Office Phone

_____ Home Phone

Distribution: All company offices, managers, and supervisory personnel.

Exhibit G-8. Executive Biographical Inventory (to be retained in the individual's personnel file)

NAME: _____

NICKNAME (FOR IDENTIFICATION): _____

ADDRESS: _____

ALTERNATE ADDRESS SUMMER, ETC.): _____

DESCRIPTION: AGE _____ BIRTHDATE _____

      PLACE OF BIRTH _____ HEIGHT _____

      WEIGHT _____ COLOR OF HAIR _____

      SEX _____ NOTICEABLE PHYSICAL TRAITS _____

      _____

HOME PHONE: _____

WIFE: _____

ADDRESS OF WIFE: _____

DESCRIPTION OF WIFE: _____

VEHICLES: _____

   LICENSE   STATE   DESCRIPTION

1. _____   _____   _____

2. _____   _____   _____

3. _____   _____   _____

CODE: FAVORITE BOOK _____ FAVORITE SPORT _____

MEDICAL EMERGENCY INFORMATION: _____

DOCTOR'S NAME: _____ PHONE: _____

SPECIAL MEDICATION: _____

Exhibit G-8. Executive Biographical Inventory (to be retained in the individual's personnel file) *(continued)*

(BACK OF CARD)

HOUSEHOLD MEMBERS:

1. NAME: _____ RELATIONSHIP: _____
    ADDRESS: _____
    DESCRIPTION: _____

    _____

MEDICAL EMERGENCY INFORMATION: _____

    _____

2. NAME: _____ RELATIONSHIP: _____
    ADDRESS: _____
    DESCRIPTION: _____

    _____

MEDICAL EMERGENCY INFORMATION: _____

    _____

3. NAME: _____ RELATIONSHIP: _____
    ADDRESS: _____
    DESCRIPTION: _____

    _____

MEDICAL EMERGENCY INFORMATION: _____

    _____

FINGERPRINTED? _____

BLOOD TYPE: _____

LOCATION IF NOT IN FILE: _____

RECENT PHOTOGRAPH: _____

LOCATION IF NOT IN FILE: _____

Appendix F
How to Establish Notice

SOURCES OF DATA

Local Police Departments

Check with the crime prevention bureau, department of statistics, administration, or public information officer (PIO). Some departments use software programs to print color maps of crime incidents for selected distances around a particular address. Check with other agencies such as transit police for information on crimes committed in their jurisdictions.

News Media

Newspapers, TV, and radio reporters, as well as their archives are good sources of information. These can be researched in person at the publication's office, through a local library, or by using on-line searching.

Subpoena

This can include police records, crime prevention or physical security surveys completed by police, security, or insurance auditors, insurance loss runs, and electronic mail records.

State and FBI Unified Crime Reports

The FBI compiles crime data from across the nation and reports it by city, region, category, age, and other categories. A copy of "Crime in the Untied States" can be found at the local library or at the FBI and other Internet sites.

ATF/FBI Arson and Bomb Reports

Publications from these agencies contain information on the prevalence of arson and bombing across the United States. The National Fire Protection Association (Quincy, MA) also maintains data on suspicious fires.

Victimization Studies

Victimization studies rely not on arrest or conviction information but on surveys of the general population's experience with crime. See "National Crime Victimization Survey" Washington, D.C., Bureau of Justice Statistics.

Valid Internal or External Surveys

Survey the employee population about its experience with crime in and around the business. Ensure that the results are statistically valid.

Centers for Disease Control and Prevention (CDC)

The CDC maintains information on a range of topics that include violence in the workplace, the use of firearms, and other violent crimes.

Local College Campuses

Although most college campuses are required by law to maintain crime data, crime committed on college campuses may not be reflected in local reporting sources.

Canvassing

Anecdotal information from interviews with patrons, employees, and community members are useful as a double check and can lead the investigator to sources others may miss. Speak with:

- Neighbors
- Competitors
- Fire and ambulance crews
- Union representatives
- Security officers
- Postal carriers
- Regular delivery drivers and suppliers (Federal Express, UPS).

Public Library

Many of the sources listed above can be found at the public library. You can also research past news articles for information at the library or connect through its Web site to clipping services.

Surrounding Businesses or Corporations

Examine their incident reports and records and interview longtime employees who would have knowledge of crime, such as the human resources director, security manager, and insurance/risk manager (for insurance loss reports).

Bureau of Justice Statistics

The National Incident-Based Reporting System NIBRS), Criminal Victimization in the U.S., Violence and Theft in the Workplace, and Sourcebook of Criminal Justice Statistics are some of the useful databases and publications available from the Bureau of Justice Statistics in Washington, DC.

INCIDENT CLASSIFICATIONS

The following list can be used to help track the occurrence of crimes and incidents. Additional subheadings or subclassifications for crimes committed by employees (internal) or from crimes and incidents committed by customers or guests (external) can be included, depending upon the needs of the firm. Robbery can be further divided by including theft by pick pocket (not robbery in some states), purse snatch, or some other division.

Arson
   Actual
   Suspected
Assault
   Simple
   Aggravated (weapon)
Attempted rape
   By employee
   By nonemployee
   Sexual

Burglary
  Attempted
  Forced entry
Computer-related crimes
  Attempted break-in
  Disclosure of passwords
Embezzlement
  Money laundering
  Kickbacks
  Technology transfer
  Extortion
  Forgery
  Counterfeiting
  Misappropriation of funds
Domestic violence "spillover"
Insurance (worker compensation) fraud
Homicide
Kidnapping
  Perpetrator known to victim
  Perpetrator unknown
  Executive or key employee
  Attempted
  Threatened
Theft
  Auto
  Proprietary information
  From auto
  Funds
  Product
  Diversion
  Misappropriation
  Raw materials
  Precious metals
  Personal items
Disturbance
Disorderly conduct
Sabotage
  Suspected
  Product tampering
Vandalism, Malicious Mischief
  Vehicles
  Tagging, graffiti
Suspicious circumstances

Indecent exposure
Possession or disclosure of objectionable material
Sexual harassment or unwanted advances
Tailgating
Corporate rule violations
Parking violations
Vehicle violations
Vehicle towed
Fire access blocked
Other vehicle code violations
Substance abuse
   Possession
   Sales
   Under influence
Hit and run
Property damage
Robbery
   Strong arm
   Weapon
   Force/fear
Suicide
   Actual
   Attempted
   Threatened
Access control
   Attempted entry
   Unauthorized entry
   Badge missing/stolen
   Misuse of badge/card
   Loaning access control card
Bombing
   Explosion
   Incendiary
   Threat
   Intelligence/information
Trespassing
Prostitution
Gambling
Gang activity
Alarms
   Security
   Fire
   Environmental

Process control
Maintenance
  Lighting
  Fencing
  Locks/doors
  Glazing
  Doors/gates/windows open
  Shrubbery/landscaping
Escort requests
Police contacts
Solicitation/special interest
Telecommunications Fraud
Misuse of company equipment/services
Obscene/harassing phone calls
Demonstrations/picketers
First aid/medical
Safety hazards
Terrorist threat
Stalking

Appendix G
Handling Media Inquiries

Most crisis management/public relations disasters result from a firm's inability to communicate effectively with the media rather than from the incident that propelled them to public scrutiny. The following is a basic list of media interview do's and don'ts:

- Do establish a warm, friendly, businesslike attitude.
- Do prepare a brief, three-to-five-sentence message introduction.
- Do answer Who, What, When, Where, Why, How.
- Do prepare to respond openly to criticism.
- Do anticipate questions and develop answers.
- Do speak slowly after silent moments.
- Do keep answers short — use silence effectively.
- Do ask questions that test understanding/acceptance.
- Do be sensitive to time constraints/deadlines.
- Do speak candidly, but accurately.
- Do repeat or rephrase questions for an audience before answering.
- Do use your own words when answering questions.
- Do use "communications bridging" tactics to change the focus of a question to an issue you wish to make and away from the topic a reporter wishes to make.
- Do lead the media "conversation."
- Do commit to follow up with answers.
- Don't frustrate a reporters need for basic answers.
- Don't use highly technical jargon.
- Don't talk to or at reporters–talk with them.
- Don't cite competitors by name if your statement is derogatory.
- Don't make financial or product projections.
- Don't expect every media person to be well prepared or friendly.
- Don't be afraid to say you can't answer a question.
- Don't say "no comment." The public equates this term with dishonesty and deception. If the media does not get a comment from you or from the company spokesperson, they will seek out someone who will. Most often this person, such as an employee of the firm, will have nothing to offer but speculation. Rephrasing your response in a manner that avoids "no comment" is acceptable, but phrasing it in a positive manner gets better results.

Instead of answering "We can't make a statement until we have read the legal documents" try "We will be happy to make a statement after we read the legal documents."

- Don't use trigger words from a question in your answer.
- Don't attempt to influence editorial reporting by promising or referring to advertising.

BIBLIOGRAPHY

Max Ckonjevic, FBIC, CGCP. Presentation to the "Survive Conference." San Francisco, 1997.

Lawrence Barton. *Crisis in Organizations: Managing and Communicating in the Heat of Chaos,* Southwestern, 1993.

Peter Schwartz. *The Art of the Long View.* Doubleday Dell, 1991.

Appendix H
Security Systems Specifications

June 1999

Dear Mr._____

The XYZ Company invites you to participate in the bidding process to provide an integrated intrusion detection/fire detection, access control, and closed-circuit television system at the facilities located in Torrance, California.

Attached to this request for proposal (RFP) is the specification which provides the requirements for the system integration. A bidders' conference and a job walk will be held at [time] on [date]. The bidders' conference and the job walk will be held at 2727 Sepulveda Street, Torrance, California. Responses to the RFP are due by [time] on [date]. Contract award will be approximately 30 days following receipt of the RFP. Should you decline to participate in the bidding process, please advise me as soon as possible. If you have questions regarding the specification prior to the bidders' conference and job walk, please call John Doe, Security Manager, XYZ Company, at (310)2794005.

Sincerely,

Richard Murphy
President & Chief Operating Officer

Enclosure

INTRODUCTION

A specification is a detailed, exact statement of particulars, especially a statement prescribing materials, dimensions, and quality of work for something to be built, installed, or manufactured.[1] A specification for a security system is a part of a request for proposal (RFP) and should provide the bidders as many details as possible. The need for a selection/evaluation team to prepare the RFP is mandatory and should consist of security, finance, procurement, facilities, operational personnel, and other functions deemed appropriate. The selection/evaluation team is normally chaired by security. The selection/evaluation team jointly prepares the specification and jointly reviews the responses to the RFP.

Prior to issuing the RFP, a bidder's questionnaire should be sent to a select group of suppliers that perform the type of work being requested. The questionnaire should ask questions that are designed to qualify bidders who can perform the desired work as well as eliminate those who cannot. Questions asked may include, but need not be limited to, the size of the company, the length of time in the business, and references (past and present) where similar work was performed. To aid in the evaluation process, a form should be used that assigns weighted values to the questions asked in the questionnaire. Another form should be prepared that assigns weighted values when evaluating the responses to the RFPs. Evaluation criteria includes pricing as well as overall responsiveness to all elements of the RFP. These forms will aid the selection/evaluation team in the selection of the successful bidder.

Following transmission of the RFP but prior to the receipt of the responses, a bidders' conference and job walk should be conducted. The bidder's conference provides the bidders with equal opportunities to ask questions about the project. The job walk familiarizes the bidders with the facility as well as the location of the system and devices.

A transmittal letter is required to accompany the RFP. The transmittal letter identifies the project schedule including (a) the date, time, and location of a bidders' conference and job walk, (b) the date and time that the responses to the RFP are due, and (c) the expected date of contract award.

The format of the specification will be tailored to the facility and should include, but need not be limited to the following subjects:

Introduction.   This section defines the overall system to be procured, e.g., access control, closed-circuit television, intrusion detection, or an integration of a number of systems.

Scope of Work.   The scope of work identifies all work to be performed by the contractor such as construction, electrical, conduit, systems hardware, software, training, and the supplies to be provided.

---

[1] *The American Heritage Dictionary of the English Language,* Third Edition.

System Requirements. System requirements identify how the buyer expects the system to perform, as well as all any specific requirements that are unique to the project.

User Requirements. User requirements are those operational provisions that the buyer desires incorporated into the system, such as software particulars, specific format of input and output data, hardware system capabilities, and hardware type.

REQUIREMENTS SPECIFICATION FOR AN INTEGRATED ELECTRONIC SECURITY SYSTEM

Introduction

This specification outlines the requirements for an integrated intrusion detection, access control, fire detection, and closed circuit television (CCTV) monitoring system for the premises identified in the Request for Proposal letter. All quotations must ensure that any inability to comply with these requirements are clearly stated in the quotation submission.

Scope of Work

The quotation is to include (a) the integration of access control, intrusion detection, fire detection, (b) all necessary hardware, (c) photo-identification badges, (d) installation of all hardware, (e) ergonomic console, (1) training of systems operators pertaining to hardware and software, and (g) commissioning of the system as specified including all wiring and equipment. Fire detection will be in accordance with all applicable regulations. The location and the number of intrusion detection devices, access control devices, and cameras are contained in the attached drawings. The location and size of the proprietary central monitoring station is also contained in the attached drawings. The quotation should include the contractor's recommendations pertaining to the above requirements.

System Requirements

Intrusion Detection/Fire Detection. The intrusion detection and fire detection systems will be integrated into a console located at the security control center. The access control and intrusion detection/fire detection systems will be stand-alone.

Access Control/CCTV

A. The access control system will be a personal computer (PC)–based system.

B. The supplier will provide a console in sufficient size to house all equipment (access control, intrusion detection, fire detection, and CCTV monitors) as well as provide for future expansion. The attached drawings indicate the size and location of the future control center.

C. Current light requirements will be taken into consideration when specifying the type and location of cameras. Where required the supplier will provide the light-level requirements.

D. The supplier will provide data on both a film-based system and a video-imaging photo-identification system.

E. The photo-identification badge will incorporate the following characteristics:
   1. Colored coded to designate area access visually, e.g., color background and/or colored bar.
   2. Company logo on the front.
   3. Color photograph on the front (size to be visible from a short distance).
   4. Employee's name on the front (size to be visible from a short distance).
   5. Signature block on the rear.
   6. Name and address of the company on the rear.
   7. Statement on the rear that if the badge is found to return it to the address indicated.
   8. Clips will be utilized to affix the badge to the outer-most garment, chest high, on the person. Necklaces will be provided for use by those who do not wish to use the clip.
   9. The badge shall include 10 fields to incorporate personal details, e.g., name, social security number/employee number, department number, card number, and expiration date.

F. The badge will incorporate the following two technologies:
   1. Magnetic stripe
   2. Proximity.

G. The badge technology will be compatible with the existing time and attendance system.

H. Initially, approximately 1,000 photo-identification/access control badges will be required.

I. For comparison purposes, cameras, monitors, recorders, multiplexers, switchers, quads, or other peripheral equipment will be Brand X or Brand Y. For comparison purposes, cameras and monitors will be quoted black-and-white and color.

J. The supplier will specify all building requirements, e.g., conduit, door hardware, and electrical, as needed, that are not included in this specification.

K. The system should provide for modular expansion of the hardware as well as cardholder capacity for future needs.

L. Access monitoring shall be able to detect and report the following conditions: (a) valid request, (b) lost card, (c) wrong time, (d) wrong door, (e) invalid card, and (f) unknown card.

M. The system should include battery back-up support.

N. The system database shall encrypt the operator passwords to prevent unauthorized viewing.

0. The system will provide for antipassback.

P. The system shall be compatible with other industry standard office equipment and software programs, in particular the latest version of Microsoft Word.

Q. Door monitoring shall include the ability to report door-forced-open and door-held conditions.

User Requirements

Access Control

A. The requirement is for a Microsoft Windows NT–compatible user presentation.

B. The system will include comprehensive on-line help screens that relate to the currently active window.

C. A print-screen command will be required for all screens.

D. System operators shall be associated with a log-on password and user ID.

E. The system shall have the capability of restricting cardholder by dates, times of day, and reader locations.

F. The system will provide an audible alarm at the console for all unauthorized ingress/egress from any door.

G. The system shall provide a detailed audit of the arrival and departure times at any of the card readers. The report will include the ability to sort by any of the 10 personal details.

H. History reporting shall be incorporated to provide the ability to review all system alarms, access control activity, and operator actions. Report capability shall be through operator's display, printer, or magnetic media. Sort capability shall include any of the 10 personal fields. In addition, the data in the system will be archived from the system to a digital media to ensure it is preserved.

I.   In order to provide for shorterm usage, each card record shall have a start and end date validity period. Upon expiration of the valid period, cards shall become automatically inactive without operator action.

J.   The system will provide a means to back-up the system's database.

Closed-Circuit Television (CCTV)

A.   Cameras will be pan/tilt/zoom as well as fixed; however, they shall be able to provide clear and recognizable images.

B.   External cameras will be able to view the entire perimeter of the buildings.

C.   Cameras are to be installed in weatherproof housings where the elements dictate.

D.   The system will provide an audible alarm at the console for all unauthorized ingress/egress from any door.

E.   Nine-inch monitors at the control center will be used for each access control point indicated on the attached drawings.

F.   A 19-inch monitor will be utilized for "pull-down" images from any of the 9-inch monitors.

G.   All images will be recorded on a 24-hour digital media.

H.   The number of cameras and monitors are contained in the attached drawings. The location and size of the monitoring location (control center) are also contained in the attached drawings.

CONCLUSION

The specification example contained in this chapter pertains to an upgrade of an existing system and is provided only as a guide. The example is not wholly designed to be applied in every situation. Each facility and each system are unique and should be addressed accordingly. Security systems and devices as well as related software are complex and the state-of-the-art changes rapidly. If the knowledge of state-of-the-art systems and devices as well as related software are not available within the organization, assistance should be sought from an independent and objective outside source. Reliance solely on the input from suppliers is not recommended.

Compliments of Robert B. Iannone, CPP Security Consultant.

Appendix I

Sample Introduction Memorandum: Disaster Recovery Planning

MEMORANDUM FOR IVA BUCKS, CHIEF FINANCIAL OFFICER

Representatives from Corporate Security will meet with key personnel from XYZ Corporation to facilitate the development of a disaster recovery plan by asking a series of questions designed to give us a better idea of your department's day-to-day operations, interdependencies, and the impact a loss of your function may have on the company over time. Senior management considers this a priority project and expects the full cooperation of all participants. Each team leader or department manager is responsible for the completion of his or her portion of the plan, with help from Security. Security employees will provide participants with a questionnaire and instructions for you or your team to list the answers to their questions.

The development of a disaster recovery plan is simple. You will be asked to accomplish the following:

1. Identify your department's critical functions or processes;
2. Determine the most cost-effective strategy to recover these functions or processes;
3. List detailed instructions that implement the strategies and that reduce the need for decision making during implementation;
4. List critical resources needed to implement the strategies.

Critical functions can be defined as a process, service, equipment, or duty that would have one of the following impacts on the company if the function is lost or if access to it is denied:

1. Affect the financial position of the company;
2. Have a regulatory impact;
3. Reduce or destroy public/customer image/confidence or sales.

Functions that can be postponed for a month or longer without suffering the above impacts are generally not considered in the plan.

Recovery strategies can include:

1. Transfer of operations to, or increase capacity at, another company site;
2. Contract the work to a third party or competitor;
3. Prearranged alternate workspace;
4. Agreements with vendors to supply preconfigured replacements for equipment within an expedient time frame;
5. Working at home.

If you have any questions, or if you need help with the software, contact [name] at extension [number].

Sincerely,

Eugene Tucker, CPP, CFE
Corporate Security

INDEX